Judge Jesus

Judge Jesus

Approaching Jesus's Messianic Judgeship in the Gospel of John from an Early Jewish Perspective

JEREMIAH L. STALLMAN

Foreword by C. Fred Smith

WIPF & STOCK · Eugene, Oregon

JUDGE JESUS
Approaching Jesus's Messianic Judgeship in the Gospel of John
from an Early Jewish Perspective

Copyright © 2021 Jeremiah L. Stallman. All rights reserved. Except for brief quotations in critical publications or reviews, no part of this book may be reproduced in any manner without prior written permission from the publisher. Write: Permissions, Wipf and Stock Publishers, 199 W. 8th Ave., Suite 3, Eugene, OR 97401.

Wipf & Stock
An Imprint of Wipf and Stock Publishers
199 W. 8th Ave., Suite 3
Eugene, OR 97401

www.wipfandstock.com

PAPERBACK ISBN: 978-1-7252-9843-9
HARDCOVER ISBN: 978-1-7252-9844-6
EBOOK ISBN: 978-1-7252-9845-3

09/09/2021

Scripture quotations from the Apocrypha are from the New Revised Standard Version Bible, copyright © 1989 The Division of Christian Education of the National Council of the Churches of Christ. Used by permission.

All other Scripture quotations are from the New American Standard Bible, copyright @ 1960, 1971, 1977, 1995 The Lockman Foundation. Used by permission.

To my wife, who put up with my grumpiness through this whole thing.

Contents

Foreword | xi

1 Introduction | 1
    Why This Study is Needed | 2
    Seeing Things from an Early Jewish Perspective | 3
    Limits of This Study | 6
    Current State of Research | 7
        Review of Second Temple Research | 7
        The Parables of Enoch | 8
        Son of Man | 9
        Judgment Literature | 11
        The Son of Man in Johannine Research | 12
    Conclusion | 19

2 The Themes of Judgment and Messianic Expectation in the Apocrypha and Pseudepigrapha | 21
    Introduction | 21
    Ben Sirach | 23
        Dating and Background | 23
        Judgment | 24
        Messianic Expectation | 26
    Wisdom of Solomon | 28
        Dating and Background | 28
        Judgment | 29
        Messianic Expectation | 30
    Jubilees | 30
        Dating and Background | 30
        Judgment | 31
        Messianic Expectation | 33

    1 Enoch | 34
        The Book of the Watchers | 35
        The Astronomical Book | 37
        The Book of Dreams | 38
        The Epistle of Enoch | 40
    2 Maccabees | 41
        Dating and Background | 41
        Judgment | 42
    Sibylline Oracles | 43
        Dating and Background | 43
        Judgment | 44
        Messianic Expectation | 45
    Testament or Assumption of Moses | 46
        Dating and Background | 46
        Judgment | 47
    Psalms of Solomon | 48
        Dating and Background | 48
        Judgment | 50
        Messianic Expectation | 51
    Conclusion | 55

3   The Themes of Judgment and Messianic Expectation at Qumran | 58
    Introduction | 58
    Dating and Background | 59
    Judgment | 60
    Messianic Expectation | 62
    Conclusion | 65

4   The Danielic Son of Man and Its Development in Second Temple Judaism | 67
    Introduction | 67
    Daniel 7:13–14 | 68
        The Son of Man in Daniel | 68
    The Parables of Enoch | 71
        Dating and Background | 71
        The Eschatological Themes of the Parables | 79
    The Son of Man in 4 Ezra | 87
        Dating and Background | 87
        Judgment and Messianic Expectation in 4 Ezra | 88

Testament of Abraham | 90
Conclusion | 91

5 The Audiences and Their Messianic Expectations Represented in the Gospel of John | 92
    Introduction | 92
    The Audiences Represented in the Gospel of John | 93
        Jews | 94
        Pharisees | 94
        Sadducees and Chief Priests | 95
        Samaritans | 96
        Crowd and Disciples | 97
    Messianic Expectation Represented in the Gospel of John | 97
        Messiah as Prophet | 98
        Messiah as King | 99
        Messiah as Coming from God | 100
        Messiah/Son of Man as Living Forever | 100
    Conclusion | 101

6 Jesus's Representation as the Son of Man in the Gospel of John | 102
    Introduction | 102
    The Son of Man Sayings in the Gospel of John | 108
        John 0:50 | 108
        John 2:12–13 | 109
        John 4:26 | 112
        John 5:26, 52, 61 | 113
        John 7:27 | 115
        John 8:34 | 116
        John 11:22, 33 | 117
        John 12:30 | 118
    Conclusion | 119

7 Jesus's Teachings on Judgment and Judgeship in the Gospel of John | 120
    Introduction | 120
    Judgment and Judgeship in the Gospel of John | 121
        John 2:9–20 | 121
        John 4:20–29 | 127
        John 11:19–35 | 134
    Conclusion | 136

8   Conclusion | 139
        Summary and Conclusion of This Study | 139
        Hermeneutical Implications | 142
        Why Study Second Temple Literature? | 143
            Background Information | 143
            Theological and Religious Belief | 144
            Interpretive Keys | 144

APPENDIX
An Example of Further Study: Sheol, Hades, and Hell | 147

Bibliography | 149

Foreword

I HAVE BEEN FRIENDS with Jeremiah Stallman for more than ten years now. We have served in the same church, taught adult Bible classes together, and enjoyed many a fine meal, over which issues of biblical interpretation, theology, and church life have been richly and deeply discussed to our mutual pleasure and improvement. I supervised his master's thesis and then served on the defense committee for his dissertation, on which this book is based. This is to say that I know Jeremiah Stallman quite well. He is a scholar of the first order, who quickly grasps the significance and multiple dimensions of just about any matter that comes up. Careful attention to detail, commitment to biblical authority, and love for the church guide all his scholarly work. Even a casual perusal of the text here will reveal his thoroughness in addressing the relevant issues raised.

Judge Jesus is an important and relevant book for our time, for several reasons. We all know that the worldview today's readers bring to the table is very different from the worldview of the original Jewish audience. This fact lies at the heart of what Stallman addresses here. His focus in this regard is singular, and this is a strength of the book. He seeks to help the reader understand biblical teaching regarding Jesus's messiahship as hearers would have understood it in their own time. Stallman offers the reader an analysis of specific Second Temple-era documents that were well known in Jesus's day, which shaped their understanding and expectations of the Messiah and his role. For example, while the phrase *son of man*, which features prominently in *Judge Jesus*, evokes a picture of Jesus in the minds of modern readers, first-century Jews heard the phrase very differently. They did not have two thousand years of cultural change, church tradition, and doctrine though which to filter the term. By referring to himself as Son of Man, Jesus intended to reshape his readers' existing understanding of the term and their understanding of him. For today's readers, knowing how

Jesus's hearers understood this phrase helps us to overcome our own cultural blinders. Stallman's book makes a real contribution to our knowledge of Jesus in this regard, because, instead of seeing him only through the lens of modernity, we see him more as his own first disciples saw him.

One major strength here is the section where Stallman looks at the Son of Man sayings in John's Gospel and their relationship to the Parables of Enoch. This gets much attention because, as he points out, the Parables is the only document between Daniel and the Gospels that uses the term son of man. His critical interaction with J. Harold Ellens is a major benefit for readers. Stallman critically engages Ellens's interpretation of John's Gospel as a refutation of the Enochic tradition regarding the son of man. Stallman rightly points the reader to John's purpose of commending Jesus as Savior to readers who were already familiar with the Parables. John sought not to refute Enoch but to reshape the reader's understanding of the term Son of Man, as the term was now being applied directly to Jesus. Stallman next examines all the Son of Man sayings in John, one by one, showing that Jesus's role as judge was at the forefront but, even so, was not the only messianic role that John emphasized. This section alone makes *Judge Jesus* an essential book for anyone pursuing a deeper understanding of the New Testament, especially of its Christology.

Jesus as Judge comes into greatest focus in the last chapter. Stallman shows here, in several passages in John's Gospel, how Jesus redefines the judge, the mode, and the place and purpose of judgment, as well as how judgment and salvation are closely linked in this Gospel. It is this redefining of these elements that is worthy of our attention. Stallman points out that Jesus's redefinition of the scope of both judgment and salvation, to include the gentiles, was an afront to Jewish nationalist assumptions. Those judged are condemned for not believing in the Son, not simply for sinful actions. Much of this is well known to readers of John today, but Stallman confronts us anew with how different it was to Jesus's hearers. The reader comes away better prepared to read John in its original context and to appreciate John's peculiar emphases with a fresh eye. Again, this enhances our understanding of the New Testament and refines our Christological conclusions.

This is why *Judge Jesus* is such an important book. We become not only better scholars of the New Testament but better disciples of Jesus Christ insofar as we see him as his first disciples, as well as his first critics, saw him. Having so much better a window into the way first-century readers understood the themes of judgment, messiahship, and kingship, among

Foreword

other themes, is of immense value to the contemporary scholar. Those of us who teach New Testament and theology classes will find this book essential to the way we present Jesus to our students, as well as to the way we understand and relate to him as Judge, as Son of Man, as God's anointed.

This book will recall to mind themes familiar in John's gospel but also highlight how unfamiliar John's presentation of those themes was in the mid-to-late first century. Stallman helps the reader to see these against the backdrop of Second Temple writings, many of which were familiar to Jews of that day, shaping their self-understanding as the people of God. I am happy to commend Stallman's work here, not only as a friend but as someone who is deeply involved in rightly interpreting and teaching the Scriptures myself—and as someone who knows too well how easy it is for Christians to assume that our way of reading the Bible is the same as other Christians' reading in all times and places. Stallman's work is an important corrective to these cultural blinders that we all share. It should be read, reread, and pondered by all who teach God's word.

C. Fred Smith
Assistant Professor of Biblical Studies at Liberty University
and author of *Developing a Biblical Worldview: Seeing Things God's Way.*

1

Introduction

THE MODERN CHRISTIAN READER of the Gospel of John tends to interpret the Gospel through a twenty-first-century mindset, full of well-nuanced descriptions of Jesus influenced by the rest of the New Testament and nearly two thousand years of Christian interpretation. The original readers of the Gospel of John had a different interpretive lens through which they would have understood the words of Jesus. John's audience was comprised of both Jews and gentiles.[1] This study will focus on John's Jewish audience, due to the Jewish nature in which the Gospel was written and due to John presenting an audience of Jews, who would have initially interpreted Jesus's words through their own Jewish mindset. The overall goal of this study is to not just establish how John's first Jewish audience would have understood Jesus's teachings within their own beliefs and traditions, but also to demonstrate to the modern interpreter of the Gospel of John that a deep study of early Jewish beliefs and traditions concerning messianic expectation, including of the role of judge, illuminates and amplifies Jesus's teachings concerning his own role as Messiah and judge.

Jesus presents himself as having the role of judge in the Gospel of John.[2] For the modern Christian, this is not a problem, since Jesus's claim as judge fits with other New Testament teachings concerning his role as

---

1. Craig L. Blomberg indicates a gentile and Jewish audience based on John's provenance and date written, but argues that John's main audience in mind seems to be Jews, due to the heavily Jewish nature of the Gospel of John (Blomberg, *Historical Reliability*, 41–44, 61–63). See also Köstenberger, *Theology of John's Gospel*, 70–72, 422–35.

2. John 3:17–19; 5:19–30; 8:15–16; 9:39; 12:31, 47–48.

judge and with the Christian belief that Jesus is God. However, the question is rarely, if ever, asked concerning how John's Jewish recipients react when Jesus boldly proclaims to the religious leaders at the temple that "not even the Father judges anyone, but He has given all judgment to the Son" (John 5:22) and later, "He gave Him authority to execute judgment, because He is the Son of Man" (5:27). Were these claims by Jesus something completely foreign to the Jews, or was there a precedent in their own messianic expectation for the messiah to be given the right to judge? In the writing of his Gospel to his own audience, it seems that John assumes his audience would have been familiar with the early Jewish beliefs concerning the expected messiah and his role as eschatological judge.[3] This project will specifically explore early Jewish literature, with special consideration of early Jewish beliefs on messianic expectation and the role of judgment. These Jewish beliefs will then be the lens through which the words of Jesus in the Gospel of John will be explored, in order to reveal just how radical Jesus's words would have been to John's first-century Jewish audience. Thus, the modern reader of the Gospel of John will better understand John's presentation of Jesus's words concerning his role as messianic judge through an early Jewish interpretive lens.

WHY THIS STUDY IS NEEDED

Within the last two decades, there has been a significant increase in Second Temple Jewish studies, especially as they relate to New Testament interpretation. However, there still remains a vast need for these studies in New Testament commentaries, introductions, teaching materials, etc. The scholarly community is aware of their existence and is overall familiar with the implications and importance they hold for New Testament biblical studies. The well-informed pastor will add these implications to his sermon. Many biblically literate people in the church are not aware of early Jewish sources and may see extrabiblical sources in a negative light. Another reason for this study is to point the biblically literate (and biblically illiterate) church community to the fact that early Jewish documents are necessary to help the church understand more fully the teachings of Jesus.

Another reason this study is needed is because there is very little interaction in early Jewish studies as they relate to the Gospel of John. Various

---

3. Chapters 5 through 7 will explore in depth how John represents the major Jewish messianic expectations of his day.

Introduction

scholarly works have focused on early Judaism and the Synoptic Gospels or early Judaism and the Pauline Epistles, but very few scholarly works consider early Judaism and the Gospel of John. Furthermore, this author is unaware of any scholarly sources that extensively consider John's representation of Jesus as messianic judge in light of early Jewish belief. Thus, there is a great need for increased scholarship in this area of interpreting various aspects of the Gospel of John in light of early Jewish beliefs.

SEEING THINGS FROM AN EARLY JEWISH PERSPECTIVE

The modern reader of the Gospel of John does not read and understand the presentation of Jesus's teachings in the same way that John's original audience understood them. The author of the Gospel of John writes to a first-century audience that would likely have understood John's Jewish references and the words of Jesus's teachings from a first-century Jewish perspective. A first-century Jewish reaction to the teachings of Jesus is not the automatic response of the twenty-first-century reader of the Gospel of John. Since its initial distribution to its earliest readers, there has been nearly two thousand years of interpretation, primarily through a Western European Christian point of view. Although there is nothing wrong with this approach, most Western interpreters of the teachings of Jesus in the Gospel of John do not consider how a first-century Jew would have heard and reacted to the teachings of Jesus. The modern reader does not read these inherently Jewish teachings through the lens of a first-century Jew, who would have been one of the primary recipients of this Gospel when it was first written. Thus, the modern reader must understand Jesus's teachings in "their town" before interpretation is made in "our town."[4]

There is then a gap between the modern reader and the implied reader. Most modern readers do not consider deep Jewish backgrounds and thought processes when reading through how John presents the teachings of Jesus to a first-century Jewish audience. Köstenberger and Patterson delineate the difference between the two readers as they note:

> The reader is the actual reader of the narrative. This is a label that properly applies to a contemporary reader. The *implied* reader is the one or ones for whom the author composed his work. It

---

4. "Their town" and "our town" are terms used by J. Scott Duvall and J. Daniel Hays in their five-step principlizing process in determining an applicable biblical principle from the text to the modern reader (Duvall and Hays, *Grasping God's Word*, 39–47).

is necessary to understand this distinction, because while the original readers of the text are no longer alive, the message was originally intended for them. Understanding this original context permits the interpreter to gain more insight into the original purpose of the author.[5]

Original meaning is a key piece that the interpreter of the text needs to seek. The original meaning that John intended for his words would have been understood by his target audience, because John would have been familiar with his audience and their beliefs. Klein, Blomberg, and Hubbard state, "Of course, if we are seeking the meaning the author/editor intended for the original recipients, that meaning *must* be what they could have understood at that time, not some meaning later readers would determine based on later historical and theological (or scientific) understanding."[6] It is the later reader's responsibility to seek out and understand as much and as closely as possible how the implied reader would have understood John's presentation of Jesus' teachings.

The contention then is the identity of the original audience in order to know where to focus one's efforts to research the background of this audience. Craig Blomberg argues for one of the original recipient groups to read this text as Palestinian Jews living in Asia Minor, where John was originally writing.[7] He argues that John writes a sharp polemic to Christians with Jewish backgrounds who were experiencing Jewish opposition. John was reassuring them that their faith in Jesus Christ was properly placed. Thus, John had an acute focus on a Jewish audience in the writing of his Gospel. Andreas Köstenberger also argues that the original audience first and foremost had diaspora Jews and gentiles attracted to Judaism.[8] Köstenberger argues that this Gospel is partially written as reactionary, as a response to the destruction of the temple, since John presents Jesus as the new temple.[9] Although gentiles would have also been part of John's audience, the primary indicators within the Jewish nature of the text indicate that John's first priority was to reach a Jewish audience and comprehensively prove to them that Jesus was indeed the long expected Messiah—not just Messiah but God himself in the flesh.

---

5. Köstenberger and Patterson, *Invitation to Biblical Interpretation*, 391.
6. Klein et al., *Biblical Interpretation*, 49–50.
7. Blomberg, *Historical Reliability*, 41–44, 61–63.
8. Köstenberger, *Theology of John's Gospel*, 70–72, 422–35.
9. Köstenberger, *Theology of John's Gospel*, 84–85.

Introduction

In order for "our town" to best understand "their town" when it comes to understanding Jesus's statements in John 5:22 and 27, we must explore the many facets that would have influenced their state of belief. This study will explore key passages in early Jewish texts for beliefs concerning their views on judgment, which included judgment criteria, recipients of judgment, imminent and eschatological elements of judgment, judgment as it relates to the coming messiah, God's role in judgment, the messiah's role in judgment, and various early Jewish views of messianic expectation. Understandably, there is no certainty that John's audience would have had access to all of the documents that the modern reader has. However, a comparison of these texts with themes found in the Gospel of John will reveal that, at a minimum, there would have been a verbal tradition with which first-century Jews were familiar. This study will also explore the historical and social settings that influenced the composition and content of each document.

The study will then focus on John's immediate Jewish audience, which is the original implied reader. This study will investigate the composition of Jesus's audience represented in the Gospel of John, which is also representative of John's Jewish audience. This study will delineate what each group within John's audience would have likely believed about the messiah and judgment, based on historically known information. This study will then exegete Jesus's own teachings concerning his fulfilment of Jewish messianic expectation and his role as imminent and eschatological judge, in light of John's Jewish audience's preconceived Jewish beliefs. The final step of this method will indicate to the modern reader just how radical Jesus's teachings would have been to the first-century Jewish ear and inform the modern reader that he or she will have a much more robust understanding of the teachings of Jesus by first seeking to understand the words of Jesus through a first-century Jewish mindset.

Knowing as much as possible about the beliefs of the original Jewish recipients of the Gospel of John will aid the modern reader in understanding how they would have understood and received the teachings of Jesus as John presents them. The author of the Gospel of John would have had the religious and cultural background of his audience in mind when he penned the words of this Gospel. The Jewish nature of this Gospel indicates that both the author and his target audience were Jewish or familiar enough with Jewish rituals, customs, and beliefs. Knowing key Jewish beliefs will aid the modern reader to read the Gospel of John through the interpretive lens of the original Jewish audience. First-century Jews would have understood the words of Jesus through their own preconceived beliefs on the topics of judgment, messianic expectation, and the messiah's role as eschatological judge.

LIMITS OF THIS STUDY

The Second Temple literature discussed will mostly consider sources written prior to AD 100, since scholarly estimates place the authorship of the Gospel of John around AD 80–100. Early Jewish documents that date after Jesus's ministry (after AD 30) will only be considered to show continuity of Jewish belief in first-century Judaism concerning the expected messiah's role in judgment. One of the limitations with some of the early Jewish sources is Christian interpolation in these documents. Thus, caution will be taken in the examination of certain texts such as 1 Enoch and the Testament of Moses to distinguish an early Jewish belief from a later Christian interpolation.[10] This study will seek to find the root Jewish beliefs regarding the expectation of a messianic judge and dismiss later Christian interpolations on the text that do not inform original Jewish belief.[11] Dating of the primary Jewish sources will play a large role in determining original Jewish belief at the time that Jesus taught. Another challenge of the dating is linking the document to a certain historical and social setting, because the content and emphases of most, if not all, of the early Jewish documents were influenced by historical and social settings. These settings influenced what was said about the type of messiah expected, as well as the extent of judgment, whether God was the one judging or judgment was a role of the messianic figure.

One of the largest limitations of this study is the limited number of early Jewish sources. Some of the key sources contained within the Dead Sea Scrolls are highly fragmentary, such as 11QMelchizedek and 4Q246 (the Son of God text). The primary sources for this study will include but are not limited to: Daniel, 2 Maccabees, Sirach, the Sibylline Oracles 3, the Psalms of Solomon, Jubilees, the Testament of Abraham, the Apocalypse of Abraham, the Testament of Moses, 4 Ezra, 2 Baruch, 1 Enoch, the Dead Sea

---

10. The OT pseudepigrapha as collected and edited by James H. Charlesworth specifically deals with which parts of early Jewish documents are later Christian interpolations (Charlesworth, *Old Testament Pseudepigrapha*). See especially the introductions to each translated document.

11. This will be heavily explored through chs. 2 through 4.

INTRODUCTION

Scrolls, and the Gospel of John. There is only so much that can be gleaned from early Jewish sources concerning what John's Jewish audience would have believed about the role of the Messiah as judge. The limit on the number of sources means that there is a lack of knowledge concerning some areas of what may or may not have been the exact beliefs of John's Jewish audience; but, overall, these documents give enough information to paint a more than sufficient picture of what a first-century Jew would have believed concerning judgment, the messiah, and the messiah's role as judge.

CURRENT STATE OF RESEARCH

Review of Second Temple Research

Several authors over the past few decades have offered various surveys on Second Temple texts found in the Apocrypha and Pseudepigrapha.[12] Each of these surveys has a different focus and goal in mind. For example, some New Testament scholars give the survey with the intent of showing how the Jewish texts inform New Testament study.[13] Others have sought to be

---

12. Lester L. Grabbe offers a chronological survey of Jewish literature from the Persian period (539–333 BC) through the end of the first century AD (Grabbe, *Judaic Religion*, 11–126). This portion of his study focuses on the historical events that would have directly influenced each of the writings. That survey will be of great value for this study, because it will help to trace chronologically Jewish thought concerning messianic expectation, the topic of judgment, and the identity of the one doing the judging. That source will help show the progression and change of belief and what events led to those changes. The second half of Grabbe's study considers special topics, and ch. 13 will greatly inform this study, as Grabbe considers what early Jewish texts said concerning messianic expectation and the type of messiah put forth in each text (Grabbe, *Judaic Religion*, 271–91).

Shaye J. D. Cohen offers a synthesis of religion, literature, and history of Judaism as it developed from 164 BC to AD 300. His work considers this period from a Jewish perspective, which will aid in this study, because part of the goal is to understand Jesus' steachings through a Jewish lens (Cohen, *From Maccabees to Mishnah*).

James C. VanderKam gives a three-part introduction to early Judaism including history, literature, and societal structures (VanderKam, *Introduction to Early Judaism*). This text will provide necessary background and dating information for many of the early Jewish texts considered in this study.

13. Larry Helyer analyzes Jewish texts based on a few different approaches (Helyer, *Exploring Jewish Literature*). He considers some texts in light of historical events, which makes up the largest body of his book. He also considers literature that fits into certain genres such as apocalypticism. He further considers literature from geographic locations (Qumran) and from individuals (Philo and Josephus). For each work that he analyzes, he seeks to give a basic introduction, dating and composition, purpose, features, topics, and its relationship to the New Testament. For this study, the overview of each Jewish text

more objective and informative.[14] These surveys will be of great use for this study, as they will give key background information on specific early Jewish texts such as date, provenance, historical and religious setting, and the overall impact that each document may have had on other documents and especially the shaping of the Jewish mindset regarding specific topics that will be explored in depth in this study.[15]

The Parables of Enoch

The Parables of Enoch is an instrumental piece of Second Temple Jewish literature that informs or begins to inform first-century AD messianic perspectives and expectation.[16] Scholarship on the Parables has increased significantly over the past two decades, and this study seeks to add to the conversation. The Parables contains many links to each of the four Gospels. Leslie Walck has significantly added to recent scholarship on the Parables by comparing the use of the son of man in the Parables of Enoch to its use in the Gospel of Matthew. His overall goal is to show the similarities between the two, with special consideration to the judgment scenes in both. Although this work focuses on Matthew, the research done on the Parables will greatly inform this current study.

James A. Waddell offers an intriguing study on how the messiah is presented in the Parables of Enoch, compared to how the Messiah is portrayed in the writings of the apostle Paul.[17] Although this book considers the writings of Paul as its end goal, chapter 3 focuses on how the messiah is pictured in the Parables of Enoch. Especially important for this study is

---

will inform the various subsections on specific sources used to build a case toward the expectation of a messianic judge.

14. See Docherty, *Jewish Pseudepigrapha*.

15. This review of literature will not consider secondary sources for every Second Temple text utilized for this study. This study will only review literature associated with the Parables of Enoch, since this text gives the greatest input for messianic expectation found in the Gospel of John regarding the expectation of a messianic judge. Secondary sources for all other Second Temple sources will be considered in the various subsections of chs. 2 through 4.

16. Dating of the Parables is crucial to this study, since that source greatly informs messianic expectation, especially as it relates to Messiah as Judge. A subsection of ch. 4 will argue for a dating of the Parables that predates the ministry of Jesus, which gives a precedent of a messianic judge as part of messianic expectation.

17. Waddell, *Messiah*, 48–103.

the section of chapter 3 that considers the functions of the messiah, such as salvation and judgment, since both topics are in view in Jesus's discourse on his self-portrayal as messianic judge in the Gospel of John.[18]

Gabriele Boccaccini presents a comprehensive collection of essays surrounding recent scholarship of the Parables of Enoch, especially as this text relates to early Jewish messianic expectation.[19] The essays in this book add significantly to the discussion of the identity of the messiah or son of man in Second Temple Judaism. Unfortunately, one aspect that is lacking from these essays is the influence of the Parables on the New Testament. Although this aspect is lacking, the information conveyed will greatly allow the conversation to move in that direction, as is the case with this study.

Son of Man

The Son of Man debate has been going on since the Protestant Reformation.[20] Although there is wide interpretation on the meaning of Son of Man, the focus of this study will be upon how the title was referenced in texts that predate the ministry of Jesus. These references will be compared to and contrasted with how Jesus uses the title Son of Man in the Gospel of John, especially in relation to Jesus as messianic judge. Unfortunately, much of the scholarship concerning the interpretation of the Son of Man in the Gospels focuses on the Synoptics.[21] However, J. Harold Ellens writes a helpful book concerning the use of Son of Man in the Gospel of John.[22] Ellens exegetes each of the uses of Son of Man in John and comments on

---

18. See also Leslie Walck's discussion on the characteristics of the Enochic Son of Man in the Parables of Enoch (Walck, *Son of Man*, 156–64).

19. Boccaccini, *Enoch and the Messiah*. Since the Parables of Enoch is one of the key sources in this current discussion, most if not all of the essays or the research presented in the essays will be utilized to inform the arguments of this section of the study.

20. Burkett, *Son of Man Debate*, 1–2. Burkett offers an extensive look at the development of the debate over the past three centuries. His main goal in this book is not necessarily to give a historical survey of the debate, but to show the many different ways that Son of Man was understood in early Jewish texts and into rabbinic texts.

21. One of the examples of Son of Man studies in the Synoptics is Walck, *Son of Man*. Walck does a comparative study on how Son of Man is used in the Parables of Enoch and Matthew, offering thorough exegesis on key passages in which the Son of Man is mentioned. The exegesis of 1 Enoch will prove to be highly useful for this study, since the Parables sheds the greatest amount of light on the Jewish expectation of the Son of Man that predates the ministry of Jesus.

22. Ellens, *Son of Man*.

the theological and christological significance of each use. One of his most helpful chapters for this current study is his consideration of how Son of Man is used in all four Gospels, in light of how it is used in Second Temple Judaism.

Lester L. Grabbe offers a brief yet detailed overview of how the definition and understanding of the son of man developed in Second Temple Judaism.[23] Grabbe explores how son of man was understood eschatologically. He considers Dan 7, the Parables of Enoch, and 4 Ezra 13. His comments on the first two sources will inform the current study, especially since Jesus's discourse on his claim as messianic judge has eschatological judgment in view.[24] Grabbe draws a distinct connection between the son of man in the Parables of Enoch and the four Gospels, especially Matthew, as opposed to just the Danielic tradition of one like a son of man.

Benjamin E. Reynolds traces the use of son of man in early Jewish sources (Daniel, 1 Enoch, 4 Ezra, 2 Baruch) and New Testament passages (the Synoptic Gospels, Acts, Revelation).[25] Reynolds's study emphasizes the apocalyptic characteristics of the Son of Man in John. The apocalyptic features of the Messiah ranked high in Jewish expectation. Reynolds brings out each of these features in his exegesis and interpretation of key Gospel of John passages. In fact, he speaks directly to one of the key passages that will inform this current study in chapter 6, where he discusses the son of man as apocalyptic judge. His study focuses on an end-times view of the son of man, which would have been a key feature in the beliefs of John's Jewish audience. One thing that this current study will seek to bring out is Jesus presenting himself as not only the apocalyptic or eschatological judge, but also as an imminent judge, who is already judging the thoughts and intentions of his audience.

---

23. Grabbe, "Son of Man."

24. Concerning 4 Ezra and 2 Baruch, both sources will be mentioned only briefly, due to the fact that they postdate the ministry of Jesus. Depending on the dating tradition of the Gospel of John, both sources also predate John. Both of these sources lend evidence to the fact that there was a developed Son of Man tradition in Judaism in the first century AD. These sources will be utilized to show precedence, not influence.

25. Reynolds, *Apocalyptic Son of Man*.

Introduction

Judgment Literature

The focus of this study is what the Jews would have expected concerning the messiah as judge and what this role would have looked like. Although this is the primary focus, the topic of the Jewish view of judgment will be explored, as it relates to who the Jews viewed as the one doing the judging (God, a human figure, angelic being, the messiah) and who were to be the recipients of the judgment (the unrighteous, Romans, Greeks, all gentiles, compromising Jews, fallen angels, etc.). This study will show that the recipients of judgment in the teachings of Jesus is unexpectedly different from who his audience, the Jews, expected it to be.

Recent scholarship that links the topic of judgment from early Jewish texts to New Testament texts is scarce. Two of the main sources that this study will consider link early Jewish sources on judgment to the apostle Paul's view of judgment in his epistles. Kent L. Yinger focuses his comparative judgment study on judgment according to deeds.[26] His main contribution to the topic is a pointed survey of Second Temple Jewish texts that speak to the topic of judgment. His method is to show how this motif comes up in these texts, as opposed to looking at judgment topically and following different aspects of it. His goal is to show what Paul and his Jewish audience would have believed about judgment when the topic is presented in various epistolary passages. Although he does not speak directly to judgeship, his survey of Second Temple sources will contribute to an understanding of what judgment would have looked like to John's Jewish audience, since the type of judgment presented by Jesus in the Gospel of John informs the type of judge that Jesus is presenting himself to be. Yinger's emphasis is to show judgment according to deeds; in a sense, there is a deed that Jesus tells his audience they must do in order to be saved.

Another recent study that discusses the topic of judgment and relates early Jewish thought to the Pauline Epistles is put forth by Chris VanLandingham. VanLandingham singles out specific ideas about judgment and shows how each Jewish source speaks directly to that topic.[27] He addresses many of the same passages as Yinger but in greater detail and adds to judgment the topic of justification, how these relate to the covenants that God made with Israel, and then how they relate to God's covenant with the church. This study will provide great insight on what the early

---

26. Yinger, *Paul, Judaism, and Judgment*.
27. VanLandingham, *Judgment and Justification*.

Jews believed about judgment and who would be saved. This will provide some of the needed information regarding the contrast that Jesus provides his audience, which will show just how radical Jesus's teachings on judgment and salvation were to his audience. Although the topic of judgment is an instrumental piece of this study, one aspect of judgment that is lacking in the area of comparative early Jewish and New Testament studies is the identity of the judge, especially in light of what Jesus teaches about his own judgeship.

Stephen H. Travis presents a study on the topic of divine retribution as it is presented by every New Testament author.[28] After a brief background of the topic in the Old Testament and Second Temple literature, Travis focuses primarily on how divine retribution is traced throughout the New Testament. The reason this study is useful when considering Jesus as judge is because the longest held Jewish belief concerning the person of judgment in was that judgment belonged solely to God. However, this study will demonstrate that the one doing the judging began to shift in Jewish thought between the first century BC through the end of the first century AD. This study will also reveal the nature and character of divine judgment as seen in the teachings of Jesus and the teachings of Paul. These teachings are important for the current study, because the nature and character of divine judgment that Jesus poses to his audience in the Gospel of John will greatly contrast with what was expected from God and his messiah.

The Son of Man in Johannine Research

The review of Johannine research focuses on two verses in the Gospel of John, 5:22 and 5:27. The two main themes for this study are Jesus as judge and the use of Son of Man in the immediate context of 5:27 and the broader context of John's Gospel. One of the main goals of this review is to see what background information various commentators bring to light concerning the Jewish background for the ideas of a messianic judge and of Jesus's usage of the Son of Man title in the Gospel of John. The reason for this is to understand how John's Jewish audience would have understood Jesus's words in 5:27, when Jesus says, "And He gave Him authority to execute judgment, because He is the Son of Man."

The following reviewed sources have been placed in general chronological order for the purpose of tracing thought and research development

---

28. Travis, *Christ and the Judgment*.

Introduction

of Jesus as judge and his use of the title Son of Man in the Gospel of John, especially in 5:27. One of the things this review will bring to light is those commentators who bring out the Jewish and possible messianic background of the son of man as judge, predating its usage in the four Gospels.

C. K. Barrett points to the uniqueness of the Son of God as the reason that this particular instance of Son of Man in John is anarthrous. His overall view on its use here points to Jesus's special position in all of humanity.[29] Francis Moloney follows this line of thinking and holds that Jesus's use of Son of Man in John accentuates his humanity.[30] However, many Johannine scholars lean toward the notion that this title points to both Jesus's humanity and divinity, because of the way it is used elsewhere in the gospels.

C. H. Dodd conflates the use of the titles Son of God and Son of Man as, in essence, two sides of the same coin.[31] Dodd also supports the notion that the title Son on Man as used in John has its background from the common tradition found in the Synoptics.[32] He points out that there is little reference to this title in pre-Christian Judaism other than Dan 7:13–14 and 1 Enoch.[33] Like other commentators, Dodd points to the Synoptics for the main origin for the use of Son of Man. The problem with this is that one then must seek to explain the origins of Son of Man in the Synoptics. Commentators only defer the problem by pointing to the Synoptics for origin understandings.

Rudolf Schnackenburg brings out that the kind of judgment mentioned in John 5, according to the Jewish mindset, was one of God's supreme acts of sovereignty and was thus something reserved for God alone. He states that John 5:22 is part of Jesus showing his equality with God.[34] He also demonstartes the Jewish messianic background of son of man in Dan 7 and 1 Enoch. For his interpretation of Dan 7:13–14, he shows how judgment is not a part of this passage, but only power and authority.[35] By the end of this section, he remains inconclusive as to the origin and Jewish understanding of the link between son of man and judgment. He points to

---

29. Barrett, *Gospel According to St John*, 218.
30. Moloney, *Johannine Son of Man*.
31. Dodd, *First Epistle of John*, 244.
32. Dodd, *Interpretation of Fourth Gospel*, 241.
33. Dodd, *First Epistle of John*, 241–44.
34. Schnackenburg, *Gospel According to St John*, 2:107.
35. Schnackenburg, *Gospel According to St John*, 2:107.

1 Enoch but does not explore further the implications of this early Jewish text.[36]

Unlike Schnackenburg, Leon Morris holds that there is not a Jewish precedent for the messiah to hold the function of final judgment. He holds that John is presenting a new and distinctive teaching concerning the role of the messiah in judgment.[37] The problem with this conclusion is that Morris fails to consider early Jewish sources for not just son of man thought but also Jewish expectation of judgment and of the messiah.

Delbert Burkett focuses on the ascending-descending concept of the Son of Man. He advocates for the reader of John not to try to push for any single category for each use of the title but to let each one speak individually.[38] Burkett develops this thesis throughout his commentary concerning each individual usage of Son of Man, but he ends up missing what John is trying to do as a whole with how he weaves this title throughout. John is notorious for building complex multifaceted meanings into the words and phrases that he repeats throughout, and Son of Man is one of many.

D. A. Carson rejects the notion that the anarthrous usage points to Jesus's humanity and that Jesus can judge mankind because he himself became human. He rejects this notion on the basis that this is a condition indicative of all humankind.[39] He also says that the usage here is used to point to Dan 7:13–14. However, Carson does not stop with Dan 7 and recognizes there is ambiguity of how the title has been used in the past. He says, "Jesus could therefore shape the title to suit his own understanding of his role."[40] Carson identifies three aspects of the title Son of Man as representing not only Jesus's divinity and humanity but also the self-revelation he imparts upon humanity, which is the basis for judgment coming upon mankind. Rejection of this revelation brings condemnation.[41]

Gerald L. Borchert sees the roll of judgment in John 5:22 and 5:27 as eschatological.[42] He also mentions the use of Son of Man had a certain Jewish expectation behind it, though he does not go into detail as to what that

---

36. Schnackenburg, *Gospel According to St John*, 2:112–13.
37. Morris, *Jesus Is the Christ*, 100–01.
38. Burkett, *Son of the Man*.
39. Carson, *Gospel According to John*, 257.
40. Carson, *Gospel According to John*, 257.
41. Carson, *Gospel According to John*, 257–58.
42. Borchert, *John 1–11*, 241.

expectation would have looked like.⁴³ Concerning the anarthrous nature of the use in 5:27, Borchert points to Colwell's rule, but goes further by saying that it is likely on purpose to point the author to Dan 7:13–14.⁴⁴ He holds that the relationship between the Son of Man and the Ancient of Days in Daniel parallels the Son-Father relationship in the Gospel of John.⁴⁵

Herman Ridderbos focuses on the eschatological tension of John 5:19–30 between realized and inaugurated eschatology. Concerning Jesus's statement in 5:27, he does point the reader to Dan 7:13 but focuses more on the power of the Son to give life than the right of the Son to judge and bring condemnation.⁴⁶ In John 5, Jesus holds salvation and judgment in close tension with each other. While the Jews had clear views about each one and who the recipients of each would be, Jesus's speeches on judgment and salvation in John reveal the irony of the Jewish situation and belief about who will be judged and for what reason.

Rodney A. Whitacre also considers Dan 7 and 1 Enoch behind the statement in John 5:27. He points to the implications that this title and the situation of the conversation might have had on his listening audience. He says, "So Jesus is saying that if they recognized him as the eschatological 'Son of Man' and if they understood this identity aright, they would know they were facing their judge."⁴⁷ Thus, Whitacre is one of the few commentators who seeks to show the mindset of Jesus's Jewish audience.

George R. Beasley-Murray asserts that the Son of Man tradition put forth in the Gospel of John follows the tradition put forth by the Synoptics, as opposed to early Jewish tradition.⁴⁸ He follows a similar view to that of Dodd, but the fact remains that one still needs to explain the background usage in the Synoptics, which in essence closely mirrors John's usage.

Raymond E. Brown seeks to give background to the origin of Jesus's title Son of Man by considering its use in Ezekiel, Dan 7, and 1 Enoch 37–71. He posits that there is one main thread from which the title originates, and that some in Jesus's audience were unfazed by his use of the title, which indicates they were familiar with the title and its previous use and

---

43. Borchert, *John 1–11*, 241, fn37.

44. Borchert, *John 1–11*, 241, fn37. Part of Colwell's rule states that "Definite predicate nouns which precede the verb usually lack the article" (Colwell, "Definite Rule," 20).

45. Borchert, *John 1–11*, 241, fn37.

46. Ridderbos, *Gospel of John*, 195–201.

47. Whitacre, *John*, 132.

48. Beasley-Murray, *John*, 77.

understanding by early Jews.[49] The supposition of familiarity is a crucial piece to this entire argument, because John mainly gives only one side of the conversation, Jesus's. The modern reader is unaware of the preconceived ideas concerning the role of the messiah or son of man in judgment. Understanding the beliefs of the audience helps one to better understand the words of Jesus. The goal is to see the beliefs of those on the other side of the conversation.

Craig S. Keener comes the closest to achieving this goal in his commentary and gets to the heart of the issue behind the passage by proposing that Jesus's saying that authority to judge was being passed to the Son was meant to be unnerving to his audience.[50] Keener points out the delegation of judgment by God in other early Jewish sources such as 1 Enoch and the Testament of Abraham. He says that although there is a Jewish precedent for the delegation of judgment, the prevailing view in Early Judaism and into the Rabbinic materials is that God judges alone without the aid of or delegation to another.[51]

John Ashton also makes some significant observations and points to John's Son of Man as one whose true home is in heaven and possibly even a divine figure, with Dan 7:13–14 as the backdrop. He shows how the use of this title is something no ordinary human being would dare to claim.[52] He distinguishes the use of this title from Son of God, which he sees as messianic. Concerning the judgeship given to Jesus in John 5:27, as it relates to the use of Son of Man, Ashton points to the uniqueness of the phraseology in this verse because it is the only instance of Son and Son of Man used next to each other, and it is the only anarthrous use of the title in the entire Gospel, which he says points directly to the anarthrous use of the title in Dan 7:13.[53] He also points to the emergence of Jewish thought in 1 Enoch, 4 Ezra, and 2 Baruch, showing the link of this title to a messianic heavenly figure. He concludes that the Son of Man is a conflation of both the Enochic and Danielic traditions.[54]

Andreas Köstenberger sees the Son of Man as "a human figure with a transcendent origin . . . where God will uniquely reveal himself in a striking

---

49. Brown, *Introduction to Gospel of John*, 252–56.
50. Keener, *Gospel of John*, 1:651.
51. Keener, *Gospel of John*, 1:651–52.
52. Ashton, *Understanding the Fourth Gospel*, 240.
53. Ashton, *Understanding the Fourth Gospel*, 259–61.
54. Ashton, *Understanding the Fourth Gospel*, 261–66.

INTRODUCTION

and supernatural way."[55] He points out that the Johannine Son of Man in several of the instances is in relation to being lifted up, in reference to the crucifixion, similar to how others use this title in the Synoptics.[56] His reference to the use in John 5:27 concerns the divine prerogative to judge. He does not mention the use of this title as messianic, and the background text he references is Dan 7:13, which he says refers to judgment as a key feature of the Danielic son of man.[57] Later, he notes that this title highlights the tension between Jesus's humanity and divinity.[58]

J. Ramsey Michaels indicates that the Son avoids the responsibility of judgment.[59] He does recognize an irony of this passage when he says, "Ironically, the very words he speaks (v. 23) carry out the 'judgment' that he says God has given him (v. 22)."[60] Michaels rejects the notion that there is anything significant about the fact that Son of Man in John 5:27 is anarthrous. In fact, he directly quotes Colwell's rule to validate his position.[61] He points to possible background passages such as Dan 7 and 1 Enoch and says it is clear that the use of Son of Man in John points John's audience back to these sources, but this is not due to the lack of the definite article.[62]

Urban von Wahlde rightly sees judgment belonging to God and compares John 5:22 to Deut 32:39–41, but he does not explore further the background of God handing over the right to judge.[63] Concerning the relation between John 5:27 and Dan 7:13, he notes that the son of man in Daniel is only given power, not the specific power to judge. Further, it is not until 1 Enoch that judgment is something handed over to the son of man.[64] Concerning aspects of judgment, he notes how John points to both present and future judgment.[65]

---

55. Köstenberger, *Theology of John's Gospel*, 191.
56. Köstenberger, *Theology of John's Gospel*, 386–87.
57. Köstenberger, *Theology of John's Gospel*, 388.
58. Köstenberger, *Theology of John's Gospel*, 529.
59. Michaels, *Gospel of John*, 313.
60. Michaels. *Gospel of John*, 314.
61. Michaels, *Gospel of John*, 319. Michaels cites Colwell, "Definite Rule," 20. Carson also points to Colwell's rule as a likely reason for this usage to be anarthrous (Carson, *Gospel According to John*, 259).
62. Michaels, *Gospel of John*, 320.
63. Von Wahlde, *Gospel and the Letters*, 2:232.
64. Von Wahlde, *Gospel and the Letters*, 2:235.
65. Von Wahlde, *Gospel and the Letters*, 1:490–93.

Frederick Dale Bruner rightly points to two prevalent Jewish beliefs that only God gives life at the beginning and only God judges at the end.[66] The focus for Bruner in John 5:22 is on Jesus's claim to divinity. Concerning the use of Son of Man by John, Bruner points to Jesus as fulfilling both Jewish beliefs. He sees Jesus as the Son of Man represented in Ps 8 as one who gives life. However, Bruner says that the focus in John 5 is on the second Jewish belief concerning God's judgment as seen from Dan 7. He says that this title refers to Jesus's lowliness as well as exaltation. Bruner asserts that the Son of Man in John mostly refers to the Danielic son of man who receives power and authority.[67]

Richard Baukham does not see the son of man as messianic and points to John 9:35–37 to support his argument. He sees the title as just a self-designation, meaning no more than "the man."[68] However, the emphasis of 9:35–37 does not at all point toward this notion, since Jesus's self-designation in this passage as Son of Man causes the one healed to worship him. One identified as only "the man" would not garner this response. Concerning the use of the Son of Man in John 5:27, Baukham rightly points out that this directly alludes to Dan 7:13.[69]

Colin Kruse focuses on Jesus's judgment as eschatological and not much concerning Jesus's judgment as immediate. He does not tie this to messianic expectation. Judgment is a divine prerogative. He mainly points to Daniel for the background for the title of son of man and briefly references Ezekiel, 1 Enoch, and 4 Ezra. He does point to the fact that this title had messianic implications in late writings.[70]

Johannes Beutler says, "The judgment is actually reserved exclusively to the Son so that God himself does not take part in it."[71] Beutler rightly picks up on the notion of both realized and eschatological judgment in John 5:24–27, though he mostly emphasizes eschatological judgment from the passage. Concerning 5:27, he also points out that John references Dan 7:13–14. However, he says that Daniel is not emphasizing the judgment

---

66. Bruner, *Gospel of John*, 314.
67. Bruner, *Gospel of John*, 114–15.
68. Bauckham, *Gospel of Glory*, 177–78.
69. Bauckham, *Gospel of Glory*, 178.
70. Kruse, *John*, judgment excursus, 126–27; 5:22, 27 comment, 174–75; Son of Man excursus, 92–94.
71. Beutler, *Commentary*, 155. He seems to miss the Father-Son dynamic. It still is God doing the judging.

aspect of the son of man but his dominion until the end of time. Beutler also interprets the Danielic son of man as Michael and Jesus taking over the title for himself.[72] One thing that Beutler does not bring into his study is early Jewish interpretation of judgment and son of man.

Overall, most commentators point toward Dan 7:13–14 as the likely origin of Jesus's use of Son of Man in John 5:27. Many also rightly point to 1 Enoch for a continuation of the view of the son of man, especially his relation to judgment.[73] Only a few point past the Gospel of John to 4 Ezra and 2 Baruch in order to show that there was a continuation of the son of man tradition in Jewish thought and belief. Concerning the role of judgment, most of the commentators considered for this study observe that this passage points to Jesus's claim to divinity. Some point out the messianic implications of Jesus's claim by juxtaposing it with his use of Son of Man in John 5:27. Only a few commentators go beyond this passage and seek to show the implications of Jesus's words to his audience and the audience's possible reaction to those words. This is one of the main things that this current study will seek to explore as it unfolds what Jesus teaches about himself in the Gospel of John concerning his role as messianic judge.

CONCLUSION

As this study progresses, it will become more evident to the reader just how complex and multifaceted Jewish belief grew to be concerning the themes of judgment and the messiah. Chapter 2 will explore the main Jewish documents that informed the early Jewish views of judgment, the criteria and recipients of judgment, the role God plays in judgment, the role the messiah plays in judgment, and what kind of messiah the Jews expected. Chapter 3 will give insight into the themes of judgment as they relate to messianic expectation in the Qumran Community. Chapter 4 will focus on the Jewish son of man tradition as it first appears in Daniel and its evolution in Jewish tradition to the end of the first century AD. Chapters 5 through 7 will consider how all these themes play into Jesus's teachings about himself in the Gospel of John. These chapters will compare early Jewish thought to the teachings of Jesus and demonstrate just how radically different Jesus's teachings would have been to the Jewish beliefs of John's

---

72. Beutler, *Commentary*, 154–56.

73. The notion that John would have been familiar with early Jewish beliefs in 1 Enoch and 4 Ezra will be explored in detail in chs. 5 through 7.

Judge Jesus

first-century audience. The overall intent and goal of this study as originally stated will be to aid the modern reader in understanding the teachings of Jesus through the lens of the original Jewish audience.

2

The Themes of Judgment and Messianic Expectation in the Apocrypha and Pseudepigrapha

INTRODUCTION

CONTAINED WITHIN THE TEACHINGS of Jesus in the Gospel of John are themes of judgment that would have been familiar to John's Jewish audience, such as judgment according to deeds (John 3:19–21; 5:29), punishment for those who do evil (5:29), reward and eternal life for those who are righteous (5:21, 24), eschatological judgment (5:27), imminent judgment (3:18), the Messiah taking on the role as judge (5:22, 27), judgment of the world (12:31a), and judgment of the ruler of this world (12:31b). John's representation of Jesus's audiences also reveals certain beliefs concerning messianic expectation, which would have influenced his role as a messianic judge, such as declaration of telling all things (4:25), unknown origin (7:27), Davidic line (7:42), and that he will remain forever (12:34). These would all be eschatological themes with which John's Jewish audience would likely have been familiar, and by the first century AD, it is likely that certain eschatological beliefs would have been highly developed. Although there were varying beliefs among the different Jewish sects, it is likely that each sect knew each other's beliefs (see Matt 22:23; Acts 23:26).[1] The beliefs that John represents of Jesus's audience are rooted in Old Testament

---

1. Chapter 5 will expound on some of the nuances between the various Jewish parties that John represents in Jesus's audience.

Scripture, but there are numerous developments and interpretations specific to early Judaism and found in early Jewish literature that would have had a greater impact on their preconceived views concerning end-times events and messianic expectations.[2] This chapter focuses solely on those early Jewish beliefs from Jewish texts concerning judgment and messianic expectation that would have influenced a first-century AD Jew above and beyond what was written in the law and the prophets. Each of the above-mentioned themes from Jesus's teachings in John will be explored, and this chapter as well as the next will reveal the beliefs that John's initial Jewish audience would have likely held concerning each theme.

The early Jewish beliefs concerning judgment and messianic expectation that this chapter will consider were developed over a span of two and a half centuries. Each text has its own set of circumstances that influenced its writing and content. Thus, each text will be looked at individually with dating and background to understand the *Sitz im Leben* and the eschatological themes surrounding judgment and messianic expectation (if present). One thing that will be observed is that by the first century AD, beliefs concerning judgment and messianic expectation are developed with much greater detail, with a conflation of the two. It will be seen that as early Jewish literature develops, God's judgment and the arrival of the messiah become intertwined, to the extent that some sources reveal a messianic figure as the one who executes God's judgment. This highly developed eschatology in early Jewish literature lends credence to the notion that John's Jewish audience would have also held similar well-developed eschatological beliefs.

One of the main themes surrounding judgment in early Jewish literature is judgment according to one's deeds.[3] Concerning the contrast of the righteous and the wicked in early Jewish apocalyptic literature, Travis says, "The righteous are those whose basic loyalty to God and his covenant is not a question, and who will therefore be acceptable to him at the final judgment. The wicked are gentiles who oppress God's people, or apostate Jews

---

2. Early Judaism or Second Temple Judaism refers to the time period from the completion of the rebuilding of the temple (516 BC) destroyed by the Babylonians to its final destruction by Rome (AD 70). Early Jewish literature refers to Jewish documents written within this time frame and will also encompass some documents composed after the destruction of the temple. These documents include, but are not limited to, canonical Scripture, the OT Apocrypha, and the OT Pseudepigrapha. For a fuller discussion on early Judaism and documents considered as early Jewish literature, see VanderKam's *Introduction to Early Judaism*.

3. See Travis, *Christ and the Judgment*, 26–52, and Yinger, *Paul, Judaism, and Judgment*, 64–142.

The Themes of Judgment and Messianic Expectation

who by the seriousness and persistence of their sins have forfeited their place in the covenant."[4] Good or evil deeds become one of the measures by which one would be considered as either righteous or wicked. John represents Jesus as using these criteria of good and evil deeds, but in a manner the Jews would not have expected (cf. John 3:19–21; 5:29).

The identity of those being judged plays a major role in judgment passages of early Jewish literature. Most early Jewish sources break people into two major categories, the righteous and the wicked. Each source will further nuance who falls into each category. In many sources, the wicked are directly identified, while there is more an assumption of the identity of the righteous. In the Gospel of John, Jesus also defines the identity of the righteous and the wicked. Understanding what John's Jewish audience thought about who were righteous will help one to better understand the impact of Jesus's words when he redefines the righteous, who will receive eternal life, and the wicked, who will be judged by the Son of Man. This chapter will not only discuss the development of Jewish thought towards God and the messiah's role in judgment, but also will show the development of the identity of the righteous and the wicked in early Judaism, which will better inform the mindset of John's Jewish audience and how they would have reacted to Jesus's teachings in John 5.

BEN SIRACH

Dating and Background

The emphasis throughout the Wisdom of Ben Sirach is on the relationship of wisdom to the Torah.[5] The author was a scribe by profession, writing in Jerusalem, most likely in 198–175 BC, just prior to the reign of Antiochus IV (175–164 BC).[6] His writings, although Jewish in nature, were influenced by Hellenistic culture that surrounded him. Sirach seeks to continue the already established Jewish wisdom tradition, but in spite of the Jewish focus, the work contains some Hellenistic influences as well. In this text, one finds hardly any mention regarding the Davidic dynasty or other kingly

---

4. Travis, *Christ and the Judgment*, 29.

5. David A. deSilva remarks on this emphasis as a guiding feature of *Sirach* (DeSilva, *Apocrypha*, 161–210).

6. Larry R. Helyer gives an original publication date of around 180 BC, due to the lack of references of the turmoil surrounding the Maccabean revolt (Helyer, *Exploring Jewish Literature*, 94).

rule, since there was foreign rule in Israel at the time. The Jewish rule that is present is the Aaronic priesthood, which is why Sirach spends a lengthy portion on it. This will factor into any potential messianic emphases of this text.

Sirach was quite influential to the Judaism of the latter portion of the Second Temple period. This text not only had an impact on other Jewish texts, but it also helped to shape the Jewish mindset in various ways.[7] John and his Jewish audience were likely familiar with the themes presented in this text. One theme that Sirach considers is judgment according to one's deeds (Sir 16:14). In the Gospel of John, Jesus will use similar language of being judged according to one's deeds (John 5:29), but his explanation of a good deed will be dramatically different from an early Jewish view of judgment according to one's deeds. This text, as well as all the others examined in this chapter, will build a case for what John's Jewish audience's mindset and beliefs may have looked like.

Judgment

The emphasis on judgment in Sirach focuses on one's present life. The judgment one receives in the afterlife is not a major theme in this text. Concerning judgment in the present life, Sirach says, "Everyone receives in accordance with his or her deeds" (Sir 16:14; cf. 16:12b; 17:23; 28:1). The view that God rewards the righteous and punishes the wicked in this lifetime reflects the prevalent view of judgment throughout early Jewish literature, and the theme, though nuanced, appears throughout the New Testament as well. One thing that will change as Jewish literature develops from this point to the time that John writes his Gospel is the nature of the deeds that are being judged and even the identity of those who are being judged. Understanding both these aspects and their development throughout two centuries of writings will be instrumental in understanding John's presentation of Jesus's words and the effect these words may have had on John's early Jewish audience.

7. DeSilva notes just how influential Sirach was on early and rabbinic Judaism. He shows how it was quoted or referenced by both the Jerusalem and Babylonian Talmuds and by many other rabbis (DeSilva, *Apocrypha*, 205–6). Collins shows that fragments of Sirach have been discovered at Qumran (2Q18). He argues extensively for the influence of wisdom on the Qumran community. Although the text of Sirach is represented by only two fragments, it is likely that the text influenced the beliefs and thinking of those at Qumran (J. Collins, *Jewish Wisdom*, 112–31).

The Themes of Judgment and Messianic Expectation

Jesus Ben Sirach was writing his wisdom literature at a time and place when Jewish persecution was not as prevalent as it would be within just a few short decades after he wrote. Although Sirach was written during a time of foreign rule, his writing was not influenced by the coming waves of violence and injustice that came with Antiochus IV's tyranny. His writings reflect a more peaceful situation and tend to be more general when talking about those whom God will judge. The language used is also not as harsh and severe, as will be seen with the texts that arise during the Antiochus IV's reign and later Roman occupation.

Sirach gives warning to the sinner in various passages (Sir 16:12b; cf. 16:14; 17:23; 28:1). He emphasizes that this sinner is also able to receive forgiveness and able to avoid the judgment toward which he is heading (5:4–7; 28:2–7).[8] Skehan and Di Lella summarize the concept of divine retribution as presented in Sirach when they say, "Keeping the commandments and fearing the Lord brought prosperity, happiness, and longevity to nation and individual believer; failure to observe the Law brought adversity, distress, and early death."[9] One must also note that this warning of judgment was directed towards national Israel and not against gentile nations, as will be the case with later Jewish literature. Sirach places the responsibility of judgeship in the hands of God himself (35:15, 22, 25).[10] He outlines how the one in the earthly office of judge ought to conduct himself (ch. 45), but there is no indication that anyone other than God himself will ultimately judge between sinner and righteous. There is no indication that God shares in eschatological judgment nor passes it to another to fulfill its requirement.

---

8. Randall A. Argall shows how Ben Sirach argues that judgment upon one's sin happens in this lifetime and, if not at this lifetime, then immediately after one's death (Argall, *First Enoch and Sirach*, 220–23).

Collins shows how Ben Sirach argues that one can obtain atonement for sin either through sacrifice or through good works (cf. Sirach 2:7–11; 5:5–7; 18:1–15; 21:1–3; J. Collins, *Jewish Wisdom*, 91).

9. Skehan and Di Lella, *Wisdom of Ben Sira*, 83.

10. Argall expands upon the divine warrior motif found in Sirach 35–36. He argues that this motif comes from the divine warrior passages from Second and Third Isaiah and that the warrior in this passage will win the battle for Israel against their foreign enemies and render vengeance upon the nations (Argall, *First Enoch and Sirach*, 211–20).

Messianic Expectation

Ben Sirach acknowledges that the promise of the kingship remains with the house of David, as he says, "Also His covenant was with David, the son of Jesse, of the tribe of Judah; the inheritance of the king is his son's alone" (Sir 47:11; cf. 45:25; 47:1–22). Concerning the division of the kingdom, he states, "Nevertheless God did not forsake His mercy, nor did He suffer any of His words to fall to the ground. He will not cut off the posterity of His chosen, nor will He destroy the offspring of them that love Him; and He will give to Jacob a remnant and to the house of David a root from him" (47:22).[11] Skehan and Di Lella recognize that these two verses are an expression of messianic hope.[12] Rogers notes that Sirach was well aware of the covenant promise made to the house of David, with an expectation that one day there would yet again be a Davidic ruler sitting on the throne of Israel.[13]

Although Sirach acknowledges the promise to David, there is still debate as to whether Jesus Ben Sirach's writings looked toward a coming messiah. The messiah is often viewed as a key figure in the eschatological age. In light of this, John J. Collins points to the fact that the only explicitly eschatological passage is the second coming of Elijah in Sir 48:10.[14] Another idea or term associated with the messiah is *anointed*, this being the term used throughout early Jewish literature to define and describe the messiah. It is also the term that causes debate among scholars as to whether a text is deemed messianic. Sirach uses the term anointed throughout the last six chapters. However, each use of anointed refers to the four main Old Testament offices that would have received an anointing as one set aside for service such as the priest (45:15, 23–26; 49:1–3; 50:1–21), judges (46:1–2), prophets (46:13, 19; 48:1–14, 17–25; 49:8–10), and kings (47:1–25; 49:4–7,

---

11. Kenneth E. Pomykala explores whether or not these passages indicate a messianic hope. His analysis and exegesis of the text leans toward the fact that Ben Sirach uses David's cultic practices to point toward the legitimacy of high priestly cultic practices, as he wants to legitimate the cultic practices of his own time (Pomykala, *Davidic Dynasty Tradition*, 131–52). Even if these passages argue for seeking legitimacy in the current cultic practices, the language used in the passages indicates there was a strong notion in Judaism that yearned for a pure Davidic monarchy. A messianic figure may not necessarily be in view, but there is every indication of a longing for a restoration of the Davidic monarchy in its original intended form.

12. Skehan and Di Lella, *Wisdom of Ben Sira*, 526–28.

13. Rogers, "Promises to David," 288–89.

14. J. Collins, *Jewish Wisdom*, 108.

The Themes of Judgment and Messianic Expectation

11–13).[15] Further, Simon the high priest is referred to using royal verbiage, but the cause of this language may be indicative of the fact that there was no Davidic king over Israel, and this was the only anointed office that held any power and authority in Jewish life at the time Sirach was writing (ch. 50).[16] Helyer notes, "Ben Sira is enamored with the priestly office and ritual. His description of Simon's officiating reads like an eyewitness account and thus affords a valuable window into temple worship in the second century B.C."[17] Thus, with relative peace at the moment of writing, it is not surprising that the high priest would be looked to for not only spiritual guidance but also kingly guidance, since he would have been the closest thing the Jews would have had concerning a national leader. This does not mean that Sirach abandons Davidic hope and the Davidic promise. In fact, he says, "But the Lord will never give up his mercy, or cause any of his works to perish; he will never blot out the descendants of his chosen one, or destroy the family line of him who loved him. So he gave a remnant to Jacob, and to David a root from his own family" (47:22). This possibly indicates that Sirach holds out hope that the Davidic kingship will one day be restored, but the remainder of the book shows that Sirach puts a greater emphasis on present leadership, the high priesthood, as opposed to future Davidic leadership.[18] Although Sirach does not purport messianic expectation, he does define the ideal person who lives righteously according to the law and

---

15. Chester notes that there is undoubtedly an upholding of the divine promise of the Davidic dynasty (ch. 47). It fades into the background as Sirach exalts the high priesthood of Simon (ch. 50) (Chester, *Messiah and Exaltation*, 331–32).

16. Dunn argues that the priestly messianic expectation found in Sirach influenced multiple branches of early Judaism, which included Maccabean Judaism and the Judaism found at Qumran. Later, he argues that the gospels do not directly make Jesus out as fulfilling a priestly messianic figure, because of his obvious non-Levitical lineage, but he does say that it is because of this expectation that the author of Hebrews argues for Jesus as a great high priest after a different priestly lineage (Dunn, "Messianic Ideas," 367–68, 373).

Lucass indicates that the emphasis in Sirach is not only the elevation of the high priest as the highest office but speaking of the priest in similar terms as God when he is emerging from the inner sanctuary (Sirach 50:5–7) (Lucass, *Concept of the Messiah*, 127).

17. Helyer, *Exploring Jewish Literature*, 100.

18. Collins notes that Sirach 49:4–5 refers to the end of the Judean royal line without any hint of future restoration (J. Collins, *Jewish Wisdom*, 108). See also Pomykala, *Davidic Dynasty Tradition*, 147. Collins further notes that Sirach likely saw the covenant with David as inferior to the covenant with Aaron, which is likely due to exaltation of and satisfaction with the "priestly theocratic regime" (J. Collins, "Messianism," 98).

lives according to God-given wisdom, which comes to have an influence on identifying the ideal messianic candidate.

Since Sirach's overall concern is how to live rightly according to the Torah, there is a greater stress on living righteously and not falling into doing wicked deeds. The anointed figure present to aid in this would be the Aaronic priesthood. Thus, the messianic figure in this text was present to aid one in gaining reward for righteousness and avoiding judgment for wicked deeds in the current lifetime.

WISDOM OF SOLOMON

Dating and Background

The Wisdom of Solomon was likely composed in Alexandria, Egypt, around the first century BC.[19] Wisdom follows a similar theme of the high place of wisdom as it was seen in Sirach. The work itself is heavily Hellenistic yet thoroughly Jewish in its theological themes. Authorial intent suggests that the author desired his readers to live upright lives that followed the law while living in a time and place that made it increasingly difficult to do so. This intent lies behind why the author spends the first six chapters dealing with living lawfully and upholding justice. These chapters also serve as a stringent reminder to the Jewish community of the judgment waiting for those that do not seek proper justice. Unlike Sirach, this work has a greater emphasis on punishment for the wicked and reward for the righteous. Sirach views punishment and reward for deeds in this lifetime, while Wisdom extends this notion of reward and punishment into the afterlife. This notion follows with other Jewish works that were written during the first century BC and first century AD.[20]

The first six chapters of this work show a contrast between the righteous and the impious or sinners and reward or punishment waiting for

---

19. DeSilva notes there is a wide debate on the dating of Wisdom. Scholars place the dating from 220 BC to AD 100. The dating does not change the overall message of this text, but it would influence the notion of when certain Jewish theological ideas came into vogue, especially concerning ideas of judgment and punishment in the afterlife. However, the language and message of this text most likely places it in the first century BC. DeSilva leans toward a date toward the beginning of the Roman domination within the first century BC, due to textual indicators that line up best with Jewish thought on early Roman occupation (DeSilva, *Introducing the Apocrypha*, 137–38).

20. Cf. Wis 5:13–16; 2 Macc 7; Jubilees 23:30–31; 4 Macc 18:23; 1 Enoch 22:9–10, 46:3–4, 51:1–10; 4 Ezra 5:31, 7:1–99; 2 Baruch 30:1–2, 50:2–3, 51:12.

The Themes of Judgment and Messianic Expectation

each group in the afterlife. Concerning the message of this text, DeSilva says, "The unknown author focuses the hearer on the judgment of God in order to demonstrate that forsaking the path of God-fearing and lawful conduct that leads to immortality means utter folly and loss."[21] The references to judgment often speak of future afterlife judgment that will come upon the wicked because of the evil deeds committed in this lifetime. The author also offers a contrasting picture of the righteous person who seeks to live uprightly in pursuit of eternal life.

Judgment

On the same note of Sirach, the judgment and identity of those being judged remains general.[22] Individuals are judged by the very sins that they have been committing (Wis 11:16; 15:18—16:1; 18:5). It seems that the author has the idea of *lex talionis* in mind concerning the nature of judgment. It is also retributive and received in this lifetime (11:9; 12:22; 16:5–14). The judgment described in Wisdom is not eschatological in nature, though the author does point toward a day of final judgment and an already determined verdict based upon deeds performed in one's lifetime (3:10, 18; 4:19–5:14).[23] The author indicates that the kings of the earth whom God has placed in positions of authority but have abused their God-given power will receive an especially harsh judgment (6:1–11). Judgment of those in high leadership positions will remain a common theme throughout early Jewish literature, especially gentile kings.[24] God is identified as the one judging the unrighteous (1:9–10; 6:3).

---

21. DeSilva, *Introducing the Apocrypha*, 131.

22. Gowan also notes that defining what the righteous life looks like is also spoken of in general terms, with no reference to it being defined by any detail (Gowan, "Wisdom," 230). This does not mean that the author does not make clear distinctions between the righteous and the wicked, but the defining features are general.

23. Reiser notes that this text represents both the Jewish notion that there will be a final day of judgment and the Greek notion of the assignment of reward and punishment that comes immediately after death (Reiser, *Jesus and Judgment*, 43–46).

Luca Mazzinghi explores the usage of "punish" and "benefit" that are juxtaposed throughout Wisdom of Solomon and concludes that these concepts are closely associated with what was waiting for the individual at the time of death based upon if he or she lived a righteous life or not (Mazzinghi, "Antithetical Pair," 237–41).

24. Cf. 1 Enoch 38:5, 46:4–5, 53:1–7, 90:30–33; 1QM 12:13f; Psalm of Solomon 17:41.

Messianic Expectation

Messianic expectation is arguably a theme that is not found in the Wisdom of Solomon. However, this does not mean that there is not a Davidic nature to this book. The book itself is being written from the perspective of Solomon. Although this book was written at a time when the Davidic monarchy was dissolved, the prayer of chapter 9 looks at the Davidic kingship as a present reality. This seems to indicate that although there was no current Davidic king, the idealistic Davidic king remained an ever-present reality. The description of the ideal righteous person in chapters 2–5 may also be an indication of an expectation for the ideal Davidic king. Although these elements are present in the text, it does not mean that this text can or should be labeled as messianic.

Although messianic development is not a focus of this text, there is a noticeable shift of when judgment was to take place, from this lifetime to sometime after death. Judgment also becomes more spelled out concerning for what one may be judged, as well as the identity of those being judged.

JUBILEES

Dating and Background

Jubilees was composed sometime between 160 and 130 BC and is a retelling of Genesis and Exodus.[25] The time period in which this text was written is significant due to the political and religious events that were taking place. This time frame saw the violence of Antiochus IV and the end of his reign of terror as he was defeated during the Maccabean rebellion, which gave birth to the Hasmonean dynasty of Jewish self-rule. Jubilees was written in an era of uncertainty and foreign oppression. VanderKam argues that this text reflects the struggles between the Jews and the Seleucids and even between the Jews that sought to maintain a pure Judaism against those who freely accepted Hellenization.[26] The author of Jubilees seems to argue against the Hellenization of Judaism. Thus, the passages concerning judgment would be highly influenced by these historical events. These passages in their context would be directed toward Jews who embraced Hellenism and against

---

25. Helyer broadens the dating from 175 BC to 100 BC, but no later than that, because of internal indicators (Helyer, *Exploring Jewish Literature*, 120–21).

26. VanderKam, *Book of Jubilees*, 139–41.

The Themes of Judgment and Messianic Expectation

the Seleucids who imposed the Hellenistic culture and violence toward the temple and toward those who sought to practice a pure Judaism. Although this is the immediate context, it is during this era that Jewish authors really started to specifically define those who would be judged, which started to include compromising Jews.

Concerning the genre of Jubilees, Docherty says, "Biblical interpretation often aims to bring a scriptural text up to date and relate it to the issues facing a contemporary audience. This goal, called actualization, is clearly in evidence in Jubilees, providing some clues to its historical setting."[27] This text serves as a rewriting of Genesis and part of Exodus, but it also serves to fill in the gaps of the text with added details and background. In a way, it serves as a commentary on the text. It is from these additions and interpretations of Genesis and Exodus that one can surmise the dating and background information but also the religious, cultural, and political leanings of the author. The book itself is considered apocalyptic, but unlike other apocalyptic works, Jubilees does not contain fantastic visions of future judgments and heavenly scenes such as 1 Enoch. However, there are thematic parallels with 1 Enoch concerning the deeds of people that lead to judgment (see Jubilees 4:16–25; cf. 1 Enoch 5:1–2; 7:20–9).[28] God's covenant relationship with Israel lies at the center of Jubilees, which lends to the view of judgment that it portrays, especially the binding of those who led God's children astray (Jubilees 10:1–2; 11:4–5; 12:20). God's judgment is seen as particularly reserved for a final day of judgment for these individuals and angelic beings.

Judgment

Throughout Jubilees, God is the one who judges (Jubilees 9:15; 16:9; 24:30, 33; 36:10), and he judges fairly and according to one's deeds (5:15–17; 21:4; 33:18). A theme of judgment is present from the very beginning of the book (1:5–29). In the first chapter, the judgment seen remains against Israel and serves more as a warning to not continue in the sins of previous generations that caused God to bring judgment upon Israel. However, there remains a hope of restoration for the elect of Israel and a hope that peace will be renewed in Israel (1:29). A prevalent event surrounding the theme of judgment in early Jewish literature is the Noahic flood and the

---

27. Docherty, *Jewish Pseudepigrapha*, 16.
28. Docherty, *Jewish Pseudepigrapha*, 17.

events leading up to it that caused this great judgment. Jubilees 5 makes brief comments on Gen 6:1–8 and interprets the sons of God as angels who took the daughters of men and bore children. It was from these offspring that sin and wickedness multiplied upon the earth (Jubilees 5:1–3).[29] God was especially angry with the angels, who were then bound in the depths of the earth until the final judgment (5:6, 10). Yinger rightly argues that the universal Noahic judgment is prototypical and acts as a model of the final judgment to come.[30] Thus, the author of Jubilees has in mind the immediate judgment of the flood, but there is also a final judgment beyond the events of the Noahic flood, still to come. Yinger continues to show how the judgment in this passage is all-inclusive (5:15) and that there will be judgment for the great according to the greatness of their deeds and for the small according to their smallness.[31] However, this passage concludes on a positive note, with salvation for those who are repentant. These will receive forgiveness and mercy at the final judgment (5:17–18).[32] Peter Enns nicely summarizes the message of salvation in Jubilees as he says:

> The author of *Jubilees*, from first to last, is concerned to emphasize God's promise to never forsake his *people*. *Israel as a people* will always remain because God is faithful. Transgression of eternal commands, however, will result in individual punishment and forfeiture of one's individual covenant status. The fact of Israel's election, however, remains sure. In fact, it is precisely the fact that God destroys individuals while maintaining the whole that demonstrates to the people that he is *faithful to the covenant*: the actions of individuals cannot affect God's purpose and plan—Israel's existence is his doing.[33]

The book of Jubilees gives an account of what an angel revealed to Moses during the forty-day period he was on the mountain.[34] Docherty notes that although Jubilees has many elements similar to other apocalypses in

---

29. 1 Enoch 7–36 expounds upon Gen 6:1–7 in great detail and the subsequent imprisonment of the angels that caused mankind to sin.

30. Yinger, *Paul, Judaism, and Judgment*, 65–66.

31. Yinger, *Paul, Judaism, and Judgment*, 66–68.

32. VanLandingham says that this passage indicates the mercy of God is only given to the righteous or the repentant, but he also says there is possibly a view that comes out of this that God's mercy is deserved because of these qualities (VanLandingham, *Judgment and Justification*, 77).

33. Enns, "Expansions of Scripture," 97.

34. Wintermute, "Jubilees," 35.

The Themes of Judgment and Messianic Expectation

the same era, it lacks extensive eschatological speculation.[35] Chapter 23 contains the lengthiest section on future judgment. This chapter represents why judgment is coming, which is because of all the evil works of man (Jubilees 23:17–18, 22). There is nothing that can save the wicked on that day of judgment (23:24). This judgment will cause many to return to a path of righteousness (23:26).[36] Even Satan will have been judged (23:29). Mercy will be shown only to those who love God (23:31). The executor of this judgment is seen to be God. Judgment against sinners is based on their evil deeds.[37] This is an eschatological judgment, but there is also an element of divine discipline, since there are those who are turned back to righteousness. Those who are saved are those who love God, and within this there is a form of righteousness.

Messianic Expectation

There is no direct indication of messianic expectation or messianic figure in Jubilees. In fact, the author points to the fact that it is the law that will bring the people back to the way of righteousness as opposed to a messianic figure in other early Jewish texts (Jubilees 23:26). Andrew Chester notes concerning this verse, "There is no messianic figure here or elsewhere in Jubilees, and the judgment and restoration are carried out by God himself, but the striking point is that observance of Torah is set as the precondition and characteristic of belonging in the new age that God brings about."[38] Although there is not a direct messianic reference in Jubilees, James VanderKam looks for messianic interpretation in this text in light of the priestly messiah of Qumran.[39] Interpreting Jubilees in light of earlier Qumran documents which leaned toward a priestly messiah causes 23:26 to make sense, in light of the fact that the priests were the ones who were

---

35. Docherty, *Jewish Pseudepigrapha*, 17.

36. Kugel indicates that this judgment is focused on the sins of the Israelites and on the Israelites not keeping the covenant of God. Thus, there is an inward focus instead of an outward focus on the gentiles or the nations being judged, as later Jewish literature will begin to indicate (Kugel, *Walk through Jubilees*, 131–32).

37. Reiser notes that although the notion of judgment according to deeds is in view, there is also in mind that God as judge is no respecter of persons, judging the small according to their small deeds and the great according to their great deeds (Reiser, *Jesus and Judgment*, 73–74).

38. Chester, *Messiah and Exaltation*, 531.

39. VanderKam, "Jubilees and the Priestly Messiah," 353–65.

supposed to be the teachers of the law. This also could possibly explain why there is not any emphasis on the Davidic monarchy. In fact, VanderKam stresses the fact that the patriarchal figure of Levi holds a greater position in Jubilees than the patriarchal figure of Judah.[40] VanderKam also makes sure that his readers understand that "it should be stressed that *Jubilees* never speaks of a messiah nor does it present Levi in an eschatological setting."[41] Further, VanderKam states, "The claim which will be presented here is not that Levi or a descendant of his is being pictured messianically in *Jubilees*. The point is that the remarkable transformation of Levi in this book reveals a prior stage in the theological evolution which culminated in the Qumran belief in a sacerdotal messiah."[42] Even though there are not direct messianic references in Jubilees, there are notions that the author was pointing his reader to the fact that the Levitical priesthood would play a role in bringing the hearts of the people back to God by means of the Torah prior to the coming final judgment of God.

1 ENOCH

The book of 1 Enoch is a compilation of five works collected into one unit over a two- to three-hundred-year time frame.[43] The completed collection of the book of 1 Enoch consists of the Book of the Watchers (chs. 1–36), the Parables of Enoch (chs. 37–71),[44] the Astronomical Book (chs. 72–82), the Book of Dreams (chs. 83–90, within which is the Animal Apocalypse [chs. 85–90]), and the Epistle of Enoch (chs. 91–108). The eschatological and messianic views espoused by each of the authors varies, some quite significantly. Therefore, each of the five books needs to be considered individually to evaluate properly the nature of judgment and messianism (if present). The book of 1 Enoch from start to finish has judgment as its theme. This judgment is usually seen as eschatological and universal (cf. 1 Enoch 10:12;

40. VanderKam, "Jubilees and the Priestly Messiah," 359.
41. VanderKam, "Jubilees and the Priestly Messiah," 359.
42. VanderKam, "Jubilees and the Priestly Messiah," 359.

43. The oldest texts date possibly as far back as the third-century BC (Book of the Watchers), and the majority of scholars place the last work (Parables of Enoch) into the late first-century BC to the early first-century AD. See the section on dating of the Parables in ch. 4 for a more detailed analysis.

44. The Parables of Enoch will not be evaluated in this chapter but will be fully evaluated in ch. 4, since it contributes significantly to the Son of Man argument that informs how Jesus utilizes the title in the Gospel of John.

16:1; 22:4, 8; 25:4; 27:2; 45:4–5; 72:1; 91:9, 15–16; 97:5; 103:8). This text sees judgment as something that happens postmortem, but there is a final day of judgment that all humankind will face, and the severity of judgment is largely based upon one's deeds (see 95:5; 100:7).[45] Although judgment is seen to be according to works, salvation is given by God through his mercy and grace (cf. 92:4–5). Other than in the Parables and a few other distinct places, one item lacking in 1 Enoch is specific judgment prophesied against specific historical figures or groups of people. One reason for this is that these first four books of 1 Enoch were composed early on in early Judaism, and thus far, only one main enemy had arisen in this period. Later judgment literature reflects judgment upon the Romans, the gentiles, Herod, the high priesthood, and other Jews whom certain Jewish sects deemed as unrighteous. The content of 1 Enoch influences the development of many of the other early Jewish writings.

The Book of the Watchers

Dating and Background

The Book of the Watchers possibly dates back as late as the third century BC.[46] The work itself does not give any indication of its provenance. Although its origin and author are unknown, it serves as an introduction to 1 Enoch as a whole and even becomes a foundational and introductory piece of Jewish literature with theological themes that echo throughout much of early Jewish literature. The Book of the Watchers paired with the Astronomical Book serve as pieces of literature that help shape Enochic Judaism, which Jackson identifies as an offshoot of early Judaism that arose at Qumran.[47] The Book of the Watchers carries with it the theme of im-

---

45. Yinger indicates that this judgment according to one's deeds falls upon both the wicked gentiles and the apostate Jews. He also argues that these judgment passages are written in order to give the righteous in Israel hope that they will eventually receive justice and vindication for the evils committed against them (Yinger, *Paul, Judaism, and Judgment*, 70–73).

46. VanderKam notes that this dating comes from the fact that the oldest copy at Qumran dates between 200 and 150 BC, meaning that the original likely dated prior to this dating, since the text itself did not originate with the Qumran community (VanderKam, *Introduction to Early Judaism*, 91).

47. David R. Jackson argues for three paradigm exemplars that define the Enochic Judaism of the Qumran sect. These paradigm exemplars are largely defined by the theological and astronomical content of the Book of the Watchers and the Astronomical Book

minent judgment, which is a prevalent theme throughout the remainder of 1 Enoch.[48] Except for the Astronomical Book, the theme of judgment pervades the entirety of the collection of 1 Enoch. This is seen from the very beginning of the book in the first chapter, where a day of tribulation is announced. This book also gives an alternative view on the origin of human sin and shows how God judged the introducers of that sin with the Noahic flood. A theme of salvation is also present in this text. The author indicates that God has not forgotten the righteous but has created separate places for different kinds of souls to receive their just reward based upon their deeds in the present life. This theme is prevalent throughout, in order to give hope to righteous Jews seeking reward in this present life. On this subject, Docherty says, "The expectation that God will soon come in judgement is expressed from the first chapter of 1 Enoch to the last, although no one systematic picture is given of this event. This theme of judgment is presented as a positive rather than a fearful message, as it is intended to console those who may be enduring suffering and oppression with the belief that something better awaits them."[49]

Judgment

The first verse of the Book of the Watchers sets the tone for not just this book but for the pervasive theme of judgment throughout all of 1 Enoch. The first verse not only announces judgment on all the enemies of God but also the salvation of the righteous.[50] In a way, 1 Enoch is written to the Jews as a message of encouragement to persevere through times of tribulation (1 Enoch 1:8).[51] God was going to judge the wicked very soon and deliver

---

(Jackson, *Enochic Judaism*).

48. Helyer notes that the Book of the Watchers looks at the origin of the problem of evil. He says that this problem goes far beyond human sin, and the BW seeks to show that there is a cosmological origin to sin, found in the angelic rebellion. The judgment announced is rooted in this angelic rebellion (Helyer, *Exploring Jewish Literature*, 84–85).

49. Docherty, *Jewish Pseudepigrapha*, 130.

50. Bauckham notes that chs. 1–5 have no exhortation to the wicked to repent but are simply an announcement of judgment with no possibility of forgiveness (Bauckham, "Apocalypses," 144).

51. Reiser notes that ch. 1 represents both a passing of sentence and forensic judgment, thus a twofold judgment on all sinners; but the righteous are excused from it (Reiser, *Jesus and Judgment*, 52–53).

The Themes of Judgment and Messianic Expectation

the righteous. If the judgment did not come in this lifetime,[52] it would definitely come in the afterlife (22:10–14), which is seen at the end of the Book of the Watchers, when the angel reveals to Enoch the separate places in the afterlife where souls are sent, depending on how they led their lives on earth (1:9; chs. 21–22).[53] This book also speaks of God himself being the one who comes with his armies from heaven to bring judgment on the earth (1:4, 6–7).[54]

The author moves from the announcement of coming judgment (chs. 1–5) to a retelling and interpretation of Gen 6:1–4 of the events that led to God bringing the first judgment upon the earth (chs. 6–11). This second section looks back on what was commanded to be judged during the Noahic flood, but also serves as a warning of the kind of judgment to come. Throughout the next several chapters, Enoch is shown the punishment that will happen to the fallen watchers and the children that they begat with the daughters of men. He is shown their place of eternal incarceration.

The Astronomical Book

Dating and Background

The Astronomical Book dates to a similar time frame as the Book of the Watchers. Unlike the Book of the Watchers, this book is the only one of the five that does not have judgment as a primary theme.[55] This book seeks to

---

52. VanLandingham notes that the Jews likely viewed the identity of the righteous as the Jewish people. The righteous Jews remain in constant contrast to the wicked throughout 1 Enoch (VanLandingham, *Judgment and Justification*, 87).

53. Reiser argues that 1 Enoch 22 shows that at the time of death, the individual will go to the place allotted him or her, based on his or her life. There will not be a time of judgment for the individual after death, because his or her fate had been determined by the time of death. This contrasts with later Jewish sources that see an initial judgment taking place at the time of death, which is usually prior to the ultimate day of judgment that takes place at the very end of time. The concept of initial judgment is also a major piece of judgment seen in John 5: Jesus presents an unexpected initial judgment, as he defines his version of initial judgment and the criteria for that judgment (Reiser, *Judgment and Jesus*, 56–57).

54. Argall argues that the divine figure in the introduction is the divine warrior figure that has its origins in Canaanite mythology and is later adapted by the Hebrew Scriptures in Second and Third Isaiah. He argues that the theophany present embodies all the major characteristics of this warrior motif (Argall, *First Enoch and Sirach*, 167–184).

55. Jackson extensively argues that one of the results of the sins depicted in the Astronomical Book, as espoused in Enochic Judaism, is that, since the cosmology is off due

give intimate knowledge of the cosmos, including the various positions of sun and moon. This book shows Enoch as one privy to such information as to how the solar calendar was set up. Interestingly, this text does not give a theological interpretation to the movements of the celestial entities and the calendar fulfillment each year. However, it does influence certain theological themes in Jubilees and Qumran literature that deal with eschatology and Judgment.

Judgment

In chapter 80, the angel Uriel reveals to Enoch that as a result of sin on the earth, rainy seasons will grow shorter (1 Enoch 80:2), plants that bear fruit will not grow at their normal time (80:3), the celestial entities will have a changed course (80:4–7), and so there will be punishment and destruction for the sinners (80:7). This is an interesting discourse, an interlude of sorts fixed between chapters on the ordering of the luminaries and how the solar calendar is supposed to be ordered. Other than this short discourse, there is no other mention of judgment, nor is there a judgment scene as there is in the rest of the books of 1 Enoch.

The Book of Dreams

Dating and Background

The Book of Dreams can be divided into two parts. The first part consists of a predictive dream had by Enoch early in his life concerning the impending flood (chs. 83–84). The second part consists of the Animal Apocalypse (chs. 85–90) that speaks to the events surrounding the tyranny of Antiochus IV Epiphanes, where each animal represents a different historical figure or entity.[56] Both dreams have judgment on the wicked as a pervasive theme. However, the Animal Apocalypse gives the vision of a messianic figure, and creation reverts back to the form God had originally intended for it.

---

to the sins of the watchers, the liturgical calendar is now off, which will ultimately be a piece that leads to God's judgment and be corrected in the final day (Jackson, *Enochic Judaism*, 139–196).

56. Helyer notes that this vision is written in the form of an allegory; if one is familiar with the historical events, it is easy to follow the allegory and what each animal represents (Helyer, *Exploring Jewish Literature*, 136).

The Themes of Judgment and Messianic Expectation

Judgment and Messianic Expectation

The first dream (chs. 83–84) consists of Enoch telling his son Methuselah the vision he has had about the coming destruction of the earth and the judgment God is going to pour out upon all of his creation. Although this vision has the great flood in mind, the author seems to be connecting this great day of judgment to a future eschatological day of judgment. For the author, this serves as a warning to his audience and is not just a look back upon the judgment God dealt to the earth in the past. This is evident from the last verse of this dream (1 Enoch 84:6), which asks God to once again bring his judgment upon the earth but also to save the righteous.

The second dream starts in a similar fashion, but the content of the dream is different, because the author is now reflecting upon biblical history as well as current events. The end of this vision reveals that the author believes that God's judgment and justice upon the wicked is imminent, and he will soon come and deliver the righteous. Chapter 90 considers current events of the author, the defeat of the Seleucids by the Jews. Halfway through the chapter, historical events are no longer considered and the author switches to his interpretation of eschatological events, which are viewed to happen soon after the events of his current day. He moves to a heavenly throne scene, where there is judgment pronounced against those who sinned against God by their actions against Israel.[57] Their punishment is to be thrown into a fiery abyss (1 Enoch 90:20–27; see also 91:9–10). The author then turns to show that all things are being made new, now that those who have done the wicked deeds have been punished (90:28–36).[58] Interestingly, the author introduces a messianic figure to the scene (90:37), but this figure remains in the background, and the author does not develop him beyond a vague introduction and a statement that this figure becomes their leader (90:38).[59] Unfortunately, this messianic-type figure introduced

---

57. Patrick A. Tiller indicates that the judgment scene here follows other Enochic angelic judgment scenes. He also notes that this scene shows a traditional Jewish judgment scenario that traces back to the book of Jeremiah (Tiller, *Commentary*, 368).

Bauckham notes that there are concrete social distinctions on the identity of the sinners in 91:19, who are identified as the powerful, rich, arrogant, unscrupulous, and oppressors of the poor. He also specifically says that they are not identified as gentiles but as Jewish apostates (Bauckham, "Apocalypses," 146).

58. Reiser notes that the final judgment scene contains various forensic elements, but there is no formal procedure (Reiser, *Jesus and Judgment*, 61).

59. Tiller notes that, contrary to the figure in Dan 7, this figure is represented as human, due to the fact that the author represents him as an animal, which follows from

by the author does not give much indication of the type of messiah that the author was expecting.[60] However, the author does give the reader a great deal of insight into what he believed about the judgment of God, those who would be judged, and the severity of the punishment. This passage also reveals that in Jewish belief, there starts to arise an association of sorts, which places the messiah as an eschatological figure in association with the final judgment. This text remains vague, but other texts such as the Parables of Enoch and the Psalm of Solomon 17 will start to develop this messianic figure further, especially as it relates to his role in the eschaton. The author reveals what he believes about those who will receive salvation and what their reward will look like. Ultimately, just like the rest of 1 Enoch thus far, this is a message that was supposed to give hope to those Israelites who had suffered under the hand of the Seleucids or other enemieswho were oppressing them. This showed the Jews that punishment of the wicked would definitely take place, even if the punishment did not take place in their lifetime. This message gave hope to the righteous Jews who were steadfast, maintained the law, and did not waver, because they believed that their deliverance was sure and their reward would be waiting for them in the end.

The Epistle of Enoch

Dating and Background

The Epistle of Enoch begins with one of its most noteworthy pieces, the Apocalypse of Weeks. The remainder of the Epistle gives various ethical exhortations, which largely deal with topics of social justice. The Apocalypse of Weeks indicates that history is broken up into ten periods called weeks. Concerning the date of composition, Docherty notes, "The seventh epoch runs from the Babylonian exile to the author's own time in the era of the Hellenizing emperor Antiochus IV Epiphanes (93.9–14). This marks the turning point of history, since it will be followed by future judgement and the extension of God's reign over the whole earth forever (91.14–17)."[61]

---

all of the other human figures being represented as animals in this apocalypse (Tiller, *Commentary*, 383–89).

60. Oegema argues that this messianic figure is likened to the figure of Michael in Dan 8–12. Although there is not much detail on this figure, the imagery would cause this angelic imagery to come to the mind of the reader (Oegema, *Anointed and His People*, 68–69).

61. Docherty, *Jewish Pseudepigrapha*, 137.

The Themes of Judgment and Messianic Expectation

This would put the date of composition probably just before the defeat of Antiochus IV Epiphanes, since judgment was still future. Concerning two of the characteristics of the apocalypse, VanderKam says, "A noteworthy feature of the apocalypse is its periodizing of history, implying that all is already predetermined in heaven, supposedly long before most of the predicted events took place. Also, the writer never mentions a resurrection before the judgment but consoles the readers with the thought of judgment on evil and a future life forever free from its influence."[62] Overall, this text keeps in form with most of the rest of the eschatological themes seen throughout the rest of 1 Enoch, which see judgment and punishment for the wicked and reward and life for the righteous.

Judgment

The Epistle of Enoch opens with a pronouncement of judgment against sin and its ultimate destruction (1 Enoch 92:5). The author also emphasizes mercy and salvation for the righteous (92:1–4), which reiterates the pattern found throughout 1 Enoch that this message is meant for the righteous to have hope and not necessarily as a warning for the wicked. This introduction leads into the Apocalypse of Weeks, which divides historical epochs into ten distinct sections, at the end of which is the tenth week, which will bring everlasting judgment (91:15). This apocalypse does not go into detail as to what this judgment will look like nor the identity of those who will receive judgment. The author's intent is to show the righteous what they should expect their reward to look like. The rest of the Epistle of Enoch acts as a guide to show the unrighteous person the things for which he will receive judgment through a series of woes. This section also sees a contrast with the righteous, who are admonished to stand firm and to continue in their righteousness, because an eternal reward awaits them.

2 MACCABEES

Dating and Background

The book of 2 Maccabees focuses on the events and matters surrounding Judas Maccabeus, as opposed to 1 Maccabees, which records the events of several members of the early Hasmonean dynasty. This book records

---

62. VanderKam, *Introduction to Early Judaism*, 104.

the events from the ascent of Antiochus IV Epiphanes (175 BC) to Judas Maccabeus's victory over general Nicanor (161 BC). The intent of this book is recorded in the first three chapters, as the author seeks to get the Jews in Egypt to embrace the festival of Hanukkah.[63] As opposed to 1 Maccabees, 2 Maccabees gives more concerning the theological interpretation of events that are outlined in 1 Maccabees, as well as more detailed accounts of the persecution and martyrdom experienced by the Jews under the tyranny of the Seleucids. Despite the brevity of this text, it gives helpful insights into the theological mindset of the common Jew during this part of the Second Temple period, especially regarding matters of the afterlife, reward for the righteous, and punishment for the wicked (see ch. 7). Second Maccabees brings out the persecution that came upon the righteous. Since it seemed like the righteous were not receiving their reward in this lifetime, an eschatological view of reward and punishment begins to develop. The author sees the soul itself as immortal, and there is immediate reward for the righteous after death. Second Maccabees 7 tells the story of a righteous family who was martyred, with one of them confessing his hope that he will be resurrected one day because of his righteousness. Doran notes that the author of 2 Maccabees is trying to draw a contrast between those who are martyred—the brothers who are righteous for keeping God's law—and the king, who is wicked and opposes God.[64] God will raise these martyrs to eternal life with a future resurrection, and the king will receive eternal punishment.

Judgment

Second Maccabees gives the reader two aspects of judgment that God will bring about upon the wicked. The first form of judgment is in the form of *lex talionis*, where the sins that the individual committed will be the same things with which the person will be punished. Thus, this form of judgment is something received in this lifetime (see 2 Macc 4:38; 5:9–10; 9:5–12; 13:8). An example of this is found in 9:5–12, when it is reported that Antiochus Epiphanes is struck with a severe intestinal disease. The author says the reason for this affliction was because "he had tortured the bowels of

---

63. Helyer notes that the emphasis in 2 Macc is on the topic of a belief in divine intervention which includes the miraculous and supernatural (Helyer, *Exploring Jewish Literature*, 161).

64. Doran, *Second Maccabees*, 156–7.

others with many and strange inflictions" (9:6). The author's reasoning is that now God was torturing Antiochus in a nature similar to which he had tortured many of the Jews.

The second form of judgment is actually spoken by the seven brothers being martyred in 2 Macc 7. The words of the seven brothers and their mother give the reader much insight to what the common Jews believed about judgment and salvation in the afterlife. The brothers and their mother hold fast to their beliefs that they will be saved, have renewed life, and a resurrected body, as long as they not break the laws of God. On the other hand, they boldly tell Antiochus the misfortune and judgment awaiting him from God. The fourth brother tells him that there will be no resurrection to life for Antiochus (7:14). The fifth brother speaks of the torture waiting for Antiochus and his descendants (7:17).[65] The sixth brother tells him that he will not go unpunished (7:19). The seventh brother has the most to say about the coming judgment upon Antiochus, as he boldly says, "You have not yet escaped the judgment of the almighty, all-seeing God. For our brothers after enduring a brief suffering have drunk of ever-flowing life, under God's covenant; but you, by the judgment of God, will receive just punishment for your arrogance" (7:35–36).[66] Although it can be argued that this can refer to judgment in this lifetime, the overall emphasis leans towards an afterlife, with eschatological judgment in view. This passage gives one insight into what the common Jews of the time period would have believed concerning judgment and punishment in the afterlife.

SIBYLLINE ORACLES

Dating and Background

The Sibylline Oracles are a collection of Jewish, Christian, and other sources whose composition spans several hundred years, with the earliest one composed as early as the second century BC. The Oracles were viewed as

---

65. Bartlett indicates that this torment is seen in how Antiochus IV's death is described in ch. 9. He also indicates the death that his children died: his son was murdered by the supporters of Demetrius (14:2; cf. 1 Macc 7:4), his alleged son Alexander Balas was beheaded (1 Macc 11:17), and Alexander's son was killed by Trypho (1 Macc 11:39–40; 13:31) (Bartlett, *First and Second Books*, 272–73).

66. VanLandingham notes that the postmortem judgment described here indicates whether one's verdict is resurrection to eternal life or annihilation, as opposed to a conscious, eternal punishment (VanLandingham, *Judgment and Justification*, 137).

prophetic in nature and typically thought to be the utterances of an older woman who had prestige. The overall messages in the Oracles lean toward gloom and judgment. Docherty notes, "Their ongoing relevance was secured by the ease with which the often vague or opaque sayings could be reworked or added to in different circumstances."[67] For purposes of this study, only Oracle 3 will be considered, because it is the only one that can be definitively dated before the composition of the Gospel of John. This oracle has both Greek and Jewish elements and follows the typical pattern of other pagan oracles of the era, predicting disaster, followed by a change in the world. Concerning the reason that Jews in Egypt adopted this pagan form of writing, Docherty again notes, "Jews, especially those living in Egypt, adopted the sibylline genre in order to provide a sense of authority and antiquity for their history and religion. They made important adaptations to the form, however, placing more emphasis on ethical teaching and eschatological expectation, and weaving in scriptural allusions."[68] The contents of Oracle 3 reflect much of the theological themes that were popular in early Judaism. The sibylline oracle was another avenue for the Jews to express their thoughts about the conditions of their current situation in a somewhat enigmatic, way without drawing direct attention from those against whom the oracles were spoken.

Judgment

Collins notes the sporadic nature of these oracles with an overall theme of woe and disaster being proclaimed.[69] In the Sibylline Oracles, a few different aspects of judgment are represented. One of them is the idea of imminent or impending judgment, which takes an earthly form and has the ring of an Old Testament judgment against the nations.[70] Docherty says, "One of the most characteristic features of the sibylline genre is the frequent announcement of impending judgement and disaster for specific people or cities (e.g., 3.205–10, 300–80, 493–544; 5.54–135, 160–213, 287–359,

---

67. Docherty, *Jewish Pseudepigrapha*, 79.
68. Docherty, *Jewish Pseudepigrapha*, 79.
69. J. Collins, "Sibylline Oracles," 317–20.
70. Bauckham notes that there is a more universalistic scope to the judgment of God in this oracle. Both Jews and gentiles will be held accountable under the same standards and punished under the same law of God (Bauckham, "Apocalypses," 186–87).

The Themes of Judgment and Messianic Expectation

434–46)."[71] There is also the theme of future or eschatological judgment. Oracle 3 is especially striking and reflects a great deal concerning messianic expectation and how the coming eschatological king will come and reign and judge (3:652–656).[72] There is also a notion that God will judge the earth (3:741–43) and establish a righteous kingdom on earth, where God is ultimately the king over all (3:767–808).[73] From these oracles, one has a sense of imminent judgment and even an eschatological judgment. It is likely that the author sees the imminent earthly judgment as an immediate precursor to the eschatological day of judgment that God will bring just prior to setting up an eternal kingdom on earth. The purveyor of that judgment overall is God, and there is a sense that the king sent by God will perform the earthly portion of the final judgment. Although judgment is a major theme of Oracle 3, this oracle, along with the theme found in the Jewish literature surveyed to this point, serves as encouragement for the righteous that God will judge their enemies and save the elect (3:702–31).

Messianic Expectation

The passage concerning messianic expectation that scholars point to is Oracle 3:652–56, where it is said that "God will send a king from the sun" (v. 652). This is typically linked historically to Ptolemy VI Philometor, who reigned over Egypt from 163 to 145 BC. Concerning a Ptolemaic king as a messianic figure, VanderKam says, "It may seem strange that a Ptolemaic king would be hailed in what appear to be quasi-messianic terms, but the third sibylline oracle is a good reminder of what at least some Jews may have understood a messianic leader to be: a human king who would effect God's will in the perilous and frightening times of the author."[74] Docherty notes, "It would indeed be a significant theological development for a

---

71. Docherty, *Jewish Pseudepigrapha*, 82.

72. Reiser indicates that the judgment oracles follow Isa 65–66 and Ezek 38–39. He says that in Isa 65–66, the emphasis of judgment makes a distinction between Israelites; but in the Oracles, the distinction is between Israel and the nations, in which the nations are judged and Israel is seen as righteous (Reiser, *Jesus and Judgment*, 100).

73. Oegema does a side by side comparison of 3:767–808 with Isa 11:1–12 and argues for the messianic nature of this passage, based on the fact that Isa 11 is typically classified as messianic. The author of the Oracles 3 uses Isa 11 allegorically for his own interpretive purposes to match his current historical context (Oegema, *Anointed and His People*, 83–85).

74. VanderKam, *Introduction to Early Judaism*, 109.

Jewish author to hail a gentile ruler as a divinely sent savior."[75] Although it is not typical, it is not unheard of in Judaism for a gentile king to be seen as a messianic deliver of sorts or considered as God's anointed. The Persian king Cyrus is referred to as the Lord's anointed in Isa 45:1, as the king to decree that the Jews were allowed to return home from exile and rebuild the temple in Jerusalem (cf. 2 Chr 36:22–23; Ezra 1:1–11; 6:3). The Jews were not lacking in enemies, and they did not have a nation or king of their own during this time frame. It should not be unexpected that a powerless people would look to a powerful king, who viewed them favorably, to be sent by God to deliver them from their enemies. The interesting part of this passage is that this gentile king is the one being used by God to usher in the final judgment and eschatological kingdom, as opposed to a Davidic king or messiah.

TESTAMENT OR ASSUMPTION OF MOSES

Dating and Background

The Testament of Moses follows along testament genre and records a pseudepigraphal account of the final words of Moses. Historical indicators within the text help to place the date of authorship, such as clear allusions to the reign of Herod the Great and possible references to the temple prior to its destruction in AD 70, thus an early first-century AD authorship. The work itself is a very short document that gives snippets of prior historical events, which give the reader a notion of what the Jewish author was feeling theologically and politically at the time of composition. Although this text falls into the testament genre, there are apocalyptic elements, which consist of divisions of history and an eschatological scene in chapter 10 that has God saving his covenant people Israel and delivering them from all of their enemies. Although this work is short, it represents much of the frustration that the Jews had with various enemies during this era and their hope for swift deliverance and judgment on all their enemies.[76]

---

75. Docherty, *Jewish Pseudepigrapha*, 83.

76. Helyer notes that this document comes from a pietistic group, who believed that it was important to follow the Mosaic law at all cost, as opposed to a violent defense of one's faith. Thus, this document emphasizes a rejection of militant nationalism (Helyer, *Exploring Jewish Literature*, 142–43). See also J. Collins, "Date and Provenance," 32.

The Themes of Judgment and Messianic Expectation

Judgment

Chapter 10 provides the reader with an eschatological judgment scene that follows with what other Jewish literature has witnessed up to this point.[77] Since this is likely a first-century AD document, it gives a clearer glimpse of eschatological thought present at the time that Jesus gave his teachings concerning the nature of judgment and his role as judge. There remains a similar pattern of the judgment of the wicked and salvation for the righteous. The judgment of God will be upon the devil (Testament of Moses 10:1) and the nations and enemies of God (10:2, 7). Even the earth and the heavens will be affected by this judgment (10:4–6).[78] The nation of Israel is the one named as the nation that God will raise up and save (10:7–9). Verse 2 indicates an elevated angelic figure.[79] There is not much indication as to the role of this figure, except that God will be a part of the final judgment. Verse 7 then shows God appearing as judge. The appearance of the figure in verse 2 possibly indicates a Jewish belief that there would be a vice-regent of sorts aiding God or receiving from God the right to judge a portion of or possibly all of creation. In its brevity, the Testament of Moses gives light to what the Jews in first-century Israel would have expected concerning the final judgment. This text indicates that the Jews believed that this judgment on all of their enemies was imminent, which is seen by the fact that the judgment scene of chapter 10 immediately follows the historical events of chapters 6 and 7, which are likely speaking of the reigns of Herod the Great and his sons, most likely the events that had just happened in the life of the original author. This time period witnessed both the height of the expectation of the final judgment and the height of messianic expectation, themes that began to intertwine with each other, as will be witnessed in the Psalms of Solomon, various documents at Qumran, and the Parables of Enoch.

---

77. Kugler notes that this text is quite deterministic in its outlook, with a severe division between the righteous and the wicked. This text also indicates that one will be terminally punished for failure to maintain the covenant relationship with God. He goes even so far as to say that this text indicates that one could unelect oneself by a failure to keep the law (Kugler, "Testaments," 195–97).

78. G. Anthony Keddie argues that though the gentile nations are included in judgment, the priestly ruling class of Israel are the primary recipients of judgment in the Testament of Moses (Keddie, "Judaean Apocalypticism," 301–38).

79. Reiser argues that this figure is similar to Melchizedek, found in 11QMelch, or even the angel Michael (Reiser, *Jesus and Judgment*, 86).

Chester argues that this figure is likely Michael, who is given a militant role (Chester, *Messiah and Exaltation*, 376).

PSALMS OF SOLOMON

Dating and Background

The Psalms of Solomon date to the late first century BC, with a completed compilation no later than the early first century AD.[80] The work itself has clear references to Pompey, which aid in dating. This Roman occupation also helps one understand the Jewish mindset behind the Psalms and why there a militant messiah is presented in Psalm 17. The Psalms have a heavy Davidic messianic theme that focuses on judgment and deliverance. Beyond the fact of Roman oppression present in the Psalms, Docherty notes that Hasmoneans were also in view of those who were going to be judged: "The community of devout Jews behind these poems were vehemently opposed to the Israelite rulers of the time, the Hasmonaeans, regarding them as corrupt, violators of the Temple cult, and illegitimate because they were not descended from the line of David."[81] The theological position that they take would have been on the minds of John's Jewish audience, especially the claim John presents in Jesus's teachings concerning his messiahship.

The Psalms speak against both Roman occupation and Hasmonean rule, often directing comments toward specific leaders.[82] The comments in the Psalms reflect an opposition to religious leaders and certain temple conduct. Docherty points out that the views expressed in the Psalms are very closely linked to the views of those at Qumran concerning apostasy in leadership. It is a possibility that the authors may have been from this community.[83] Regardless of the authorship, the content of the Psalms suggests that there was mounting messianic and eschatological expectation for a Davidic deliverer to come and make right the perversions that were happening in the leadership both politically and religiously. Part of the understanding built into the messianic figure portrayed is that this Davidic messiah would be an instrument of judgment. In fact, the psalmist goes so far as to say that the judgment is coming as punishment because of the many sins of

---

80. This dating comes from a series to references to specific historic events in Pss 2, 8, and 17 that take place between 80 and 30 BC.

81. Docherty, *Jewish Pseudepigrapha*, 69–70.

82. Trafton identifies the sinners in Psalm of Solomon 17 as referring to the Hasmoneans (Trafton, "What Would David Do?," 162).

83. Docherty, *Jewish Pseudepigrapha*, 74. Reiser puts this work as a Pharisaic composition that was originally written in Hebrew and later translated into Greek (Reiser, *Jesus and Judgment*, 47).

The Themes of Judgment and Messianic Expectation

the leadership, such as sexual immorality, hypocrisy, arrogance, excessive wealth, lying and slander (Psalm of Solomon 1:4–8; 2:11–13; 4:1–5; 5:16; 8:9–12; 12:1–3). Thus, part of messianic expectation was for the messiah to judge the unrighteous for the sins committed. In the Psalms, the Davidic messiah is God's instrument in judgment, as opposed to the one given all authority by God to judge, as the Parables of Enoch indicates. However, this points to a growing expectation of what was expected by John's Jewish audience, as John makes certain messianic claims about Jesus.

The Psalms also speak to the salvation and protective care of the righteous (Psalm of Solomon 2:35–6; 4:25; 5:15; 6:6; 10:6–8; 11:1; 13:12; 14:10).[84] As has been seen in previous texts, this juxtaposition of righteousness and judgment is a significant piece of many judgment passages not only in the Psalms but in most early Jewish literature.[85] This juxtaposition of the salvation of the righteous and the punishment of the unrighteous is a prominent feature in the Psalms and also plays into the views of Jesus's audience represented in the Gospel of John. Part of John's Jewish audience likely consisted of the religious elite, who would have seen themselves as the righteous who were under God's protection of judgment.[86] However, John shows that Jesus radically redefines judgment and salvation in a way quite different from what people expected the messiah to teach. The Psalms not only provide necessary information concerning the messianic expectation of John's Jewish audience, but also insight into his audience's view of who will be saved and who will be judged. Both of these notions are key features in understanding Jesus's teachings in the Gospel of John to the fullest.

---

84. Reiser brings out the fact that the Psalms have an emphasis on the contrast between the punishment of the wicked and the reward received by the righteous at the day of the Lord. He also brings out that the contrast in the Psalms goes beyond a general contrast between righteous and wicked but further identifies Israel and the nations as those righteous and wicked (Reiser, *Jesus and Judgment*, 47–50).

85. Falk notes that the language of righteousness in the Psalms is not concerned with saving activity but is almost exclusively associated with judgment: in God's judgments are found his righteousness (Falk, "Psalms and Prayers," 39–44).

86. VanLandingham notes that the Psalms indicate that those who are seen as wicked may also include those who are outside a certain sect of Judaism and not necessarily be based upon one's deeds, though that is a major piece of how one is judged (VanLandingham, *Judgment and Justification*, 138–39).

Judgment

Chapter 2 contains a judgment scene that pronounces judgment on the nations that took part in oppressing Israel (esp. Psalm of Solomon 2:34–41). The author spends the majority of the chapter calling out the nations and the kings of those nations for the atrocities that they brought against his people, against Jerusalem, and against his holy temple (2:2–11, 13–14, 20, 25–28). The author also identifies that judgment is upon the people according to their deeds (2:17). In 2:17, he has both the previous sins of Israel in mind, which brought the judgment of God upon the Israelites through the means of other nations, and the deeds of the nations for going too far in the God-ordained punishment against the Israelites in their arrogance.[87] Thus, the psalmist argues that the wrath and judgment of God against these nations because of their arrogance will be much more severe and will have eternal ramifications (2:35, 39). This psalm identifies God as the true righteous king who will come down and execute judgment and wrath upon all of his enemies and the enemies of Israel (2:36). Ultimately, the psalm is written to give hope of salvation to the righteous, who will receive an eternal reward (2:37–41).[88]

The theme of God's judgment pervades much of this short psalter, with a striking messianic emphasis in the last two psalms (Psalms of Solomon 17–18). Wright notes that the reason for such a strong message of judgment is because it is "a response of devout Jews to the capture of Jerusalem by the Romans in the first century B.C."[89] There is a clear concern about the fate of the righteous and the sinners at the time of final judgment.[90] Chapter 17 represents the tangible way in which the nations will be placed in submission and ruled over by the messiah for eternity. Entailed in this would be a form of earthly judgment. DeSilva notes that the messiah will purge the sinful from the land, which entails the ability to judge what is considered

---

87. Yinger notes that the judgment on Israel is much more than just corrective bun-punitive in its force (Yinger, *Paul, Judaism, and Judgment*, 75–76).

88. Yinger indicates that the reward for the righteous is not necessarily automatic. The Psalms of Solomon present those who accept God's discipline and punishment and correct their ways as those who will receive God's mercy and the reward of eternal life. On the other hand, those who despise God's discipline will receive his wrath and eternal destruction (Yinger, *Paul, Judaism, and Judgment*, 73–74).

89. Wright, "Psalms of Solomon," 639.

90. Reiser emphasizes the concept of reward for the righteous and punishment for sinners in his discussion on judgment as seen throughout the Psalms (Reiser, *Jesus and Judgment*, 47–50).

sinful.[91] However, the place of ultimate judgment of the righteous and wicked remains in the hands of God in the last day. Docherty notes that one of the themes concerning judgment is a present punishment from God for sins, but there is also a theme of God's mercy.[92] There is an aspect of divine separation of the righteous and the wicked at the final judgment, where the righteous look forward to eternal life (3:12; 14:10) and the wicked face destruction in Hades (3:11; 12:6; 14:9; 15:10). The messiah is not in this heavenly realm, but the author of the Psalms sees him as an immediate solution to their current circumstances with their new gentile oppressors.

Messianic Expectation

Nearly two hundred years after Ben Sirach wrote, the expectation of the coming of a Davidic figure changed drastically. Ben Sirach wrote at a time when foreign occupation had been a reality for a few centuries, but oppression of the foreign power was not severe. The severity of the oppression changed drastically soon after his death and became a present reality in much of the Jewish literature from the time of Antiochus IV Epiphanes. The Psalms now have a new oppressor in view, which sparks the author to write in much more detail regarding a Davidic messiah who would deliver Israel and judge this foreign power.[93] Thus, Psalm of Solomon 17 intertwines the judgment of God with a heavy messianic emphasis upon one from the house of David coming to deliver the Jews from the oppressive gentiles.[94] Joseph Trafton cannot emphasize the importance of Psalm of

---

91. DeSilva, *Jewish Teachers of Jesus*, 151.

92. Docherty, *Jewish Pseudepigrapha*, 74–75.

93. Benedikt Eckhardt looks at the Psalms as an important historical source of information for Second Temple Judaism, especially the late Hasmonean period (Eckhardt, "Psalms of Solomon," 7–30). Eckhardt says that the Psalms do not reflect Pompey's campaign because of the retrospective language used concerning God's justice in the condemnation of the Jews (Eckhardt, "Psalms of Solomon," 24). He concludes that the Psalms "do not represent the theocratic zeal of the Jewish populace, but a small group of Jews alienated from the great majority (Eckhardt, "Psalms of Solomon," 25).

94. Pomykala puts the dating of this psalm between 61 and 57 BC, which would make it at the time of Pompey's capture of Jerusalem and the waning of the Hasmonean dynasty (Pomykala, *Davidic Dynasty Tradition*, 159).

Reiser notes that Ps 17 represents one of the first instances in Jewish literature that someone other than God himself partakes in the final judgment. This text, paired with the Parables, which Reiser says was likely written about the same time, gives merit to the idea that there was a growing messianic expectation in the first century BC that the

Solomon 17 enough, as he says, "Ps. Sol. 17 remains the longest, continuous description of the Messiah that we possess from pre-Christian Judaism."[95] Reiser shows how the messiah described in the Psalms closely resembles the description of the messianic figure in the Parables of Enoch, which is to be expected because of the similar time frame in which they were being written.[96] Although the two documents contain opposite views of a messianic type, they both have similar judgment themes that mirror the Jewish mindset of the day concerning the judgment of the wicked and salvation of the righteous. Political turmoil would be one of the key motivating factors for the authoring of this psalm.[97]

This psalm has from the very beginning a cry for a deliverer (v. 3).[98] The plea is for God to come and deliver them. Verse 5 looks back to the original Davidic covenant, showing that God specifically chose David to rule over Israel and to always have a descendant on the throne. Zacharias notes that this is the first time David is mentioned in the whole corpus.[99] A push for a Davidic dynasty is likely expressed in the light of the fact that the Hasmonean dynasty had no legitimate Davidic claim to the throne. There is a longing for the restoration of the Davidic monarchy and for a Davidic

---

messiah would have some sort of day of judgment responsibilities handed to him from God (Reiser, *Jesus and Judgment*, 50).

95. Trafton, "What Would David Do?," 157–58. Trafton notes that the section in the temple scroll concerning the king (11Q19 LVI, 12–LIX, 21) which is the longest section on kingship, is in no sense messianic (Trafton, "What Would David Do?," fn10, 158). In his essay, Trafton highlights the main verbs used in Ps 17. He considers expectations, extended expectations, and surprises in light of what messianic passages in the OT say concerning expectation of David as king and the Davidic kingship. The surprise expectations are those not supported in the OT, such as the cleansing of Jerusalem (vv. 22, 30), the gathering of the holy people (v. 26), distributing the Jews upon the land (v. 28), the disciplining of the house of Israel (v. 42), judging Israel in the Ssynagogues (v. 43), showing mercy upon the nations (v. 43), and engaging in hostile actions against his enemies (vv. 22–25, 36) (Trafton, "What Would David Do?," 166–71).

96. Reiser, *Jesus and Judgment*, 50. On the other hand, Chester argues that, although idealized, this messiah is in no sense otherworldly (Chester, *Messiah and Exaltation*, 342).

97. Pomykala points past a Pharisaic authorship and argues for an Essenic authorship, since much of the language in the psalm mirrors language used in the documents at Qumran (Pomykala, *Davidic Dynasty Tradition*, 159–60).

98. Pomykala notes that this psalm is a communal lament or complaint, meaning that this was a grievance expressed by many, not just by a select few or the author (Pomykala, *Davidic Dynasty Tradition*, 160).

99. Zacharias, *Raise Up to Them*, 18.

The Themes of Judgment and Messianic Expectation

king to be raised up to bring judgment upon all the enemies of God. This idea is most clearly expressed in verse 21 as the author says, "See, Lord, and raise up for them their king, the Son of David, to rule over your servant Israel in the time known to you, O God."[100] The author acknowledges some of the blame for the loss of the Davidic monarchy (v. 6) but puts most of the blame for the lack of a current Davidic monarchy on foreign oppressors (vv. 6–15). Zacharias notes, "Those who have not been promised anything have set up their own royal house in direct contrast to the [kingdom] of David and his descendants."[101] Verse 23 beseeches God to raise up a king for Israel. The psalmist uses the phrase the son of David to describe this one to be raised up. Verse 24 shows why there is a need for this Davidic king, which is to "shatter unrighteous rulers." The ruler over Israel during the time that this was written was Rome and possibly the Herods, who were seen as unrighteous and illegitimate rulers.

Verses 25–49 then consider the actions and characteristics this ruler will have. The significance of this psalm is that it is one of the most explicit explanations of the Davidic messiah in all Jewish literature written prior to the coming of Jesus. In verse 25, the first thing that this ruler will do is purge Jerusalem of unrighteous rulers. Zacharias notes that the rulers here are the illegitimate rulers, who are contrasted with the legitimate Davidic ruler.[102] This is not surprising, since by the writing of this psalm, there had been all kinds of unrighteous rulers over Jerusalem. It is likely that the current rulers in Jerusalem are those to whom the psalmist is referring, but one cannot help but see allusions to previous unrighteous rulers such as Antiochus Epiphanes and even the Hasmoneans, who ended their reign in unrighteousness. Most likely the author has the Herods and the Romans in mind in the current context. The psalmist has already spoken on the fact that the only ruler who can legitimately rule in Jerusalem is from the line of David, and he looks forward to when that will be a reality once again.

Verse 26 shows that this ruler will reign with wisdom and righteousness. With these two characteristics, he will rightly rule the kingdom and execute necessary justice. The psalmist also makes mention of a rod of iron, which likely refers to Ps 2, a messianic psalm. Davenport notes, "The

---

100. Pomykala notes that the phrase Son of David likely refers to messianic expectation. He later shows that this Son of David is pictured in an idealized and superhuman way (Pomykala, *Davidic Dynasty Tradition*, 162–70).

101. Zacharias, *Raise Up to Them*, 19.

102. Zacharias, *Raise Up to Them*, 25.

psalmist has modified the content of Psalm 2:9 so that now it is not the nations that are to be broken, with a rod of iron, but sinners."[103] Zacharias makes a notable point: "The actions of the Messiah towards the sinful leaders of Israel are not life-threatening, it is only their pride that he smashes."[104] The idea of the messiah ruling with an iron rod is also repeated in Revelation, referring to how Jesus will deal with the unruly nations (Rev 2:27; 12:5; 19:15). The rod itself is a symbol of how the messiah will rule and not a symbol of war against his enemies. Each reference shows how a messianic figure will deal with the ungodly nations and eventually bring them into submission. Verse 28 talks about how he will "gather together a holy people," which likely has implications of gathering the diaspora Jews who had been scattered all over the world. The Jews saw themselves as reigning and ruling with the messiah in the future kingdom in Jerusalem. Verse 30 has the king redistributing the Jews in their rightful plots of land after they have all been gathered together. The emphasis in this psalm is what it has been for the Jews since entrance in the land, which is a long life in that land as their reward for righteous living. The unrighteous are expelled from the land. The kingdom set up by this king is described as present and physical. The view presented by the psalmist looks to a restoration of Israel to how it was formerly in days of old, under the original reigns of David and Solomon, but without any form of unrighteousness. In a way, he is describing the kingdom in the ideal way in which Moses described the kingdom in Deuteronomy, as long as the people remained without sin. He is presenting a king who is without sin and who will completely abolish unrighteousness to set up the kingdom that God intended all along.

Verse 41 sees this messiah-king as one without sin, which makes him the prime candidate to be able to rule in righteousness and in wisdom.[105] Zacharias notes, "As a representative of YHWH this righteous state makes sense, and in light of the perception that the spiritual status of the king reflects the spiritual status of Israel, this sinlessness also makes sense because the Jews are now a holy people."[106] The rest of this section then describes more in depth the righteousness and wisdom of this king. He is thus the

---

103. Davenport, "Anointed of the Lord," 73.

104. Zacharias, *Raise Up to Them*, 26.

105. Grindheim specifically points out that this messianic figure is understood as completely human. There are not divine qualities ascribed, like other messianic texts. Being sinless just means that he is a unique human being (Grindheim, *God's Equal*, 136–37).

106. Zacharias, *Raise Up to Them*, 38.

The Themes of Judgment and Messianic Expectation

ideal figure to reign not only over the house of Israel but also over the rest of the nations. He is the one who will fully acknowledge God as his King and follow his Sovereign's will fully and completely and cause others to do the same.

This psalm presents what the ideal king in Israel should have looked like from the beginning. This will be the one future king who will reign and rule on earth from Jerusalem and bring everything into subjection under his feet. This view of the messiah was likely something that the author may have expected in his own lifetime or something that was about to happen shortly after. The mindset was that the messiah's coming was imminent and would be something that would take over with a great military force. In fact, this psalm may have been in the minds of the people in AD 132–35 as Bar Kokhba led a revolt against Rome. A strong military leader is what the Jews were looking for, so they could expel the Romans from them and once again rule themselves in the manner they believed God wanted.

CONCLUSION

The theme of judgment is central to early Jewish literature. Judgment according to one's deeds is a common theme seen throughout early Judaism. It reappears in the Gospel of John as Jesus speaks to what deeds merit one judgment or eternal life. There is also a notion of *lex talionis* in some of the earlier works such as Sirach and 2 Maccabees, where those who do wicked deeds receive an earthly punishment in a form similar to the wicked deeds they performed in their lifetime. However, it also seems that later literature partially abandoned this notion, because there were those who did evil deeds who did not receive punishment in their current lifetime. Thus, early Jewish literature transitions into punishment and reward being received after death and/or at the final resurrection and/or day of the Lord. The punishment received by the wicked upon death or the final judgment is seen to be predetermined, with no way out of what the individual will justly receive. The recipients of this punishment are most clearly seen to be received by the mighty, rulers, and kings who have abused their power and reached beyond their God-given authority. There is also designation for apostate Jews and those outside a certain community or sect, such as what will be seen in the following chapter, where certain Qumran texts will be considered concerning these topics. Another group that was not considered in depth were the angelic beings who forsook God, procreated with the daughters of men, and revealed heavenly knowledge to mankind. Several sources allow for the wicked to receive mercy in judgment if they repent in their current lifetime. Reward at death or the final judgment is received by those who maintain the covenant or those who are within a certain community or sect. Good deeds are important, but reward and receipt of eternal life is based upon God's mercy. The texts above have the main purpose of encouragement for the righteous who were not seeing their reward in their present lifetime. These texts encouraged them to persevere, because they would eventually receive their reward at their death or the final resurrection. The texts also encouraged them that the wicked would ultimately be punished for the evils they were committing against God's people.

Other than later documents such as the Psalms of Solomon, the Parables of Enoch, and various Qumran documents, messianic expectation is not highly developed, nor is it central to most early Jewish documents. However, this does not mean that it is not present. One aspect of messianic expectation that runs throughout is that the messiah was an eschatological figure who would appear at or just prior to the final judgment. Thus, there was a close association with the messiah and the final judgment. Davidic hope is also a common thread in Sirach, the Psalms of Solomon, and various Qumran documents. The Psalm of Solomon 17 is the most highly developed text concerning early Jewish Davidic messianic expectation that predates Jesus's ministry. This figure is a physical deliverer who acts as a warrior to deliver Israel and set up God's kingdom on earth. The Qumran documents reveal that there is a possible expectation of two messiahs, one kingly and one priestly. However, later Qumran documents point toward a Davidic or an exalted heavenly messianic figure. A servant of the Lord motif from Isaiah is also alluded to throughout early Jewish literature and is directly associated with the messianic figure in those texts.

Judgment was a major aspect of what John's Jewish audience expected with the coming of the messiah in one form or another. Jesus's teachings about his role as judge and the righteous and the wicked being judged according to deeds were not foreign concepts in early Jewish messianic expectation. Jesus teaches on reward and punishment, as well as the final resurrection of the dead. These are all eschatological themes and topics on which John's Jewish audience had well developed views. However, Jesus redefines the common Jewish belief of the expectation of a messianic judge who would receive judgment and who would receive eternal life. Chapters

The Themes of Judgment and Messianic Expectation

5 through 7 will reveal just how unexpected Jesus's teachings about himself as the eschatological messianic judge are to John's Jewish audience. Another teaching unexpected by John's Jewish audience is who Jesus says will receive judgment and the identity of those who will be rewarded with eternal life. Chapter 7 will especially reveal just how shocking Jesus's words concerning judgment are for an early Jewish audience, which lies in contrast with what has been observed thus far.

3

The Themes of Judgment and Messianic Expectation at Qumran

INTRODUCTION

THE PREVIOUS CHAPTER INVESTIGATED the themes surrounding messianic expectation and judgment throughout key early Jewish documents. Whether or not John's Jewish audience was familiar with each of the documents, the in-depth analysis of the Gospel of John in chapters 5 through 7 will reveal that John assumed his Jewish audience was, at the least, familiar with the themes within them. These themes also show up throughout various texts within the Dead Sea Scrolls. Over the past seventy years, there has been no lack of scholarship surrounding Qumran and the Dead Sea Scrolls. The point of this chapter is not to give an in-depth analysis of these themes. This chapter will show that the themes of judgment and messianic expectation were also present within the extrabiblical documents found at Qumran. This chapter will reveal a slight variation on what the Qumran community believed concerning these themes. The overall perspective that this chapter seeks to demonstrate is the consistency of Jewish beliefs concerning the messiah and judgment and that there is a link between the two within certain Dead Sea Scroll texts.

The Themes of Judgment and Messianic Expectation at Qumran

DATING AND BACKGROUND

The Qumran community was likely an Essene community established on the northwest rim of the Dead Sea and only seven miles outside the community.[1] The vitality of the community lasted from around 150 BC to AD 68. The community itself was somewhat secluded and quite exclusive as to whom they would allow into the community. The community was a separate sect of Judaism with its own religious nuances and practices. It was likely a sect that was Levitical in its origins as a group of priests and Levites who split away from the rest, due to stark disagreements with the Hasmoneans and the priests placed in office by that dynasty. This is reflected throughout the texts produced by this sect. It will be seen that those they say will receive the severest of judgments are the apostate Jews associated with the temple cult that parted from the strict Judaism of the Torah.

There were various types of literature discovered at Qumran. Represented in the Dead Sea Scrolls are all of the Old Testament minus the book of Esther, the pseudepigraphal texts of 1 Enoch (minus the Parables) and Jubilees, Tobit, and a multitude of works produced by the community, which included rule books, Bible interpretation of various kinds, religious poetry, wisdom compositions in prose and verse, sectarian calendars, and liturgical texts. The extent of the library at Qumran reveals that the community itself was quite religious and even strict in their belief and practice. The leader of the community is continually referred to as the teacher of righteousness throughout the literature that was exclusive to that Qumran community. There is no indication that this leader was seen as a messianic figure, but there is indication that they believed the teacher was a precursor to the messiah or messiahs who would follow him. The community believed themselves to be an eschatological community that was living in the end times, with the great day of the Lord to be revealed. Thus, they developed their own eschatology concerning judgment and messianic expectation. It is necessary to understand this community's thoughts on judgment and messianic expectation because John's representation of Jesus's teachings concerning messianic judgment challenge views held by the Qumran community.

---

1. Scott gives a helpful summary of the history, beliefs, and social structure of the Essenes and the Qumran community (Scott, *Jewish Backgrounds*, 215–29). See also Sanders, *Paul and Palestinian Judaism*, 239–328; Collins, *Dead Sea Scrolls*.

JUDGMENT

The Qumran community was an exclusivist community who saw themselves as the true remnant of Israel. As with some of the other early Jewish texts concerning being judged for one's deeds, so also the Qumran community believed that God did not base righteousness upon individual deeds but upon whether or not one was in the covenant community (1QH; 1QM).[2] Sanders notes that salvation was through entrance into the community and not through the scrutiny of one's deeds.[3] The view of judgment that this community had was overall an eschatological judgment, but it was an imminent eschatological judgment (4Q161). Reiser, while commenting on the psalms of the teacher of righteousness, observes: "The ultimate judgment and accomplished salvation are in the future, but even now the lot of the one and the other group is being decided. Hence the present is seen completely in its eschatological aspect."[4] Thus, God was going to bring about the final judgment at any moment. Travis notes that there was a sort of hatred for the outsider, and it was the outsider (Jews and gentiles) who would receive the greater portion of God's wrath.[5]

Throughout the Dead Sea Scrolls, God is the initiator of this judgment, but members of the community will be active participants in the final judgment (1QS; 1QH).[6] Travis notes, "The eschatological battle will be the time for retaliation against the sons of darkness, as the War rule

---

2. Yinger shows how the deeds represented in 1QH IV are seen as the abominable sins of idolatry and a hardened heart (Yinger, *Paul, Judaism, and Judgment*, 108–9). The emphasis of the overall message of 1QH would characterize these sins upon those who are outside the community. The community would not have seen themselves as guilty of these sins that lead to judgment.

3. Sanders, *Paul and Palestinian Judaism*, 240–57.

4. Reiser, *Jesus and Judgment*, 75.

5. Travis, *Christ and the Judgment*, 33.

6. VanLandingham notes that the receiving of reward for being righteous is not a matter of the amount of good deeds but is more black and white: one either obeys or does not (VanLandingham, *Judgment and Justification*, 118).

Falk notes that salvation in 1QH means "deliverance from the wicked, release from the guilt of sin and the weakness of humanity, and participation in the heavenly community." He also notes that there is a present reality of salvation for those who are in the community. The presented idea of salvation is much more exclusivist than other notions of salvation found in Second Temple Judaism (Falk, "Psalms and Prayers," 28–29).

Chester argues that there are clear messianic allusions in 1QH, as the text alludes to 2 Sam 22–23 and links to Isa 66:7–11, the birth of a messianic child and the birth of a new people (Chester, *Messiah and Exaltation*, 263–64).

makes plain."[7] It should also be noted that this judgment is taking place in an earthly scene and not in heaven, despite other above early Jewish sources putting the final judgment at the throne of God in heaven (e.g., Parable of Enoch). There is also thought in this community that a messianic figure from the branch of David will be the one to lead the way and free the people from those who oppress them (4Q285; 4Q161; 1QSb). He is the one who will receive the covenant of kingship (4Q252), and one of the main features included within kingship is the seat of judgment. There is a sense in which the messiah will partake in an aspect of final judgment and possibly even the resurrection (1Q521).[8] There is also a semi-ambiguous fragment which contains the title son of God as one who will partake with God in final judgment and the establishment of the kingdom on earth (4Q246).[9] The son of God does not contain a direct reference and is thought most likely to be referring to one of the archangels such as Michael, or the exalted figure of Melchizedek, or perhaps even the messiah.[10] The figure of Melchizedek takes up final judgment against the prince of darkness Belial and also has a hand in restoration at the final jubilee (11Q13). The overall picture is that God is not alone in his final judgment but has people, the messiah, and heavenly beings participate in final judgment. This translates well into Jesus's claim as messianic judge, especially with his references to the final judgment in the Gospel of John.

The commentary on Habakkuk (1QpHab) exhibits much of the eschatological views of the Qumran community. Right from the beginning, the text reveals the belief that they saw themselves as the final generation, which would see judgment come upon the gentiles.[11] This text not only shows that the gentiles were wicked but also that the current priesthood residing over the temple was wicked, so those priests would receive

---

7. Travis, *Christ and the Judgment*, 33.

8. 1Q521 is only a small fragment, and the larger context of this passage is incomplete.

9. This Son of God figure can possibly be a reference to an antichrist figure such as Antiochus IV Epiphanes or the eschatological archenemy of God. However, Grindheim argues that the title should be viewed positively as the collective people of God, an angelic figure, or a coming Jewish ruler. He more concisely argues that this figure is most likely a messianic figure who was inspired by the Danielic Son of Man (Grindheim, *God's Equal*, 137–38).

10. Vermes, *Complete Dead Sea Scrolls*, 617.

11. Oegema says that although the teacher of righteousness is not specifically mentioned in 1QpHab, the teacher of righteousness is believed to play a key post-prophetic role that leads up to the coming of the Messiah (Oegema, *Anointed and His People*, 108–09).

judgment.¹² The reason for this judgment is because they despise the law of God and because of the many sins they have heaped up over the things they have done against God's people. The author sees the teacher of righteousness and the members of the community as those who will be saved and also indicates that God will use the elect community to aid in bringing about judgment on the community. The author comments on the means of God's judgment by the use of fire and brimstone. This language is likely used to point the reader to Gen 19, where God uses fire and brimstone to judge the cities of Sodom and Gomorrah. The author seems to be saying that this is the type of judgment God is about to bring upon the wicked of this final generation. The commentary on Habakkuk is acutely focused on judgment of both the wicked nations and the wicked priests. The author wants to make clearly known the sins for which both groups are going to be judged. The author is also intent on making a clear distinction between those who are being judged and the elect whom God will save.

MESSIANIC EXPECTATION

One of the expectations for the messiah was of two different messiahs: one from the line of David as a kingly messiah and one from the line of Aaron as a priestly messiah.¹³ Hurst argues that the Qumran literature points to a kingly messiah as one from the line of David as the redeemer of Israel, while the priestly messiah functions as the leading priest alongside the primary Davidic messiah.¹⁴ The texts that support this idea are the Damascus

---

12. Yinger argues that this warning against the priesthood should not serve just as an outward warning. He sees the emphasis of this warning as internal, saying that what will happen to the priests in judgment will happen to those in the community who follow this same path of apostasy (Yinger, *Paul, Judaism, and Judgment*, 130–31).

13. Pomykala focuses on just the Davidic dynasty tradition at Qumran and focuses solely on sectarian documents that were specific to the Qumran community: 4QDibHam, 4QpGena, 4QFlor, 4QpIsaa, and 4QSerek HaMilhamah (Pomykala, *Davidic Dynasty Tradition*, 171–216). His conclusion concerning these documents is that all of the documents, with the exception of 4QDibHam, have a common Davidic messianic theme (written between 30 BC and AD 70). He notes that the characteristics of this branch of David are that one would take office in the last days as a militant leader whose power would come from God; he would have the qualities of compassion, sinlessness, holiness, wisdom, faithfulness, and purity; he would rid the nation of foreign powers and authorities, as well as apostate Jews; and his rule will extend over all nations (Pomykala, *Davidic Dynasty Tradition*, 212–16).

14. Hurst, "Did Qumran Expect," 160.

Document, the Manual of Discipline, and the Rule of the Congregation. Many other documents such as the War Scroll (1QM) and the Messianic Apocalypse also refer to the messiah. Overall, it can be concluded that there was an idea of two possible messiahs who would come at the same time, one for spiritual matters and one for political matters. Other than a few terms, there are not a lot of defining characteristics of this messiah, as has been seen with other pieces of Second Temple literature, such as the Psalms of Solomon and the Parables of Enoch.

The Damascus Document (CD) is a work containing rules and regulations by which to live within the Qumran community. This document also looked forward to the coming of an eschatological messianic figure. Prior to the presentation of the messiah, the author indicates that there will be a time of judgment, when God will execute judgment upon the backsliding members of the covenant (CD 8:1–2; 19:13–14) and retribution will be upon the wicked (8:9; 19:6).[15] In four distinct places, the CD presents the variation of the phrase "the messiah from Aaron and Israel" (cf. 9b:10; 9b:29; 15:4; and 18:7). The biggest implication from these texts is that the Jews from Qumran were expecting two different messiahs. The presence of the messianic figure in the midst of judgment indicates that the messiah is an eschatological figure. However, the CD does not go into much detail concerning the eschatological role of the messiah.[16] This view seems to be mostly unique to the Qumran community, though later Jewish texts such as the Testament of the Twelve Patriarchs picks up on this notion (cf. Testament of Reuben 6:7–12). Hurst notes that when the Testaments are talking about a messiah of Levi, they are likely referencing the Hasmonean priest-kings; but when John Hyrcanus departed ways from the Pharisees, there was a shift to just a messiah from Judah.[17] However, there is a conflicting view in the Testament of Judah, likely from a different author, who sees only one messiah coming from the line of Judah (Testament of Judah 21:1–5; 24).

The Manual of Discipline (1QS), because of wording in 1QS 9:10–11, has led some to gather the idea of three possible messiahs in the mind of the author. It states in verse 11: ". . . until there come the prophet and the

15. Reiser indicates that these passages utilize Isa 7:17 and Zech 13:7, which themselves are messianic in nature (Reiser, *Jesus and Judgment*, 78–79).

16. Oegema notes that the community behind the CD likely saw themselves as living in the period just prior to the coming of the eschatological Messiah (Oegema, *Anointed and His People*, 97).

17. Oegema, *Anointed and His People*, 162–63.

messiahs of Aaron and Israel."[18] It is possible that this supports the notion of the tripartite office of the messiah and may be in the background of the author of Hebrews, when that author asserts that Jesus is the perfect prophet, priest, and king. However, Hurst notes that there is much debate on the syntax of this one instance and its possible meaning.[19]

The Rule of the Congregation (1QSa) is likely supposed to be a preface to 1QS. It is more fully known as the Rule of the Congregation of Israel at the End of Time.[20] This is also a document that purports to have two messiahs listed. Hurst notes there is a Levitical domination of a messianic figure.[21] This document refers to the end-times messianic banquet. In this banquet, the priestly figure precedes the Davidic figure but only on who appears first. This does not necessarily mean that one is more important than the other. Hurst makes a keen observation on the reason for the prominence of a Levitical messiah: since the community itself was composed of temple priests, the natural lean would be toward a prominent Levitical figure as the main messianic figure.[22]

The Messianic Apocalypse (4Q521), also known as the resurrection fragment, was likely written in the first century BC, which suggests a messianic development within the community as they possibly moved away from two ambiguous figures from Aaron and Israel and toward one figure, who possibly began to be more defined and held more divine qualities. According to Vermes, the reference to messiah in this document is in the singular and is likely not referring to Aaron or Israel as in previous documents.[23] One significant element is that the author quotes Ps 146:6-7 and Isa 61:1 in the text, which are viewed as part of messianic expectation in this document. These passages are also quoted by Jesus in Luke 4:18 as being fulfilled by Jesus in the presence of the people.

---

18. Wise et al., *Dead Sea Scrolls*, 139. Oegema notes that this document is an earlier Qumran work, and this phrase only appears here in the earlier documents, but in the later documents it appears more often (Oegema, *Anointed and His People*, 90–92).

19. Hurst, "Did Qumran Expect," 169–71.

20. Hurst, "Did Qumran Expect," 172.

21. Hurst, "Did Qumran Expect," 172.

22. Hurst, "Did Qumran Expect," 172.

23. Vermes, *Complete Dead Sea Scrolls*, 412.
Chester argues that the messiah presented in this text is most likely a royal messiah, especially with reference to a scepter. This messiah is also associated directly with the time of eschatological deliverance. He also indicates that this messiah may also play a prophetic role like Moses or Elijah (Chester, *Messiah and Exaltation*, 251–54).

11QMelchizedek (11Q13) is an intriguing document that also cites Isa 61:1–2 in a messianic form. The author uses the name of Melchizedek in place of *El, Elohim,* and *Yahweh*. Wise, Abegg, and Cook note, "Melchizedek is said to atone for the sins of the righteous and to execute judgment upon the wicked—actions usually associated with God himself."[24] The figure of Melchizedek appears only twice in the Old Testament, Gen 14 and Ps 110. In the Old Testament, he is a mysterious figure and very little is known about him. By the first century BC, at least in the Qumran community and maybe even in other pockets of Judaism, Melchizedek is possibly viewed as a divine being and maybe even as God himself.[25] However, there is very little to support that claim other than this one passage. Within this text, there is a messianic figure who is an eschatological figure. This figure is also associated with final judgment, which indicates that the Qumran community believed the day of the Lord would be accompanied by an end-times figure other than God himself. The text says he is the one prophesied by Daniel, who will proclaim God's truth but will be "cut off." The author then quotes Isa 61:2, directly identifying this one as the anointed one, the messiah.[26] Unfortunately, this text is highly fragmented, and many of the details of the passage are missing. Thus, only speculation remains as to the overall message and content of this text. However, the rest of the documents at Qumran give helpful indications to the eschatological message of this text.

CONCLUSION

The Dead Sea Scrolls reveal an imminent eschatological view concerning the messiah and judgment. They reveal that the Qumran community believed that they were truly living in the end times and that the coming of the messiah and the final judgment were likely to happen within their lifetime. The previous sections reveal some of the difficulties in understanding some of the key documents that talk about the coming messiah and judgment, because only small fragments of these texts exist. Even without these full

---

24. Wise et al., *Dead Sea Scrolls*, 455.

25. Grindheim argues that this figure most likely represents an exalted angel who serves as a divine agent rather than one who is equal with God (Grindheim, *God's Equal*, 150–51).

26. Wise et al., *Dead Sea Scrolls*, 457.
Chester says that the one anointed with the spirit should be interpreted as a separate figure from Melchizedek and should not necessarily be seen as a royal messiah; a prophetic messiah is more plausible (Chester, *Messiah and Exaltation*, 259–61).

texts, there is still a fairly full picture surrounding what the Qumran community believed about the coming messiah, the coming judgment, and the link between the two. A difficulty is that there seems to be an inconsistency on their views of the messiah. This is not something that should cause concern, though, because the previous chapter revealed just how varied messianic views were within Judaism. The multiple messianic views represented at Qumran follow the pattern seen thus far within Judaism.

This chapter reveals that, although the Qumran community was its own unique Jewish sect, there was still an overall consistency in views on the themes of messianic expectation, judgment, and their interaction with each other. Although it is unknown just how familiar John's Jewish audience would have been with the beliefs of the Qumran community, John's representation of Jesus's teachings concerning messianic judgment challenge views held by the Qumran community, in the same way that John articulates the words of Jesus as challenging his own Jewish audience's view on the themes of messianic expectation and judgment.

4

The Danielic Son of Man and Its Development in Second Temple Judaism

INTRODUCTION

IN THE GOSPEL OF John, Jesus presents himself as the Danielic one like a son of man with characteristics that were associated with that figure. John's Jewish audience would have had preconceived beliefs about the son of man, which has origins in Daniel and becomes more highly developed in the Parables of Enoch. Jesus's teachings contain familiar themes associated with the son of man from Daniel and the Parables, such as judgeship passed from God to him (John 5:22, 27), the general resurrection with the separation of the righteous and the wicked (5:28–29), judgment according to deeds (3:19–21; 5:29), the revelation of heavenly knowledge (3:12), heavenly origin and pre-existence (1:2; 3:13), and exaltation (13:31). There is also much overlap in the themes presented in the introductions of chapters 2 and 3 concerning judgment and messianic expectation, which will also be briefly mentioned in this chapter. This chapter and chapters 2 and 3 give a combined view of the eschatological beliefs that were likely present in John's Jewish audience concerning judgment and messianic expectation. This chapter specifically considers the Jewish development of the Danielic one like a son of man, which eventually developed into a title synonymous with messiah, especially in the Parables of Enoch. This development helps inform what an early Jewish audience is thinking when Jesus uses the title Son of Man for himself throughout the Gospel of John. One must keep in mind that John strategically places Jesus's Son of Man sayings throughout his Gospel with a specific purpose in mind. In the Gospel of John, the Son of Man sayings are used in proximity to or directly pertaining to judgment or Jesus's role as messianic judge (see 5:27). This chapter will seek to elaborate upon what John's Jewish audience may have thought about the Danielic son of man and what their preconceived beliefs about him would have been. The words that Jesus uses in John likely elicited certain beliefs and imagery from both Daniel and the Parables of Enoch. Chapters 5 through 7 will then consider just how radically different Jesus' teachings are when contrasted with known Jewish beliefs. Each of the above teachings of Jesus will be considered in light of what John's Jewish audience would have believed concerning each theme.

DANIEL 7:13-14

The Son of Man in Daniel

The use of son of man in Dan 7:13 is the first appearance in Jewish literature where this title is used as a term to describe a quasi-divine heavenly figure, as opposed to it referring to a human being.[1] The phrase in Dan 7:13 is most often translated as "one like a son of man," while some translators push further and seek to translate the essence of the phrase as "one like a human being."[2] Although the latter phrase captures the essence of one like a son of man in its immediate context in Daniel, it fails to capture theological implications and future Jewish and Christian interpretations of the title. Previous uses of the phrase or title in the Hebrew Scriptures are used in connection to a human figure (e.g., Ezekiel) or the collective humankind (e.g., Ps 80:17; 144:3). Daniel becomes the first instance in Jewish literature where this title is used to refer to a heavenly figure. It is this passage that moves the son of man tradition in the direction of this title being associated

---

1. Grabbe considers the philological background of the title *son of man* throughout Hebrew and Aramaic documents, especially those in the same Middle Aramaic language category as Dan 7. The documents that fall into this category are mainly those that are found at Qumran. Each use of the Aramaic phrase consistently refers to a specific human being or humanity as a collective. In fact, Grabbe concludes without hesitation that every use of son of man in the documents considered was not used messianically (Grabbe, "Son of Man," 169–80).

2. Reiser puts forth this interpretation in *Jesus and Judgment*, 39.

The Danielic Son of Man and Its Development

with a messianic and/or heavenly figure.[3] The Jewish tradition is evidenced in the Parables of Enoch (1 Enoch 37–71) and 4 Ezra, which present the son of man as a heavenly and messianic figure who is closely associated with or directly participates in the final judgment.

Scholars debate the identity of the one like a son of man in Dan 7:13. One argument is that this figure represents the collective Jewish people. Another argument is that this one represents a messianic figure.[4] Lester Grabbe makes an argument that Daniel is referring to the archangel Michael or to Gabriel, since similar language is used to refer to them in Dan 10.[5] John Collins argues for Michael and not a messianic figure, because nowhere else in Daniel is there a reference to a messianic figure, but other places in Daniel mention the angelic figures of Michael and Gabriel and attribute human features to them. He also argues that the son of man figure in 1 Enoch 46:1 is said to have the face of an angel, and he argues that the Son of Man in the Synoptic Gospels is repeatedly associated with angels (Matt. 13:41; 16:27; 24:31; 25:31; Mark 8:38; 13:27, 41; Luke 9:26).[6] A point of contention with these passages is that they put Jesus as the Son of Man, as the key figure who will come with his angels at the end of days. The immediate context in Daniel points to this figure most likely being an angelic figure. However, New Testament interpretation of this passage very emphatically links the figure in Dan 7 to Jesus as the Son of Man who will come in the clouds with his angels. The Gospels did not just make a giant leap from the Danielic one like a son of man to Jesus's self-titling as the Son of Man. Rather, there were at least two centuries of development of thought concerning the identity of the son of man in early Judaism. This development of Jewish thought is bridged by the Parables of Enoch and the book of 4 Ezra, which indicate that the son of man tradition was still vibrant in late first-century AD Jewish circles apart from Christian influence. These

---

3. Reynolds indicates that the one like a son of man is depicted with features with which God is often associated in other OT passages. He also indicates that there is no ascent or descent language associated with this figure, which draws one to conclude that this figure was already in heaven. The kingly nature of this figure is due to the nature of the language of kingdom and dominion. This language lends one to see messianic implications in the text as well (Reynolds, *Apocalyptic Son of Man*, 29–33).

4. J. Harold Ellens extensively argues for the one like a son of man to be a human figure and not a divine figure. He rejects Collins's argument of the son of man being presented as an angelic figure (Ellens, *Son of Man*, 146–50).

5. Grabbe, "Son of Man," 181–82.

6. J. Collins, *Apocalyptic Imagination*, 101–4.

two documents support the notion that John's Jewish audience would have had a well-developed idea of a heavenly messianic figure who was also identified as the son of man. Associated with this figure were theological themes of judgment, resurrection, and salvation, about which John's Jewish audience would have had preconceived ideas on how these topics worked themselves out and how they related to the coming Messiah.

Judgment in Daniel

The eschatological and apocalyptic nature of the second half of Daniel opens with various judgment scenes and occasions. Dan 7 opens with a scene where four beasts are present, which represent the four major empires of the earth. Just prior to the one like a son of man establishing his dominion over the whole earth, judgment was to come on these four beasts. These four beasts are seen to be judged by God, and their dominion is stripped away.[7] There is also an implicit judgment in 12:1–3.[8] Although 12:1–3 is not a descriptive judgment scene, there is an implied judgment in the resurrection scene, when Daniel is shown that some will awake to everlasting contempt (v. 3).[9] This passage comes just prior to the description of historical events outlined in chapter 11, with the inference that the deeds of this evil king will ultimately be punished. Chapter 12 is mainly present to give hope

---

7. Reiser argues that 7:9–10 opens to a heavenly courtroom scene similar to the scene in 1 Enoch 14:15–23, where God presides over a college of judges and the angels are seen as associate members. Reiser notes that the scene in Daniel is fragmentary and does not give a full picture of all that is taking place in the courtroom. He also says that the judgment scene is over just as quickly as it began, and there is a swift verdict with no defense allowed for the beasts (Reiser, *Jesus and Judgment*, 39).

Reynolds brings out the contrast between the beasts represented as animals and the one like a son of man represented as a humanlike figure who receives dominion (Reynolds, *Apocalyptic Son of Man*, 28–29).

Ellens notes that although the one like a son of man is given power and dominion over the evil empires, the text of Dan 7 never indicates that the right to judge is given to this figure, unlike the figure in the Parables (Ellens, *Son of Man*, 147).

8. Nickelsburg sees this passage as a forensic judgment scene (Nickelsburg, *Resurrection, Immortality*, 11–27). However, Reiser argues that this passage does not contain the typical elements of a forensic judgment scene (Reiser, *Jesus and Judgment*, 40–41).

9. Chester gives two reasons for the importance and development of the resurrection in Jewish belief: first, it is an affirmation of physical resurrection; second, it depicts human transformation into an angelic or suprahuman mode. Dan 12 represents the beginnings of the development of this Jewish belief in a resurrection, which will be later nuanced in other early Jewish texts (Chester, *Messiah and Exaltation*, 159–68).

THE DANIELIC SON OF MAN AND ITS DEVELOPMENT

to the nation of Israel to those who fell victim to not only the evils of the king presented in chapter 11 but also the evils of the four beasts of chapter 7. Israel was being given the hope that some would awake to everlasting life. Although the judgment scenes of Daniel are not as explicit as other Second Temple documents, the theme of judgment is closely associated with the figure of one like a son of man. This association will become even more explicit in the Parables of Enoch and 4 Ezra, which associate the heavenly messianic son of man with coming judgment. The judgment scenes are much more explicit and quite specific in various passages. Therefore, it is very likely that John's Jewish audience would have had various images and preconceived ideas when Jesus makes multiple allusions to Dan 7 and 12 in John 5. His audience would not only have been familiar with Daniel but also likely familiar with the Parables of Enoch, which would have caused greater imagery links as Jesus offers his self-identification as the Son of Man and teachings on his role as messianic judge.

THE PARABLES OF ENOCH

Messianic expectation is a common theme in New Testament background studies. One question that needs to be addressed is whether or not the sources one uses for background study are valid. One of the issues in Second Temple Jewish sources is dating and background of specific sources. The dating and background of the Parables of Enoch are no exception. In fact, the debate on the dating of the Parables of Enoch is even greater because of its high potential to impact New Testament messianic expectation. Many issues that have been raised within this debate. The main goal in this section will be to focus on a positive case for a range of dates for the Parables of Enoch and to answer objections only as needed to support this positive case. This section will seek to argue for a late first-century BC to an early first-century AD composition of the Parables of Enoch and to build a case for a Herodian background of the issues contained within.

Dating and Background

Issues in Dating the Parables of Enoch

J. T. Milik argues for a third-century AD composition of the Parables of Enoch. He bases his dating on the fact that the fifth book of the Sibylline

Oracles dates to the third century AD, since the latest element in it falls in the reign of Caracalla, who was killed in AD 217.[10] Milik makes this connection based upon the similar themes shared between the Parables and the books of the Sibylline Oracles written in the third century.[11] Another indicator he brings out is the Christian elements throughout.[12] He claims that the Parables, as well as many other early Jewish documents, contain Christian variants and Christian interpolations. However, these do not necessarily signify a late Jewish or Christian authorship. It has been the task of translators and text critics to discern what was likely to be original and what was added or changed later. More evidence on his side is that the Parables is not part of the Enoch corpus discovered at Qumran. Since Milik published this volume, many Second Temple scholars have challenged his dating of the Parables. Suter notes that there is almost a universal consensus on the rejection of Milik's conclusions, but this does not mean that there is not still debate on the dating of the Parables.[13] Isaac maintains that the current dating of the Parables in first century BC (105–64 BC),[14] and many other scholars propose something in between. One can see by this gap in the dating that there is about a three-hundred to four-hundred year spread in the placement of the dating.

Milik was not without reason to want to give the Parables a much later date. There are many issues present that have caused an ongoing debate concerning the dating of the Parables. Milik's main argument for a later date and Christian composition was because it was not found in the library of Qumran. Milik boldly states, "In conclusion, it is around the year A.D. 270 or shortly afterwards that I would place the composition of the Book of Parables."[15] Charlesworth notes that for many years, many researchers thought that this was the consensus among Enochic scholars, but he says that this was in fact the complete opposite of the case. In fact, Charlesworth proclaims that "in 1977 during a congress of specialists on 1 Enoch, no one

---

10. Milik, *Books of Enoch*, 94.
11. Milik, *Books of Enoch*, 92–98.
12. Milik, *Books of Enoch*, 97.
13. Suter, "Enoch in Sheol," 415–17. Suter indicates that current scholarship puts the dates of the Parables between 50 BC and AD 117. Suter puts the Parables tradition parallel to the Son of Man tradition in the gospels (Suter, "Enoch in Sheol," 440–42). His basic conclusion is that neither tradition directly influenced the other.
14. Isaac, "First (Ethiopic Apocalypse of) Enoch," 7.
15. Milik, *Books of Enoch*, 96.

agreed with Milik that the work is Christian."[16] Charlesworth completely rejects the idea that the Parables is a Christian work, arguing, "There is no obvious 'Christian' thought in these chapters. Jesus is never mentioned and there is no allusion to him. The son of man is certainly not Jesus. The son of man is revealed, in the final scene, to be none other than Enoch."[17] Thus, Charlesworth identifies the Parables as thoroughly Jewish and predating any Christian writing.

Another issue in dating the Parables is that the earliest copies are preserved only in Ethiopic and early medieval copies.[18] No manuscripts have been found to date in the original Aramaic, and there are no early Greek translations, like there are for many of the other early Jewish pseudepigraphal works. Charlesworth offers his evidence for Jewish origins as he says, "It seems obvious that this text derives from an earlier Aramaic text. Hence, one eye should be on the Ethiopic text and another on the putative Aramaic original."[19] This is another reason why Milik leans toward a later composition date. However, Charlesworth and others have argued persuasively that a lack of external evidence should not bring one to conclude that the dating of the Parables should be late. The majority consensus remains that it is a completely Jewish work dating somewhere in the late first century BC to the early first century AD. Internal evidence paired with historical events in this era point one toward a pre-Christian dating.

Suter identifies nine obstacles that hinder a consensus dating of the Parables even after the dismissal of Milik's dating hypothesis. They are listed as follows:

1. The absence of the Parables at Qumran.
2. Is 1 Enoch 56:5–8 a historical reference or an apocalyptic myth?
3. Does 1 Enoch 56:7 require a date before the destruction of Jerusalem?
4. Are the hot springs in 1 Enoch 67:4–13 a reference to Herod the Great at Callirrhoe?
5. The identity of the kings and mighty.
6. The implications of social context for the question of date.

16. Charlesworth, "Can We Discern," 451.
17. Charlesworth, "Can We Discern," 455.
18. Charlesworth, "Can We Discern," 452.
19. Charlesworth, "Can We Discern," 452.

7. The affinity of the Parables to other literature.
8. The influence of the Parables on the New Testament.
9. The identification of the dating traditions behind the Parables.[20]

These dating issues will not be completely resolved in this book since there is still debate between many of the Parables scholars on the nature of the resolution for each of these points. However, several of these will be considered in more depth to build a case for composition dating prior to the ministry of Jesus.

Nickelsburg and VanderKam bring to light their own set of issues in dating the Parables, which mirrors many of the concerns voiced by other scholars.[21] One of the things they point out that makes the Parables more difficult to date is that there is no survey of Israel's history within which to place its contents, as there is with other apocalypses such as Dan 7–12, 1 Enoch 85–90, 2 Baruch, and 4 Ezra.[22] Alongside this contention, they identify the fact that there are only a few identifiable historical allusions, and these comprise only a few verses of the entire Parables.[23] One allusion is possibly the invasion of the Parthians and Medes in 1 Enoch 56:5–7 and the other allusion is in 67:5–13, which may refer to Herod the Great's visit to the hot springs in Kallirrhoe in an attempt to cure his health issues. These two allusions are some of the main pieces of internal evidence that scholars use to push for an early dating of the text. Charlesworth adds several more textual allusions that he will tie to Herod the Great's reign, which adds to the persuasiveness of the argument of a late first-century BC to early first-century AD composition of the Parables.[24] Nickelsburg and VanderKam also deal with its absence from Qumran, which is why some scholars date it to after AD 68, which was the destruction of the community by the Romans. They also bring out issues on how the Parables compares to other Jewish texts, as well as to the Synoptic Gospels and other early Christian literature. These dating issues will be considered in more depth to see just how much of an issue each one truly is. It is likely that the dating debate of the Parables will continue for many more decades, unless a definitive archeological find

20. Suter, "Enoch in Sheol," 417.
21. Nickelsburg and VanderKam, *First Enoch 2*, 58–60.
22. Nickelsburg and VanderKam, *First Enoch 2*, 59.
23. Nickelsburg and VanderKam, *First Enoch 2*, 59–60.
24. Charlesworth, "Can We Discern," 457–65.

finally settles the matter. However, clear concise answers to various dating issues, plus a cumulative case for various historical allusions within the Parables, will provide one with ample support to show that the Parables contributed to the first-century AD Jewish messianic expectation.

The Absence of the Parables at Qumran

The absence of the Parables at Qumran became one of the defining reasons for Milik to conclude that the Parables was a much later Christian composition. However, this absence has not hindered the most influential Parables scholars from dating this book during the Herodian dynasty. Nickelsburg and VanderKam note, "This absence is worth noting since the Scrolls preserve the MSS. of the Book of the Watchers, the Book of the Giants, the Book of the Luminaries, the Epistle of Enoch, and the story of Noah's death."[25] There may be several reasons for its absence from Qumran. It is possible that the Parables postdates Qumran. It is possible that this document was rejected by the Qumran community, due to not fitting with their nuance of Enochic Judaism. Greenfield and Stone offer a more developed argument to why one cannot necessarily give a late date to the Parables just because it is absent from Qumran.[26] There are also other books not present at Qumran that maintain pre-Christian dates, such as Esther, Judith, the Testament of Moses, and the Psalms of Solomon. Thus, one cannot argue for a later date just because it is absent from the library at Qumran. Nickelsburg and VanderKam state, "The Parables' absence from Qumran can just as well reflect a bifurcation of the Enoch tradition prior to the 'foundation' of 'the Qumran Community' and indicate the parables were composed in a Jewish setting apart from Qumran."[27] It is also possible that since the Parables' place of composition was Galilee,[28] manuscripts did not circulate down to Qumran prior to Qumran's destruction. Regardless of the reason, to date no copies or fragments of the Parables have been discovered at Qumran. Charlesworth takes a different direction on one of the possible reasons that the Parables has not been discovered at Qumran. He notes, "Over one hundred fragments remain unidentified within the

---

25. Nickelsburg and VanderKam, *First Enoch 2*, 60.
26. Greenfield and Stone, "Enochic Pentateuch," 51–66.
27. Nickelsburg and VanderKam, *First Enoch 2*, 60.
28. This is the location of composition for which Charlesworth argues (Charlesworth, "Can We Discern," 452).

Qumran corpus."[29] Related to this, he identifies the fact that only 10 to 20 percent of the entire Qumran corpus that was likely placed in the caves prior to the destruction of the community is available for study.[30] Thus, it is a possibility that the Parables was placed in the caves but did not survive in the same form as other documents have.

Elements for Dating the Book of Parables

One of the internal evidences that most Parables scholars mention to date this work is the reference in 1 Enoch 56:5–8 concerning the invasion of the Parthians and the Medes. Verse 5 specifically mentions these two nations by name, which is the only specific mention of a nation by a proper name in the whole Parables. The debate is whether this passage is a specific reference to the Parthian invasion of 40–39 BC[31] or just an apocalyptic tool to reference another historical event.[32] The issue is that names are given but no historical details that would further explicate this mention of the Parthians and Medes. Suter notes that many Parables scholars fall somewhere in the middle of this debate and say that this passage is a vague allusion to a historical event that happened within a generation or so of the author.[33] Perhaps this historical allusion alone is not enough to establish a date, but paired with other possible historical allusions, it allows one to firmly argue for an early first-century AD dating at the latest and likely prior to the ministry of Jesus.

The Identity of the Kings and the Mighty

The reference to the kings and the mighty in the Parables is rather vague and does not seem to allude to a specific group of kings. This vagueness is

---

29. Charlesworth, "Can We Discern," 456.

30. Charlesworth, "Can We Discern," 456. Greenfield and Stone also come to similar conclusions, based on the fact that only a small fraction of documents has survived (Greenfield and Stone, "Enochic Pentateuch," 55–57).

31. Bampfylde argues that this is a precise reference to the actual historical event that took place in 40–39 BC (Bampfylde, "Similitudes of Enoch," 15–16, 22–28).

32. Suter leans toward this passage as being apocalyptic myth, since the description in the passage does not meet the insignificance of the actual Parthian invasion and since some Jews actually invited the Parthians into the area (Suter, "Enoch in Sheol," 421–22). See also Suter, *Tradition and Composition*, 12, 24, 176–77.

33. Suter, "Enoch in Sheol," 422.

another feature that has allowed for the dating to be placed by many scholars into various places in history. However, Nickelsburg and VanderKam note, "A substantial amount of scholars see this passage as an allusion to the last days of Herod the Great, when the ailing king unsuccessfully sought relief from the terminal illness in the hot springs of Kallirrhoe."[34] If this is the case, then this would push the dating to no earlier than 4 BC, since his death resulted shortly after these attempts at healing. However, it is also not likely that the author would have written too much after this date, because this singular event would not have remained very significant for long; there were so many more Herodian and Roman events of significance that happened in the first half of the first century AD after the death of Herod the Great. The main pattern with apocalyptic writing is that the event purported is fresh in the mind of the writer, especially when it deals with such an obscure event as Herod's visit to a hot spring.

The Influence of the Parables on First-Century Jewish Texts

The two main Jewish texts with likely influence from the Parables are 4 Ezra and 2 Baruch. Nickelsburg and VanderKam note that the Parables and 4 Ezra contain the threads of elements from Dan 7, Davidic royal ideology, and Second Isaiah's servant theology.[35] They continue in their parallels to the extent that they conclude, "These parallels indicate that 4 Ezra is dependent on the Parables or that the Parables and 4 Ezra are dependent on a common eschatological tradition that combined in one transcendent figure elements proper to the Davidic king, the Deutero-Isaiahic Servant, and Daniel's 'one like a son of man.'"[36] Second Baruch also seems to be dependent on this tradition, especially since it shares much in common with 4 Ezra.

The Setting of the Parables

Allusions and other dating factors place the setting of this book within the Herodian era. The tendency of apocalyptic literature was to write in reaction to negative historical events, showing that the judgment of God

---

34. Nickelsburg and VanderKam, *First Enoch 2*, 61.

35. Nickelsburg and VanderKam, *First Enoch 2*, 61.

36. Nickelsburg and VanderKam, *First Enoch 2*, 61. Nickelsburg and VanderKam provide five parallel passages of dependence on a Son of Man/servant tradition.

would be upon the ones causing suffering. Concerning the setting of the Parables, Nickelsburg and VanderKam note, "This is a time of violence and oppression and of an angry and frustrated consciousness of class distinction, which looks for resolution in the coming judgment."[37] They give three complaints against the rich and powerful: the persecution of the righteous (1 Enoch 47), the excess taxation (53:2), and the seizure of property.[38] Horsley notes the heavy amount of taxation that Herod imposed upon the Jews during his reign, which would have caused a high amount of Jewish unrest and a number of revolts.[39] Concerning the seizure of land, Charlesworth argues at length for an allusion to Herod seizing the property of the Jews throughout the Parables.[40] Charlesworth adds one more interesting piece to the Herodian era background. He picks up on the references to those "who possess the earth" (38:4; 62:3–6) and the possession and rulership of the dry ground (48:8; 62:9; 63:1–10). He notes that Palestine at one time was characterized by areas of swamps and marshes and areas of dry ground. The dry ground would have been the place of vineyards and farms. This reflects the taking of the lands from the Jews that happened in the Herodian era due to high taxation. By the end of the Herodian era, many of the Jews had lost their land and in essence become tenant farmers. This would reflect the judgment pronounced upon the kings and the mighty who possess the dry land. Charlesworth makes this a new piece of his argument that places the dating within the Herodian era.[41]

The overall picture that the author of the Parables seeks to produce is that the kings and the mighty will receive their just judgment at the coming of the Son of Man for the wrongs they did against Jews (1 Enoch 63:12). In addition to these complaints from the Jews, there is also a notion that the Parables speaks against the detestable religious practices of the kings and the mighty. The Parables indicates that these rulers practiced idolatry and denied the reality of the Lord of Spirits (41:2; 45:1; 46:7; 60:6; 65:6). Nickelsburg and VanderKam note that it is possible that the author has many of the building projects of Herod in mind, such as the various cities erected in honor of the caesars and temples and monuments erected in

---

37. Nickelsburg and VanderKam, *First Enoch 2*, 63.
38. Nickelsburg and VanderKam, *First Enoch 2*, 63.
39. Horsley, *Revolt of the Scribes*, 170–73.
40. Charlesworth, "Can We Discern," 458–65.
41. Charlesworth, "Can We Discern," 458–65.

THE DANIELIC SON OF MAN AND ITS DEVELOPMENT

honor of various gods and goddesses.[42] With an early first-century AD date in mind and Galilee as a place of composition, the linking of the references in the Parables to aspects of the reign of Herod come into greater focus and help one better understand how great the desire was of the Jews to have a messiah come to swiftly rectify the situation and bring judgment upon the wicked and salvation to the righteous. This would be the frame of mind of many of the Jews as they look to Jesus as a possible messianic figure to deliver them from oppressive forces.

The Eschatological Themes of the Parables

God as a figure of divine judgement is commonplace all throughout Second Temple literature in the same way that God is the one who is Judge throughout the Old Testament. Waddell notes that the earlier Enochic literature, which predates the Parables of Enoch, puts the divine judgement only in the hands of God.[43] Waddell identifies three aspects of judging, which are "the divine figure engages in judgment, executes judgment, and sits on the throne of his glory, an act which is almost always connected to the role of judgment [in the Parables of Enoch]."[44] Collins brings out that it is clear throughout this work that the final place of the righteous and the wicked is clearly determined.[45]

The Parables presents a messianic figure who is given the place of judgment. The author bestows a few titles on this figure, such as the righteous one (1 Enoch 38:2), the chosen one (45:2–3; 51:3; 55:4; 61:8; 62:1–3), and the son of man (62:5; 69:27–29). Each of these references is associated with an aspect of judgment, and much of this refers to an eschatological judgment.[46] Waddell notes nine different instances of a messianic figure on the throne in heaven spelling out judgment (45:1–3; 51:3; 55:4; 61:8; 62:2; 62:3; 62:5; 69:27; 69:29).[47] Interestingly, this is the same place that a divine figure sits in judgment in two other places in the Parables (47:4;

---

42. Nickelsburg and VanderKam, *First Enoch 2*, 64.
43. Waddell, *Messiah*, 41.
44. Waddell, *Messiah*, 41.
45. J. Collins, *Apocalyptic Imagination*, 181.
46. Lucass emphasizes the fact that these titles do not represent different figures but refer to the same figure. These titles also reference the anointed one of Hebrew Scripture (Lucass, *Concept of the Messiah*, 146–48).
47. Waddell, *Messiah*, 90–91.

60:2). DeSilva notes how the author weaves together imagery from both Daniel and Isaiah to come up with the ideal messianic figure.[48]

The messianic figure is seen as the one who sits upon the throne of glory (45:3), which is where he will spell out judgment for the righteous and the wicked (45:5). The son of man is seen alongside the Ancient of Days (46:1), and both sit on the same throne of glory.[49] He also has a preexistent nature with the Ancient of Days (48:5-6). He is one who will judge the secret things of men (49:1-4; 61:8-9). He is the one who will judge heavenly beings (61:8) and mighty men on the earth, such as kings (48:8-9; 62:1-2). Part of this judgment is salvation for the righteous (38:1-6), and there is a transformation on the earth to make it a blessing for the righteous (45:3). Overall, the Parables gives the clearest representation of the place of judgment given to the messiah. This is significant because much of the early Jewish literature examined shows that the place of judgment remains with God. This text indicates a changing view concerning messianic thought that was developing at the end of the first century BC and on into the first century AD.

Judgment

Judgement upon the wicked is announced at the very beginning of the first parable (1 Enoch 38:1). The judgment is upon sinners because of their sins, and part of their fate is to be driven from the face of the earth. The recipients of judgment are consistent throughout. Those that are the focal point of judgment are the kings and mighty (38:5; 46:4-6; 48:8-10; 53:1-56:8; 62:1-12). The identity of the kings and mighty is not given, but the trend in apocalyptic literature was to refer to those who were immediately on the mind of the author. Current circumstances dictated that the specific people

---

48. DeSilva, *Jewish Teachers of Jesus*, 135. Lucass confirms this notion and further says that the conflation of the two messianic figures brings much more detail to the definition of the Messiah. It is highly likely that Jews by the time of Jesus would have had a detailed view on what the messianic son of man would have looked like and what his function was (Lucass, *Concept of the Messiah*, 149-53).

Grindheim brings out just how ideal this figure is by showing how he manifests a variety of divine characteristics and qualities that are usually attributed to God (Grindheim, *God's Equal*, 162-63). Reynolds goes into detail on these divine characteristics (Reynolds, *Apocalyptic Son of Man*, 47).

49. Walck notes that 46:1 is strikingly similar to Dan 7:13. This passage would have been very familiar to the author and his audience (Walck, *Son of Man*, 58-61).

who were being talked about were likely the Herodians and all those in power associated with their reign.

The judgment portrayed in the Parables is a final judgment. From the very beginning of this text, there is a notion that the unrighteous will no longer be given a chance to repent, "for their life will be at an end" (1 Enoch 38:6). In a way, the Parables is a warning to the unrighteous, giving them an opportunity to repent before it is too late (50:2). Those who do repent will receive mercy and will be numbered among the righteous, because they repented (50:3), but those who do not repent will not be given any more chances to repent. Boccaccini says, "According to the Book of Parables, the righteous are saved according to God's justice and mercy, and sinners are condemned according to God's justice and mercy; but those who repent will be saved by God's mercy, even though they should not be saved according to God's justice."[50] He also points out that this is the last opportunity for repentance in the Enochic judgment timeline in the Parables, and after this, no more opportunity will be given. This opportunity is given just prior to the final judgment. Boccaccini notes that this forgiveness is not given by the messiah but by God.[51]

Judgment is based on a weighing of one's deeds (1 Enoch 41:1; 43:2). One of the deeds that seems to carry the most weight is the denial of the name of the Lord of Spirits (41:2; 45:1–2). This seems to be the common trait of the kings and the mighty, but it is not limited to the kings and mighty. The same fate is on all who deny the name of the Lord of Spirits. Another of the deeds weighed is taking his name in vain (60:6). These are both sins that the kings and the mighty have perpetuated, since in their strength and pride, they find no reason to worship God.

The place of fate for the kings and the mighty is described as a deep valley that will consume them (1 Enoch 53:1–2). This is a place with burning fire (54:1), which is designed for no one to escape forever. This is also a place where the rebellious angels will receive punishment (54:5–6; 55:3–56:3).[52]

---

50. Boccaccini, "Forgiveness of Sins," 161.

51. Boccaccini, "Forgiveness of Sins," 161. He makes a distinction in his article to show the difference between this tradition and the synoptic tradition, where Jesus, the Son of Man, forgives sins (Mark 2:1–10).

52. Nickelsburg ties this angelic judgment back to 1 Enoch 6–11, where the angels are condemned for passing secret heavenly knowledge to men. This continues to be the reason for angelic judgment in the Parables (Nickelsburg, "Salvation without and with Messiah," 56–57).

Possession of the land is a theme that comes up throughout the Parables. For the Jews, their theology is closely tied to the land. This reference is to a specific plot of land, namely the land that was promised to Abraham (Gen 12:7; 13:14-15; 15:7; 17:8). This is the land of which the Israelites eventually took possession and divided to all twelve tribes accordingly, as recorded in Joshua. Eventually, Israel and Judah were dispossessed from the land, but a portion eventually returned under the leadership of Ezra and Nehemiah and once again possessed the land. During the Herodian era, famine and high taxes caused many Jews either to sell their land for survival or to have their land taken from them, due to delinquency.[53] There would have been bitterness and resentment toward those who unlawfully took the land from them. Therefore, it is no surprise that part of the judgment mentioned is a rightful repossession of the land by the righteous. One of the final results of the judgment is that the kings and the mighty will no longer be the ones who possess the land (1 Enoch 38:4; 48:8-9; 62:1-8; 63:1, 12; 67:12). The land itself is tied to the eschatology of the Parables. This land will be returned to the righteous, who will dwell in it forever, while the doers of iniquity will be punished and cast out.

Another reason for judgment upon the kings and the mighty is because of how they persecuted the righteous.[54] The unrighteous were the ones who shed the blood of the righteous (1 Enoch 47:1-2), and a day of reckoning is upon those who persecuted the righteous (47:4). This kind of persecution and crying out for vindication is especially seen in 1-2 Maccabees, where the indication is that those persecuted for the sake of righteousness will receive their reward at the final resurrection, and their persecutors will receive just punishment. In a way, the Parables spells out in detail what will happen to the righteous and the sinners in this last day. The persecuted righteous are vindicated and the sinners are utterly destroyed from the face of the earth.

The final judgment will be an edict given by the messiah against the kings and the mighty and all sinners (1 Enoch 62:5-6), and he will hand them over to the angels for their just punishment (62:11).[55] One of the

---

53. Charlesworth argues that this talk concerning the kings and the mighty and the possession of the land is one of the indicators that the Herodian era and events lay in the background of the Parables (Charlesworth, "Can We Discern," 458-65.

54. Nickelsburg compares the persecuted righteous ones in the Parables to the suffering servant of Isa 52-53 (Nickelsburg, *Resurrection, Immortality*, 93-98, 110-11).

55. Reiser notes that chs. 61-63 represent the most extensive description of judgment. This judgment contains forensic features, but the verdict of the wicked has already

reasons that these angels are being judged is because they were the ones who descended upon the earth and caused human beings to sin and be led astray (64:2).

Messianism

The eschatological messiah revealed in the Parables is a heavenly messiah.[56] However, Waddell notes that the messiah in the Parables is a human figure also.[57] There is no indication that his judgment will take place on the earth, nor is there any indication that his presence will be known on the earth prior to the resurrection. In fact, the revealing of the identity of the messiah does not come until the very end of the Parables. These parables are given as a warning to the inhabitants of the earth that there will soon be a final day when the messiah is revealed, and then he will judge between the righteous and the sinners. Nickelsburg ties the son of man to Ps 2, which would thus link the son of man in the Parables to a Davidic messiah.[58] He makes this link based on wording between the two sources and links found in Isaiah.[59]

The messiah is a character who makes appearances all throughout the Parables. There are a few titles that refer to the messiah, such as the righteous one, chosen one, son of man,[60] and messiah. Each title refers to the

been determined (Reiser, *Jesus and Judgment*, 66–69).

56. Grabbe notes that the representation of the messiah as a heavenly figure is a key difference of the Parables compared to much of the rest of Second Temple sources that see the messiah as an earthly figure (Grabbe, "Son of Man," 184–85). Grabbe also gives a more complete survey of Jewish views of the the messiah in the Second Temple Period, and most represent an earthly Messiah (Grabbe, *Judaic Religion*, 271–91). Lucass reasons that the shift to viewing the messiah as an exalted heavenly figure may be due to the Hasmonean usurpation of the high priesthood and the change in calendar. These two things saw a corruption in the earthly anointed one and the temple, which also corrupted the Day of Atonement as no longer effective, which caused the hope to be placed in a heavenly redeemer (Lucass, *Concept of the Messiah*, 154–55).

57. Waddell, *Messiah*, 49–51.

58. Nickelsburg, *Resurrection, Immortality*, 285.

59. Grabbe notes that the author of the Parables in chs. 46–48 alludes to the servant of the Lord texts in Isa 42:1–4 and 49:1–6. He also alludes to the Davidic oracles of Ps 2 and Isa 11. Grabbe says that these refences leave no doubt that the author of the Parables directly links the son of man to the OT promised Messiah (Grabbe, "Son of Man," 183–84).

60. Grabbe gives a helpful essay on the meaning and origin of the son of man. He contributes etymological explanations, as well as how the phrase is used in early Jewish

same individual, and by the end of the Parables, Enoch is the one identified as the son of man (1 Enoch 71:14). Thus, the narrator of the Parables is the messiah.

The messiah is one whom God is waiting until the final judgment to finally reveal (1 Enoch 62:7; 69:26).[61] There is also a possible indication that the messiah is pre-existent and remains hidden by God until the time of judgment (48:2–3, 6; 62:7).[62] The messiah makes his first appearance in the midst of the righteous as one who is about to bring judgment on the sinners. This judgment will come once the messiah begins to reveal the secret things that are to come (38:2–3). The messiah is the key figure in the judgment of sinners, kings, and the mighty. He is also the key figure who announces reward and eternal life for the righteous. God is the one who bestows this responsibility upon the messiah, as all judgment is handed down to him.[63]

One of the most astonishing developments in the Parables is that the messiah will sit on the throne of glory (1 Enoch 45:3; 51:3; 55:4; 61:8; 62:2–3, 5; 69:27–29; cf. Dan 7:9–14).[64] This is the same throne on which the Lord of Spirits sits (1 Enoch 47:3; 60:2). This is juxtaposed to the thrones of which the kings and the mighty will be dispossessed (46:4–5; 55:5). The author develops in much greater detail the place that the son of man takes in Dan 7.[65] The Parables represents just how far the Danielic tradition grew

---

texts and how the definition grew as it was used by the New Testament and other early Christian texts (Grabbe, "Son of Man").

61. Collins gives discussion to this topic and the whole idea of a heavenly messiah in more detail (J. Collins, "Heavenly Representative," 111–33).

62. Grabbe takes the position that the Parables represents the messiah as pre-existent (Grabbe, "Son of Man," 184). However, VanderKam argues against the notion of the messiah represented as pre-existent (VanderKam, "Righteous One, Messiah," 179–82).

Lucass argues for a pre-existent son of man and indicates that the son of man is just now being revealed by God and stands as a mediator between man and God (Lucass, *Concept of the Messiah*, 148–49).

63. Grindheim notes that although the role of judge is handed to him, he is not independent in his judgment but acts on behalf of God (Grindheim, *God's Equal*, 99).

64. Black notes that the messiah taking the divine judgment throne is a particularly significant shift in early Judaism, which has particular importance for the gospels, where Jesus equates himself with this messianic figure who will one day be the one who judges the righteous and the unrighteous (Black, "Messianism of the Parables," 150–55).

65. Grabbe contends that the development of the son of man in the Parables is a much more in-depth development from the Dan 7 account, but the Parables is still dependent on Dan 7 for the origins of the tradition (Grabbe, "Son of Man," 183–84). Nickelsburg closely associates the son of man in the Parables with Dan 7. He places both texts next to

over the course of one to five centuries (depending on the date one assigns to both works). By the first century AD, one can see that the messianic tradition of a divine judgment figure is well established.

The messiah is described as one who has righteousness in him (1 Enoch 46:3).[66] It is because of this exceeding righteousness that he is given the heavenly place of honor and the ability to judge the unrighteous. It is this messiah who will physically remove the kings and the mighty from their thrones (46:4–5).[67] He will crush and destroy them in his strength until they are no more.

The messiah is the one who is handed the place of judgment after he is seated on the throne of glory (1 Enoch 61:8; 69:27). This is an interesting position for anyone other than God, since he is the one throughout the Old Testament who spells out judgment upon the unrighteous. He shares neither his judgment position nor his throne with anyone. This messianic tradition in the Parables will open up the followers of Jesus to be more accepting of Jesus taking this position (John 5:22). Part of the judgment responsibilities of the messiah will be to slay the sinners and cause the unrighteous to perish from his presence (1 Enoch 62:2–3).[68] Once the kings and the mighty recognize the messiah for who he is, they will bow their faces in terror (62:5) and will "bless and glorify and exalt him who rules over all" (62:6).

Resurrection

The Parables attests to a resurrection of both the righteous and the unrighteous (1 Enoch 51:1). It is at the resurrection that the messiah will take the

---

each other to demonstrate just how closely they are tied together (Nickelsburg, "Salvation without and with Messiah," 58–59).

66. Walck interestingly notes that righteousness dwells in the son of man, but in the OT, righteousness did not dwell in an individual. Righteousness is seen to dwell in the city or a field or metaphorically, but not in an individual (Walck, *Son of Man*, 76).

67. Oegema interprets this passage as a messiah as not only an end-times judge but as a warrior messiah with military characteristics (Oegema, *Anointed and His People*, 144–45).

Chiala notes that 46:1–4 alludes directly to Dan 7 in both features and structure. This indicates that later early Jewish interpretation of Daniel viewed the figure in Dan 7 as messianic (Chiala, "Son of Man," 159–62).

68. Walck notes that the author in 62:1–3 continues his use of Dan 7 allusions but also alludes to Isa 11:2–4 in reference to the identity of the son of man (Walck, *Son of Man*, 101–2).

throne and divide out the righteous to inherit the new earth (51:2–5).[69] In the resurrection, it is the angels who gather the righteous (61:1–5). The resurrection is significant because it marks the beginning of the final judgment, and it is at the resurrection that the messiah is revealed and judgment commences, which marks the end of the possibility of the unrighteous to repent.

Soteriology

Salvation in the Parables is eschatological. The reason that salvation is needed is because of the oppression of the kings and the mighty. Salvation for the righteous comes at the hands of the messiah, who has a dual judgment role of punishing the sinners and rewarding the righteous. One thing that Nickelsburg brings out is that "the text never states why they have been chosen or what deeds or characteristics make them righteous or holy."[70] However, in the typical Jewish mindset, the righteous would be those Jews who maintained the law and did not compromise for the sake of gaining favor and power, as some Jews had done. Those Jews who compromised were listed among those who would ultimately receive judgment in the last days, but those who held fast to the law and did not compromise with the gentiles were ones who would receive reward, which included eternal life and a restoration of the land that was unlawfully taken from them. Regardless of what qualifies them for salvation, "the Son of Man is the vindicator and savior of the righteous."[71]

The narrator speaks to the fact that he has been given eternal life (1 Enoch 37:4). Eternal life is also in view for the righteous (58:3). This declaration comes prior to the telling of the three parables. The inference may be that eternal life may be granted to those who heed the message of the parables and follow the path of righteousness. The messiah is the one who is given the ability to see into the secret ways of the righteous and weigh their deeds to determine if they are worthy to receive eternal life (61:8–9).

Part of the vision reveals the final resting place for the righteous (1 Enoch 38:4). The author describes it as a dwelling place where they will live

---

69. Chester notes that 51:1–5 is a clear allusion to Dan 12:3, but this passage gives much more detail of the resurrection and final judgment event, as opposed to the vagueness of Dan 12 (Chester, *Messiah and Exaltation*, 63).

70. Nickelsburg, "Salvation without and with Messiah," 57.

71. Nickelsburg, "Salvation without and with Messiah," 58.

eternally in the presence of the messiah, and the messiah will rule over the righteous in a spirit of righteousness (39:4–8). Part of this salvation is that the righteous will be the mighty, which shows a role reversal (39:7). The current place of the mighty's reward is on the earth, but this earth will be stripped from them and returned to the righteous, which they will inherit forever. However, this reality is not yet realized, because the narrator gives a sense of longing for this to come to pass (39:8).

Part of this salvation has a new heaven and a new earth in view (1 Enoch 45:4–5). The righteous will inherit the new earth, and the messiah will dwell on the earth with them (v. 5). This will be a dwelling place only for the righteous, because sinners will never step foot on this new earth but will be destroyed from it (vv. 5–6). Not only will the messiah dwell with the righteous, but the presence of God will be in their midst (vv. 5–6). This harkens back to the garden of Eden, where the presence of God was with humans (Gen. 2). This also looks forward to the new heavens and new earth presented in Isa 65. The contents of this place include an inexhaustible spring of righteousness and many springs of wisdom from which the righteous will drink (1 Enoch 48:1). It will be a place of worship of the Lord of Spirits (48:5).

THE SON OF MAN IN 4 EZRA

Dating and Background

Although 4 Ezra is typically dated to the late first century to early second century AD, it provides coherence and additional evidence to the argument that the Jews had specific beliefs concerning the son of man as a messianic judge figure. This document, paired with Daniel and the Parables of Enoch, indicates that this was an established Jewish tradition in the late first century BC and throughout the first century AD. Thus, it is highly likely that John's Jewish audience would have been very familiar with the idea that the messiah could potentially be the heavenly son of man figure from Daniel instead of or possibly in addition to the conquering Davidic king who was seen in the Psalms of Solomon. It then remains to examine what 4 Ezra says about the son of man as messiah and his role in judgment.

The phrase son of man is not present in 4 Ezra, but there are clear allusions throughout the text that connect directly to the apocalyptic visions in Daniel and the Parables of Enoch. It is likely that the reason son of man is not used in this text is because the author does not want the description of his figure to be confused or conflated with how the Gospels use the title to refer to Jesus; the Gospels would likely have been circulated throughout the area by the time of his writing, and his audience would likely have been familiar with this title used in direct reference to Jesus. Thus, the author likely wanted his audience to see that he was directly referring to Daniel and the Parables. There is no doubt that the author was well acquainted with these two texts, as will be indicated below. The vision of chapters 11–13 follows along with the events outlined in Dan 7. In 4 Ezra 11:1 and following, there is an eagle representing the Roman empire rising from the sea, and in Dan 7:3–4, there is a great beast with wings like eagles rising from the sea, which also represents an evil empire. In 4 Ezra 12:3, the whole body of the eagle is destroyed by fire, which corresponds to the beast being destroyed and given over to burning fire in Dan 7:11. In 4 Ezra 13:1–2, there is a man rising from the sea, which corresponds to the one like a son of man coming in the clouds. Another interesting development in 4 Ezra is in 7:28–29, where the messiah is referred to in terms of sonship to God. Also associated with this messianic figure are judgment, salvation, and resurrection. Ultimately, the messianic figure presented in 4 Ezra acts on behalf of God, and it is God himself bringing about this judgment.

Judgment and Messianic Expectation in 4 Ezra

Associated with the messianic figure in 4 Ezra is his role in judgment and how it relates to God's overall role in judgment.[72] There are two main passages that deal directly with the messiah and his immediate role in eschatological events, 4 Ezra 7:26–44 and 12:31–34. Intertwined in the judgment scenes are two different visions concerning the same messianic figure.[73] Chronologically, 12:31–34 should be placed right after 7:28, because these verses add a few more details as to what the reign of the messiah will entail.

---

72. VanLandingham indicates that the judgment passages follow the Deuteronomic formula for blessings and curses, when speaking to whether one will be judged as righteous or wicked. The same theme of judgment according to one's deeds follows in this text as it does throughout Second Temple texts. He also argues that this text gives a good representation of late first-century AD Judaism concerning eschatological judgment (VanLandingham, *Judgment and Justification*, 151–52).

73. Ellens notes that this figure is given similar features as God in the OT, such as extinguishing enemies with a fiery breath, associated with clouds, and melting humanity with a distinctive voice (Ellens, *Son of Man*, 166).

They indicate that the messiah, who is from the lineage of David, will be revealed at the end times and will sit on a judgment seat to judge the wicked nations, especially the evil Roman Empire, and reestablish the Jewish people to reign with him. This messianic kingdom will be established for four hundred years (7:28).[74] At the end of his reign, the messiah will die, as will the population of the earth, and the earth will rest for seven days, after which will be a resurrection of the dead, which will give way to the final day of judgment, presided over by God himself (7:29–33).[75] These passages reveal just how imminently the Jews believed the messianic kingdom would come and be established. They believed that the messiah would swiftly come in and purge the earth of evil nations, especially the Roman Empire. These passages also indicate that there was a Jewish belief that the messiah would partake in some form of eschatological judgment.[76] This belief follows a similar course for the messianic expectation not only from Daniel and the Parables of Enoch, but also from the Psalms of Solomon and various Qumran documents. Fourth Ezra indicates that the Jewish idea of the messianic figure purported in the Parables of Enoch was not just a rogue sectarian idea about the messiah to come, but was likely a belief that was known by John, as well as by his Jewish audience. These documents would have likely influenced their beliefs about what the messiah would look like. This messianic expectation is evidenced by the fact that this same tradition was being used in apocalyptic Jewish literature a century or so after the Parables was written.

TESTAMENT OF ABRAHAM

The Testament of Abraham is a document that speaks directly to the eschatological idea that God appointed another as judge over mankind. There is much debate as to the dating and provenance of this document, since there are not any internal historical indicators that would lead one to more definitively date it. There is also debate as to whether this is a Jewish document

---

74. Reynolds notes that the description of the messiah in 4 Ezra alludes directly to Isa 11. This figure is also one that executes God's end-times judgment and is described with features typically given in descriptions of God in the OT (Reynolds, *Apocalyptic Son of Man*, 52–54).

75. Reiser notes that the judgment here is done without any favor or mercy but solely based upon one's deeds, which is keeping the law (Reiser, *Jesus and Judgment*, 115–16).

76. Chester notes that this figure, although it plays a key eschatological role, is rather limited (Chester, *Messiah and Exaltation*, 347).

(with possible Christian interpolations) or a Christian document written with Jewish elements to mirror apocalyptic and testamental literature of the era. The majority of commentators lean towards the original document being a Jewish work because "it seems very unlikely that a Christian work dealing with the subject of death would make no reference to the role of Jesus' crucifixion and resurrection in securing eternal life or would place Abel (13.2) rather than Christ in the role of heavenly judge."[77] Due to historical ambiguity, commentators place the composition of the original document anywhere between 200 BC and AD 100. This document is being considered in this study because, if it is a Jewish document within this time frame, it gives direct support to the fact that John's Jewish audience would have had a preconceived belief about the idea that God would give the responsibility of judging mankind to another. Thus, when Jesus says, "For not even the Father judges anyone, but He has given all judgment to the Son" (John 5:22), it is a statement that would have conflicted with his audience's eschatological beliefs concerning the judgment role of the Messiah.

Chapter 13 in the Testament of Abraham opens up with an eschatological judgment scene that depicts three different judgments. The first judgment is done by Abel as the judge over all creation (Testament of Abraham 13:2), then a judgment of the gentiles by the twelve tribes of Israel (13:6), then the final judgment done by God (13:7). The passage most pertinent to this study is:

> Do you see, most holy Abraham, the terrible man sitting upon the throne? This is the son of the first created Adam, who is called Abel, whom the wicked Cain killed, and he sits thus to judge all creation, and examines righteous men and sinners. For God has said, I shall not judge you, but every man born of man shall be judged. Therefore, he has given to him judgment, to judge the world until his great and glorious coming. (13:2-4)

This passage indicates that, at least by the end of the first century AD, there was a Jewish belief that God would or has already placed the judgment of humankind into the hands of one other than himself. Thus, it is likely that there would have been those in John's Jewish audience who understood Jesus's statement in John 5:22 and would have not given a second thought to this statement's claim.

---

77. Docherty, *Jewish Pseudepigrapha*, 116. Further, Chester argues that the figure of Abel should be understood as the one like a son of man from Dan 7 (Chester, *Messiah and Exaltation*, 71–73).

THE DANIELIC SON OF MAN AND ITS DEVELOPMENT

CONCLUSION

In addition to the eschatological expectation of judgment and the Messiah considered in chapters 2 and 3, early Jewish beliefs also developed concerning the one like a son of man from Dan 7. Although the identity of this figure in Daniel is debated, the Parables of Enoch and later 4 Ezra reveal that early Jewish belief by the beginning of the first century AD interprets the Danielic one like a son of man as the messiah. The son of man in the Parables is an exalted figure who receives the eschatological role of judge, which is passed to him by God. This figure engages in judgment, executes judgment, and is even given the throne of God to do so. Just like in other early Jewish texts, judgment is based on works in the present life, and the final judgment has been predetermined. The verdict of the judgment is either punishment or eternal life, which is ultimately determined at the resurrection. Again, this text was written to give hope to the righteous to persevere in the midst of the tyranny of the kings and the mighty who oppressed the people and received their reward in this lifetime. The righteous would receive their reward upon death and ultimately in the resurrection, when they were granted eternal life, and they would watch as the wicked received their just punishment for their evil works in the present life.

Fourth Ezra and the Testament of Abraham are included to show continuity of belief in the first century AD that a messianic figure would receive the role of eschatological judge and that the beliefs about the son of man in the Parables are not isolated beliefs. Although these two documents are brief, they contain similar eschatological themes of judgment and the end times.

The early Jewish beliefs explicated in chapters 2 and 3, combined with the beliefs surrounding the son of man tradition in this chapter, give a fairly full picture of what John's Jewish audience would have believed and what imagery would have come to mind, as John presents Jesus using certain terms and phrases pertaining to judgment, his role as judge, the use of his self-designation as the Son of Man and its relation to his claim as the one who has received the right to judge, the resurrection, and other surrounding eschatological themes. Jesus's teachings challenge and reinterpret every eschatological belief of John's Jewish audience. Jesus's teachings concerning judgment and his role in it reveal just how radical his teachings would have been to an early Jewish audience.

5

The Audiences and Their Messianic Expectations Represented in the Gospel of John

INTRODUCTION

THE GOSPEL OF JOHN seeks to present Jesus in a different light from the rest of the gospels. John not only wants to show his audience that Jesus is the promised Messiah to come but also that he is the divine Son of God. John's high Christology places much more emphasis on the divinity of Jesus than the other Gospels, which comes out throughout the Gospel in Jesus's discourses and his actions. One aspect of Jesus's messianism and claim of divinity that is often overlooked is Jesus's claim as messianic judge in light of early Jewish belief. As has been seen in chapters 2 through 4, there is an established precedent that shows that a claim to be the messianic eschatological judge was not a far-fetched notion for John's Jewish audience. There is in early Jewish texts an already established messianic tradition that would allow for God to pass his authority to judge to another. It should not be misunderstood the presence of this tradition somehow undermines Jesus's divinity. The Gospel of John makes it quite clear that Jesus claims equality with the Father and does what he sees his Father doing, which is why the Jewish leaders seek to kill him, not because of his messianic claims.

This chapter will consider the specific audiences and views of messianic expectation represented in the Gospel of John. The teachings of Jesus in the Gospel of John are in the context of his Jewish audience, who had their own preconceived beliefs and expectations concerning the coming messiah and his possible role in the eschatological judgment. This chapter will seek to identify the various audiences of Jesus throughout the Gospel of John and their eschatological and messianic beliefs. It is probable that John had similar Jewish audiences in mind when he penned his Gospel. It is important to understand the represented audience, because it will help the modern reader understand why John represents the words of Jesus and those to whom he is talking in the way that he does. Each audience type would have understood the words of Jesus differently. The way the original audience would have understood something gives the modern interpreter necessary keys to better and more fully interpret the way that John represents the conversations in his Gospel.

As has been seen in chapters 2 through 4, there was a broad range of belief concerning messianic expectation throughout early Judaism. This would likely have been the case with John's Jewish audience as well. Interestingly, John interacts with most of the main messianic expectations found in early Jewish thought. Knowing the early Jewish background behind the messianic views represented in the Gospel of John will greatly aid the modern interpreter in knowing why Jesus's responses to certain Jewish claims and questions are represented in the manner that John penned them. This knowledge also aids in how Jesus's words ought to be understood by a modern interpreter.

THE AUDIENCES REPRESENTED IN THE GOSPEL OF JOHN

Understanding John's Jewish audience and the beliefs that the various sects and social groups had will help one better and more clearly understand the intensity and radical nature of the teachings of Jesus. The Jewish audiences represented in the Gospel of John were likely similar in nature to those to whom John was writing. The modern interpreter will greatly benefit from knowing and understanding how these nuanced Jewish audiences would have understood John's presentation of Jesus's teachings. Most commentators consulted for this study interpret the teachings of Jesus in light of Christian belief and Old Testament interpretation. Only a handful of commentators (although the number is increasing in recent scholarship) consider Jesus's teachings in light of early Judaism and early Jewish beliefs. This study will seek to go even further and carefully consider what John's immediate Jewish audience would have been thinking upon hearing or reading John's presentation of Jesus's use of certain key words and phrases concerning his role as Messiah and judge. This study will also consider just how radically different Jesus's teachings were from John's audience's beliefs on these topics. This section will seek to provide brief background to the various Jewish sects and social groups, with special note on those groups that held to certain distinct eschatological or messianic beliefs.

Jews

The Gospel of John uses the designation Jews typically to refer to Jewish leadership, while other places John identifies the leadership as Pharisees and chief priests (John 7:32, 45; 11:47, 57). Jesus's use of the term is used in a somewhat negative fashion, often to warn his audience against the hypocritical teachings of the Jewish leadership and to show a distinction between true and false believers. John identifies the Jews as those who are opposed to Jesus and his teachings (5:16–18; 6:41; 7:1 8:48–58; 10:31).

Pharisees

The Pharisees were one of the more predominant religious sects of early Judaism and the predominant sect identified in the Gospel of John as a part of Jesus's audience.[1] They likely have their origins during the time of Ezra, with the main concern to separate themselves from all types of impurities as regulated in the Torah. Concerning what Josephus writes about the Pharisees, J. Julius Scott says, "The Pharisees maintained a simple lifestyle; they were affectionate and harmonious in their dealings with others, especially respectful to their elders, and quite influential throughout the land of Israel—although at the time of Herod they numbered only about six thousand."[2]

---

1. For further discussion on the Pharisees' history and beliefs, see VanderKam, *Introduction to Early Judaism*, 187–89; Scott, *Jewish Backgrounds*, 202–206; Josephus, *Antiquities* and *Jewish War*.

2. Outside of a few references in the New Testament, Scott gets the majority of his information concerning the Pharisees from Josephus's *Antiquities* and *Jewish War*. Here, Scott references *Antiquities* 13.10.5; 17.2.4; 18.1.3; and *Jewish War* 2.8.14 (Scott, *Jewish Backgrounds*, 203).

The Audiences and Their Messianic Expectations

The Gospel of Mark reveals not only their strict adherence to the law, but also their strict adherence to the hedge that was placed around the law so that they would not accidentally or unknowingly break the law. Mark 7:3–4 says, "For the Pharisees and all the Jews do not eat unless they carefully wash their hands, thus observing the traditions of the elders; and when they come from the marketplace, they do not eat unless they cleanse themselves; and there are many other things which they have received in order to observe, such as the washing of cups and pitchers and copper pots." This is just one example of their strict legalistic practices.

The Gospels reveal special concern for keeping the Sabbath and the regulations surrounding its keeping. One of the harshest critiques of Jesus by the Pharisees is their accusation that Jesus does work on the Sabbath, which is mainly found in his Sabbath healings (see Matt 12:10–12; Mark 3:1–4; Luke 6:6–9; 13:10–16; 14:1–5; John 5:9–16; 9:14–16).

Doctrine was also quite important to the Pharisees. Apart from strict views concerning the Torah, they had developed beliefs concerning immortality, the resurrection, messianic expectation, eschatological views, divine sovereignty, angels, demons, and spirits.[3] However, apart from a few documents linked to pharisaical composition, their religious and doctrinal beliefs are not well articulated and developed. The amount that is present in these sources paired with their interactions with Jesus indicates that they would have understood the implications of Jesus's teachings in these areas. Jesus used words, phrases, and beliefs with which the Pharisees were familiar. Jesus uses their understanding and challenges these beliefs, which is evident both from his teachings and their response to these teachings.

Sadducees and Chief Priests

Although the Sadducees are not mentioned in the Gospel of John by name, the Synoptic Gospels identify them as part of the audience paired with those who were present with the Pharisees (Matt 16:1; 22:23, 34; Mark 12:13, 18). It is possible that John's reference of the chief priests is of the Sadducees,

---

3. There are a few early Jewish texts that are of possible Pharisaic composition, which would inform their eschatological and messianic beliefs; see Testament of Moses and Psalms of Solomon. See also Acts 23:8. Due to their learned nature, the Pharisees likely studied and were quite familiar with the apocryphal and pseudepigraphal documents composed by the time of Jesus's ministry. See Wylen, *Jews in Time of Jesus*, 142; VanderKam, *Introduction to Early Judaism*, 205–6.

since the Sadducees identified themselves as coming from priestly lineage.[4] Religiously, the Synoptic Gospels and Acts give a representation of their beliefs, especially in connection to saying that there is no resurrection (Matt 22:23; Mark 12:18; Luke 20:27; Acts 23:8, also showing their denial of angels and spirits). The Sadducees were literalists who only accepted the teachings of Moses in the Torah and thus rejected other teachings, including the prophets.[5] Although they would have rejected the traditions developed from non-Sadducean literature that came out of the early Jewish writings, it is likely that they would have been familiar with the beliefs that came out of them.

Samaritans

John 4 represents Jesus's encounter with the Samaritans. This chapter also contains some of their religious views regarding worship (John 4:20) and messianic expectation (4:25). The Samaritans originated from the Jews left in the land after the Assyrian conquest and the foreigners imported into the land by the Assyrians. Inevitably, they intermarried, and there resulted a syncretistic religion of Yahwehism and the religion of the foreigners. From the return from exile to the time of Jesus's ministry, there had been several centuries of dissent and conflict between the Jews and the Samaritans in political, social, cultural, and religious areas.[6] Religiously, the Samaritans held only to the Torah, which was modified from the traditional Masoretic Text of the Jews. They also held Moses in very high esteem and reverence, even beyond what was seen by the Pharisees and Sadducees.[7] Thus, the messianic expectation of the Samaritans would have focused around the prophecy from Moses in Deut 18:15 and 18 that a prophet like him would be raised up from their own countrymen.[8] This follows with the Samari-

---

4. Wylen notes that they were priestly and aristocratic (Wylen, *Jews in Time of Jesus*, 138–39). See also VanderKam, *Introduction to Early Judaism*, 189; Scott, *Jewish Backgrounds*, 206–7.

5. See Wylen, *Jews in Time of Jesus*, 138–39; VanderKam, *Introduction to Early Judaism*, 190–91; Scott, *Jewish Backgrounds*, 208.

6. James D. Purvis brings out many of the points of contention between the Samaritans and the Jews (Purvis, "Samaritans and Judaism," 81–98).

7. Scott, *Jewish Backgrounds*, 196–200.

8. Novenson brings out the distinction between Judean and Samaritan beliefs concerning the prophet, especially as they relate to the prophet as messianic (Novenson, "Jesus the Messiah," 112–14).

tan woman's statement in 4:25 when she says, "When that one comes, he will declare all things to us." Other than this encounter in John 4, there is no other indication in the Gospel of John that Samaritans were again part of Jesus's audience, but this passage does indicate that the Samaritans had a certain messianic expectation. Interestingly, this is also one of the two places in which Jesus directly identifies himself as the Messiah, as opposed to his indirect manner with the Pharisees, chief priests, and the crowd.

Crowd and Disciples

The crowd and the disciples represent the Jewish people who were not necessarily identified with a certain Jewish sect or cultural group. These Jews would have included farmers, fishermen, carpenters, merchants, etc., from which came Jesus's disciples and the majority of his followers. These were the commoners of Jewish society and likely did not have extensive educations like the Pharisees and the chief priests. However, the Gospel of John indicates that even the crowd had certain eschatological and messianic views, which were likely taught in the synagogues on the Sabbath. There is no religious consensus by which the common Israelite in Jesus's audience can be measured. In fact, in terms of messianic expectation of the crowd, about four to five messianic views are expressed, with some of them clearly having closer ties to the messianic expectation of early Jewish literature than of the Old Testament. Other than Jesus's interaction with Nicodemus, all the statements of messianic expectation in the Gospel of John come from the common Jew and not the religious elite.

MESSIANIC EXPECTATION REPRESENTED IN THE GOSPEL OF JOHN

Messianic expectation was at an all-time high at the time of Jesus's ministry. This was also the case by the time of the writing of the Gospel of John. John's Jewish audience would have been searching diligently for the messiah. It is likely his audience would have been familiar with the claims of Christianity by this period. The Jews in John's audience would have had similar messianic expectations as the audiences represented in the Gospel. This expectation is evidenced by the early Jewish literature that was produced in the late first century BC through the mid-second century AD. The Gospel of John not only concerns itself with messianic expectation as it relates to Jesus, but also records specific Jewish messianic beliefs that John represents in Jesus's audiences throughout the Gospel. This section will consider those passages in John that exhibit someone in Jesus's audience espousing an early Jewish belief about the coming messiah that was present in the Old Testament and early Jewish literature. This section will not only give light to the messianic expectation of his audience but argue that his audience had a wide range of messianic expectations and would have expected the messiah to say certain things and make certain claims. Jesus's distinction about his own messianic role is nuanced in his teachings. It is the radical nuances to which Jesus's audience react, not the expected claim.

Messiah as Prophet

One of the messianic expectations represented in the Gospel of John is that the messiah was the prophet whom Moses prophesied would come after him (Deut 18:15, 18).[9] As was seen in the above section on the Samaritans, the expectation of the messiah to be the prophet flows naturally from strict adherence to the Torah alone (cf. John 4:25).[10] The beginning of John 6 records the sign of the multiplication of the five loaves and two fish. This sign is purposefully performed in the like manner of God providing manna to the Israelites in the wilderness, which is evidenced by Jesus's words to the crowd in 6:32, where Jesus references Moses giving bread out of heaven. In 6:14, it appears that the crowd perceives the sign as similar to the sign Moses proclaimed to the people through God, concluding that Jesus truly is the prophet who is to come into the world. Williams notes that it was

---

9. Cf. 1QS 8:15–9:11. This passage specifically mentions the prophet as one with the anointed of Aaron and Israel, thus a possible third messianic figure in view at Qumran.

Bauckham gives an extensive survey on those who identified themselves as prophets in the first century AD. He gives four common characteristics: they claimed to be prophets, they took their followers into the desert, they promised their followers signs, and they spoke of liberation and deliverance. This is why John the Baptist and Jesus's audiences ask them certain questions, because they were seeing if Jesus matched up to their standard of messianic expectation of the prophet (Bauckham, *Testimony of the Beloved*, 212–25). See also Frey, *Theology and History*, 30–31.

Williams notes that references to the prophet as an eschatological figure in early Jewish literature are quite limited. He says that this prophet in early Jewish literature is seen as speaking oracles concerning cultic regulations (cf. 1 Macc 4:46; 14:41) (Williams, "Jesus the Prophet," 94–95).

10. Keener notes that Samaritan belief would have seen the prophet as a ruler and a teacher, like Moses, and not just as a prophetic figure (Keener, *Gospel of John*, 1:619–20).

likely a Jewish expectation for a prophet like Moses to come and perform signs similar to the signs performed by Moses and securing liberation from Rome.[11] Interestingly, the crowd then seeks to make Jesus king by force, which conflates both the prophetic expectation and kingly expectation of the crowd.[12]

Another aspect of the prophet from Deut 18 that the people pick up on is his ability to teach things that he has not learned but which were taught to him by God. In John 7:15, the Jews say, "How has this man become learned, having never been educated?" The Jews were aware of who studied at their schools. The implication is that Jesus has knowledge about things of which he should not have knowledge, since he did not attend any of the rabbinic schools. The confession of the people at the end of his teachings is that he is the prophet, because of the words they were hearing him say. Paired with this is the confession of others that he is the Christ (7:40–41).

Messiah as King

A kingly messiah from the line of David is also an expectation seen on the lips of the crowd in the Gospel of John.[13] The first instance is seen from the confession of Nathanael in John 1:49, as he says, "Rabbi, you are the Son of God; you are the King of Israel." This comes right after a prophetic utterance that Jesus speaks to Nathanael, in which, like 6:14–15 seen previously, it appears the Jews were looking for a messiah as both prophet and king. In the context of the messiah as the prophet (7:40) are those in the crowd saying that the messiah was to be from Bethlehem of the line of David, which also indicates an expectation of a kingly messiah.[14] John 7:43 notes

---

11. See *Ant.* 20:97–98, 168–70, *J. W.* 259–63, as represented in Williams, "Jesus the Prophet," 100–101.

12. See Keener's discussion on the Jewish expectation of the prophet to have both a prophetic and kingly role (Keener, *Gospel of John*, 669–71). Keener points out that the reaction of the crowd to make Jesus king by force was something that was typical in this era of those who claimed to be prophets or identified themselves as a prophet. Novenson notes that Jewish tradition saw Moses in a prophetic and kingly manner (Novenson, "Jesus the Messiah," 114–15).

13. Cf. Sir 45:25; 47:1–22; Psalm of Solomon 17; 4Q161, 11–21; 4Q174; 4Q285; 1QSb 2:22–5:29; 1QM 5:1–2; 11:6–7. A king from the sun, see Sibylline Oracles 3:652–56.

14. Keener notes that John's emphasis seems to be on Jesus's divine kingship, which is different from what the crowd would have expected concerning the kingship of the expected messiah (Keener, *Gospel of John*, 487–88).

there was division in the crowd concerning Jesus. This indicates that there were multiple Jewish views concerning the expectation of the messiah and possible conflation of views as well. A similar scenario happens when the Jews are asking John the Baptist if he is the one to come (1:19–21).

Messiah as Coming from God

One of the messianic expectations that is seen in a few of the early Jewish texts is that the messiah would have heavenly or unknown origins.[15] This view of the messiah possibly appears when Nicodemus confesses that he believes that Jesus is a teacher who comes from God because of the signs that he performs. In one aspect, this follows with the Mosaic prophecy of the prophet receiving his teachings from God; but the context of John 3:1–21 moves toward the Enochic tradition of heavenly knowledge being revealed to and through the son of man. This is further evidenced by John the Baptist;s words later in the chapter, as John says concerning Jesus's origins that "he who comes from above is above all" (3:31). The crowd gives an interesting belief concerning the messiah in 7:27 when they say, "Whenever the Christ may come, no one knows where he is from." By contrast, just a few verses later, the crowd says that the Christ will come from Bethlehem of the line of David (7:42). Both 7:27 and 7:42 indicate that there were differing opinions concerning messianic expectation in Jesus's audience, but also that the crowd likely knew each other's messianic opinions, because of the debate and division concerning Jesus as the Christ (7:43).

Messiah/Son of Man as Living Forever

One last piece of messianic expectation exhibited in the Gospel of John pertains to the belief of the Christ as the son of man who is to remain forever (John 12:34).[16] This proclamation comes right after Jesus indicates

---

15. Cf. Dan 7–9; 1 Enoch 37–71; 90:37–38; Testament of Moses 10; Psalm of Solomon 17; 4 Ezra 7, 12.

Bauckham gives two possibilities of a hidden messiah: he will be a man who will not be known as messiah until God reveals him to be, or he is revealed when he comes from heaven (Bauckham, *Testimony of the Beloved*, 232–33).

16. First Enoch 37:4 sees God granting Enoch, later identified as the son of man, eternal life. The author of the Parables directly references the messiah as "the righteous one" (1 Enoch 38:2), "the chosen one" (45:2–3; 51:3; 55:4; 61:8; 62:1–3), and "the son of man" (62:5; 69:27–29).

the kind of death that the son of man is going to die (12:23–24, 32–33). Although the crowd themselves say that their teaching about the Christ remaining forever comes from the law, this teaching actually more closely follows the Enochic tradition of the son of man given an exalted status from God (cf. 1 Enoch 62:6).[17] This belief follows with the previous belief of the messiah having a heavenly origin, because a heavenly origin would indicate the messiah having supernatural characteristics, which would have included immortality and eternality.

CONCLUSION

The audiences represented in the Gospel indicate a wide variety of Jewish perspectives. It is important for the modern interpreter to know the background of these audiences, because each one has a slightly different messianic understanding. John makes some of these messianic understandings obvious, but others, such as the Samaritans, are not quite clear to a modern interpreter if he or she does not know the background.

The representation of the various messianic views throughout the Gospel of John indicates that John was quite familiar with the messianic views throughout early Judaism. Since John was familiar with these messianic perspectives, it is likely that his Jewish audience was as well. This is indicated by the fact that John does not stop to explain the embedded messianic views along the way. He assumes that his Jewish audience would be familiar with the nuanced messianic views and the specific implications that each had. Although this is the case with the original audience, a modern audience may not have this nuanced insight and preconceived beliefs. The modern interpreter will better understand the text when the text is perceived with an early Jewish mindset.

Bauckham points to the eternal dynasty promised to David in 2 Sam 7:12–13 (cf. Psalm of Solomon 17) (Bauckham, *Testimony of the Beloved*, 235–36). See also Köstenberger, *John*, 385–86.

17. 4 Ezra 7:28 indicates that the Davidic messiah would have an established earthly kingdom for four hundred years before he dies. This indicates a possible Jewish belief raised in John 12:34. The "forever" may just indicate a belief in a supernaturally long life.

6

Jesus's Representation as the Son of Man in the Gospel of John

INTRODUCTION

CHAPTER 4 MADE IT evident that there was an established son of man tradition by the time John wrote his Gospel. The Synoptic Gospels verify this. John also uses the Son of Man throughout his Gospel. However, John's usage of Son of Man is quite strategic. He uses the title in a way that is going to become pregnant with meaning. The reader will discover that there are numerous links to Daniel and the Parables of Enoch. There are also embedded Old Testament references associated with its usage. There are links that will be drawn between Son of Man and the various messianic expectations. These things and others are some of what John's Jewish audience would have likely had in mind when coming across each Son of Man reference. John strategically links the things with which an early Jew would have been familiar to the Son of Man sayings in his Gospel. These are strategically placed to paint a fuller picture of how John represents Jesus as the Messiah in his Gospel.

The modern interpreter needs to clearly understand how Jesus represents himself as the Son of Man in John in light of what his Jewish audiencalready believed, because this will much more clearly show just how radical Jesus's teachings are compared to the beliefs of his audience. Directly related to the Son of Man is Jesus's redefined role as the imminent and eschatological messianic judge. By the first century AD, there would

Jesus's Representation as the Son of Man

have been an established Jewish tradition that the expected messiah would partake in the eschatological judgment in one form or another. John presents Jesus as expressing his own teachings on this belief, which contrast with the preconceived beliefs of his Jewish audience, who are looking for immediate eschatological judgment upon the arrival of the messiah. This chapter will seek to show how the teachings of Jesus concerning his self-identification as the Son of Man and messianic judge are radically different from the beliefs and views of his Jewish audience.

There is a long-standing son of man debate concerning the origin of its use in the Gospel of John.[1] Although there is merit to entering the conversation, this study is concerned with how Jesus used this title in relation to how John's Jewish audience had preconceived ideas and beliefs about the son of man and his identity. The extent of this debate will be considered as it pertains to helping one understand how Jesus used the title in the Gospel of John. One of the things revealed by this debate is that after Daniel, the Parables of Enoch is the only document until the composition of the Gospels that uses the title son of man. Thus, there is heavy reliance in scholarship upon this document in the son of man debate. Much can be gleaned from the Parables and possible influence upon early Jewish belief concerning messianic expectation in regard to the figure of the son of man. The Parables of Enoch show the Messiah as a distinct figure from God. DeSilva notes:

> While the Parables of Enoch provide the closest comparative text for the study of Jesus' conception of the Son of Man, it is difficult to demonstrate direct dependence. Jesus seems to know and to draw upon the traditions about the Son of Man known from the Parables of Enoch but not necessarily upon those particular texts directly.[2]

---

1. Common interpretations of the Johannine origins of the Son of Man include: (1) a reinterpretation of the Synoptic tradition (Casey, *Solution to the "Son of Man"*); (2) the OT background of Dan 7 combined with Ps 8, Prov 30:1–4, and Ezekiel (Burkett, *Son of the Man*; Ridderbos, *Gospel of John*, 93; Rhea, *Johannine Son of Man*); (3) a gnostic redeemer myth (Bultmann, *Gospel of John*); (4) a reflection of heavenly man speculations (Dodd, *Interpretation of Fourth Gospel*; Higgins, *Son of Man*); (5) a combination of Dan 7, the Parables of Enoch, and other early Jewish texts (Moloney, *Johannine Son of Man*; Reynolds, *Apocalyptic Son of Man*; Ellens, *Son of Man*); (6) a representation of Jesus's humanity only where, for example, Jesus has the right to judge mankind because he is the perfectly righteous man (Barrett, *Gospel According to St John*, 262).

2. DeSilva, *Jewish Teachers of Jesus*, 139.

Both judge from the same throne, but the author of the Parables does not conflate the two as the same divine being. Jesus does. One shocking thing for the Jewish leaders to hear was Jesus's redefinition of who would receive the judgment of condemnation. Jesus points the finger at them and says that they are the ones who stand condemned unless they believe in the Son of Man.[3] The religious leaders saw themselves as the righteous, who would have had an automatic pass at the final judgment. They were the ones who remained faithful to God in the midst of Roman sovereignty and followed the law meticulously and even all the religious traditions.

Chapter 4 of this study sought only to show the presence of the son of man tradition in the first century AD and to define what those beliefs would have been and how these beliefs would have been in the mind of John's Jewish audience when Jesus is teaching concerning his role as the Son of Man and eschatological judge. The Son of Man saying in John 5:27 must be understood in the overall context of how the Son of Man is presented and defined throughout John. Francis J. Moloney rightly notes that the thirteen uses of Son of Man in John need to be understood synchronically, as he says, "The meaning of the expression in any one of them should be guided by the meaning of the other 12."[4] Thus, this section will take the overall picture of the Son of Man in the Gospel of John and show how that relates to Jesus's claim as the eschatological judge in John, in relation to how John's Jewish audience understood the role of the son of man.

---

3. DeSilva gives a helpful summary of how John uses the title Son of Man for Jesus and some of the implications that it brings. He says, "The phrase 'Son of Man' also figures prominently in speech attributed to Jesus in the Fourth Gospel. These include suffering Son of Man sayings, though in the peculiar Johannine idioms of 'lifting up' the Son of Man (John 3:14; 8:28), of eating the flesh and drinking the blood of the Son of Man (6:53), and of the hour of the Son of Man's 'glorification' (12:23; 13:31). In the Fourth Gospel, Jesus' conversation partners are prepared to speak of the Messiah also as the Son of Man: 'We heard from the Law that the Messiah remains forever, and how can *you* say that it is necessary that the Son of Man be lifted up? Who is this Son of Man?' (12:34). When Jesus asks the man born blind, 'Do you believe in the Son of Man?' John writes as though the latter would know the title independently as one more way of speaking about the Messiah: 'Who is he, sir, that I may believe in him?' (9:35–36). The Son of Man also has the eschatological role familiar from Parables of Enoch and the Gospels (especially Matthew), as he is 'given authority to execute judgment' by God (5:27). Distinctive among the Gospels is John's emphasis on the Son of Man as a preexistent being who has first descended from heaven to enter the realm of human beings and moves forward toward ascending again to heaven (3:13; 6:62)" (DeSilva, *Jewish Teachers of Jesus*, 135).

4. Moloney, "*Parables of Enoch*," 279.

Jesus's Representation as the Son of Man

John represents Jesus using specific phrases, concepts, and beliefs in his teachings that would have resonated with his audience. Jesus's using the title Son of Man throughout John would have sounded familiar to John's Jewish audience. However, Jesus takes a concept or belief from early Jewish thought and gives his own definition and interpretation of the Son of Man as it relates to himself, which is often a radical and completely unexpected conception that departs from the Danielic and Enochic traditions developed in early Judaism. In fact, Ellens notes nine stark contrasts between the presentation of the son of man in the Parables and the Gospel of John:

1. John's Son of Man is not a man who begins his career on earth and is swept up into heaven by a whirlwind, as Enoch is. Instead, he is a divine figure whose journey begins in heaven (1:1–5), and is carried out on earth, both characteristics more like Daniel's Son of Man than Enoch's.

2. John's Son of Man descends to earth to carry out his divinely designed function (1:14). This function is not to judge as in Daniel, 1 Enoch, and the Synoptic Gospels (5:27–47), but as a savior (3:12–18).

3. In John, as in Mark, Matthew, and Luke, he reveals himself on earth to be the Son of Man: to Nathanael and his companions (1:51ff), to his disciples and the crowd (12:28), and to all humanity whom he will draw to himself (12:32). In 1 Enoch he is announced the Son of Man by a special celestial decree from God to the angelic host in heaven.

4. John's Son of Man is not raised to supra-angelic status, as in 1 Enoch and the Synoptic Gospels, since in John he begins and remains superior to the angels, namely, divine.

5. Moreover, he does not become angelomorphic; he manifests however as anthropomorphic (1:14, 17ff.), as in Daniel, despite the fact that in John he is really theomorphic (Jn 1:1).

6. John's Son of Man inherently knows all the wisdom and secrets of God, whereas Enoch needs to be given a celestial tour to be taught the mysteries he must reveal.

7. John's Son of Man conveys these heavenly mysteries to humankind for the enlightenment and salvation of the whole world (1:4–5, 9–13), whereas in Daniel and 1 Enoch he does so only for executing the eschatological judgment.

8. In John he awaits no *eschaton* or final judgment, since for the Son of Man in John, as in Daniel, the judgment is already past.

However, Enoch is commissioned to judge the world at some future time and hence to bring in the *eschaton*, as is the Son of Man in the Synoptic Gospels.

9. John's Son of Man is restored, in the end, to heavenly status by God himself (John 17), whereas Enoch is at best assigned to the angelic host and, though it is unclear, perhaps reassigned to earth in carrying out the final judgment (1 Enoch 70–71), as in the Synoptic Gospels.[5]

These contrasts pertain to how Jesus uses the title Son of Man.

The key argument that Ellens contests is that the author of the Gospel presents his account as an aggressive apologetic against an Enochic son of man tradition within the Judaism of his immediate audience.[6] He argues that the Gospel author is presenting the correct interpretation of the Danielic son of man tradition, and the Gospel acts as a means to point out the false contentions of the Enochic tradition. Ellens presents his case, but unfortunately, he does not expand his argument much beyond the points listed above.

Although this is plausible, an aggressive apologetic against Enochic Judaism does not fully fit with John's overall purpose for writing, which is to argue for believing in Jesus's true identity (see John 20:31). Instead of an aggressive apologetic, it seems that John is presenting the teachings of Jesus with words and phrases for which they already had definitions for within their traditions. These remain in the background as John presents Jesus as radically redefining their preconceived beliefs concerning the true identity of the son of man. Instead of arguing against the Jewish traditions of his audience, John's main intent is to argue for the true identity of Jesus. To do this, John must define Jesus by redefining the traditions with which they are familiar.

The main contention that this study has with Ellens is with points 2 and 8 concerning the role of the Son of Man as judge and the timing of the judgment as seen in contrast between John and the Parables. The problem with point 2 is that John presents Jesus as taking on the role of judge and not just of Savior of the world. Jesus's role as judge may not be an active one in the Gospel of John, but his role as judge is certainly there in a passive sense. In John 3:12–18 and 5:27–47, Jesus speaks concerning condemnation as a verdict that has already been passed upon those who do

---

5. Ellens, *Son of Man*, 161–62.
6. Ellens, *Son of Man*, 156–164.

not believe. Jesus is taking on a role as judge, but not in the active eschatological sense as seen in the Parables. However, Jesus mentions the eventual eschatological judgment that is to come, which has greater similarities to the judgment described in the Parables. Thus, one of the functions of Jesus's coming does actually bring judgment, just not in the way that John's Jewish audience expects. The Gospel of John is not necessarily refuting this idea of eschatological judgment found in the Parables, but John is redefining it for his Jewish audience to show a distinction between Jesus's imminent and eschatological roles as judge.

The issue with point 8 is that John 5:25–29 speaks to both an imminent (see also 3:16–20) and eschatological judgment. Jesus speaks of a judgment that is presently taking place and not just a judgment that has already happened in the past. Although the past tense is used in 3:17–21 concerning those condemned, the acts of unbelief and rejection that brings the condemnation are something taking place in the present. In 5:25–29, the eschatological judgment is clearly mentioned by Jesus as he speaks about his bifurcated judgment role. Thus, Ellens's point that John represents the judgment as something that is past does not follow with how John presents Jesus's future role as eschatological judge.

This study will reveal these stark contrasts in the teachings of Jesus and the beliefs of John's Jewish audience. This study will seek to expand upon Ellens's list above and flesh out in more depth how these contrasts work themselves out throughout the Son of Man sayings of Jesus. The overall push will be to demonstrate how John's Jewish audience understood his presentation of the Son of Man sayings as they relate to his roles as Messiah and judge. John indicates that Jesus purposefully makes these contrasts in order to help his audience truly understand how one obtains eternal life and avoids both the imminent and eschatological judgment of condemnation. Most notable will be the beliefs of Jesus's religious audience who consider themselves as righteous and among those who would receive God's mercy and eternal life based on their keeping of the covenant and good deeds.[7] One of Jesus's points that he emphatically makes is that those who see themselves as righteous are the very ones who will receive condemnation.

---

7. Identity of the righteous: Sir 2:15–17; 23:27; 1 Enoch 94:1–4; 99:10; 103:99; 104:12; Identity of the wicked: Sir 41:18; 5:4–7; 10:7, 12; 1 Enoch 94:8; 96:4–5, 8; 99:2; 102:9; Jubilees 23:17–18, 22.

THE SON OF MAN SAYINGS IN THE GOSPEL OF JOHN

John 1:51

The Son of Man saying in John 1:51[8] comes in the immediate context of Jesus's conversation with Nathanael and his confession of Jesus as the Son of God and the King of Israel. Both titles have messianic implications both in the Old Testament and in early Jewish texts.[9] Nathanael's confession reveals that he was familiar with early Jewish messianic expectations. As has been previously discussed, his and others' confessions indicate that the commoners in Israel and not just the religious elite had specific views on what the coming Messiah would look like. This passage comes right after John the Baptist identifying Jesus as the Lamb of God who takes away the sin of the world (1:29), and the confession causes two of John's disciples to follow Jesus. Also, part of the context is the story of Jesus's first miracle being performed at the wedding in Cana of Galilee (2:1–12), which follows from Jesus's response to Nathanael in 1:50 that he would see "greater things than these."[10]

The Son of Man saying itself is reminiscent of Jacob's dream of a ladder in Gen 28:10–17.[11] In both passages, there is an avenue presented as provided by God between heaven and earth.[12] Burkett says, "The Son of Man is the reality depicted by Jacob's ladder, the connection between God's

---

8. Many scholars and commentators assert that 1:51 is interpolated into the text because of semantic difficulty and clumsiness of the narrative flow from 1:43–2:11. It is argued that the original context might be borrowed from Matt 16:27–28, which has the context of the resurrection or second coming, where the context of angels about to glorify the Son of Man would be more appropriate. The interpolation here is to reinforce the divine identity of the incarnate Logos of the prologue (Ellens, *Son of Man*, 34–37; Brown, *Introduction to Gospel of John*, 88–152; Keener, *Gospel of John*, 488–91; Morris, *Gospel According to John*, 150–52; Beasley-Murray, *John*, 18–30; Moloney, *Gospel of John*, 48–63).

9. Reynolds notes the strength and significance of Nathanael's and Phillip's messianic claims and how each one has understanding and origin in early Jewish Literature and the OT (Reynolds, *Apocalyptic Son of Man*, 90–92).

10. Moloney shows how this saying is in the context of revelation. In the context of Pentecost, this looks forward to the revelation of the glory which is revealed in 2:1–11. He also argues that John 1:19–2:11 is better understood being read parallel to Exod 19:7–19 (Moloney, "*Parables of Enoch*," 279–80).

11. Ridderbos says that the presence of the angels and Jacob's ladder indicates that the Son of Man has heavenly powers at his disposal (Ridderbos, *Gospel of John*, 94).

12. Thompson argues that this verse depicts God disclosing heavenly secrets (Thompson, *John*, 53).

household on earth and God in heaven."[13] In John 1:51, the Son of Man is the access point by which mankind is able to enter heaven and receive eternal life. Ellens asserts that the main use of the Son of Man here is that he is a heavenly figure naturally associated with the heavenly realm.[14] Heaven will be opened to mankind through the Son of Man, and he will reveal heavenly mysteries. Both of these are similar characteristics of the son of man in the Parables of Enoch.

John 3:13–14

The context of the Son of Man sayings in John 3:13–14 is the centerpiece of the conversation that Jesus has with Nicodemus. This passage specifically identifies Nicodemus as a Pharisee.[15] It is likely he was familiar with many of the early Jewish texts or at least the eschatological speculations that came from them, which would have included the son of man figure in the Parables of Enoch. This is the only instance in John where the title is used twice by Jesus in back-to-back sentences. This passage also reveals a multitude of information associated with the Son of Man. In this passage, the Son of Man is the revealer of heavenly knowledge,[16] having a heavenly

---

13. Burkett, *Son of Man*, 119.

14. Ellens, *Son of Man*, 39. Further, Keener asserts that the Son of Man here is being depicted as a figure greater than Jacob or any of the other patriarchs, because the angels here are dependent upon Jesus as the mediatorial figure (Keener, *Gospel of John*, 488–91). See also Reynolds, *Apocalyptic Son of Man*, 92–95.

15. See above discussion of beliefs of Pharisees.

16. Keener references 4 Ezra 4:5–9, 21, showing that there was an early Jewish tradition regarding heavenly and earthly wisdom. Earthly wisdom can be barely figured out, and heavenly wisdom has not been obtained (Keener, *Gospel of John*, 559–60).

Ellens asserts that the Son of Man as revealer of heavenly things follows with what has already been said in John thus far concerning the heavenly origin of the Logos and the Son of Man as the mediatorial figure in the Jacob's ladder allusion. He also notes that in 1 Enoch, wisdom's search for a dwelling place on earth was unsuccessful, which contrasts with Jesus's role as a revealer of heavenly wisdom as successful (Ellens, *Son of Man*, 44–46). See also Thompson, *John*, 84.

Ridderbos argues that the ascent and descent themselves refer to the divine work of redemption to be accomplished by the Son of Man. He says the ascent does not refer to receiving knowledge from heaven but can be understood as the Son's participation in divine glory (Ridderbos, *Gospel of John*, 135–36).

origin,[17] an exalted figure,[18] a judge,[19] and the Savior of the human race. Other than the Savior of the human race, which is one of Jesus's key redefinitions of the Jewish understanding of the Son of Man, these are common features of the son of man in the Parables. The contrast that Jesus brings out will be explored in greater depth in the next chapter on the judgeship of Jesus.

John 3:13 has in mind the incarnation of the heavenly Logos from 1:1–18.[20] This references the heavenly origin and preexistent nature of the Son of Man.[21] This also maintains the allusion to Jacob's ladder in 1:51.[22] The heavenly origin of the Son of Man further alludes to the early Jewish interpretation of the Danielic one like a son of man as seen in the Parables of Enoch. Although Nicodemus may not have been familiar with how Jesus uses Son of Man in 1:51, this would have conjured up imagery and beliefs

---

17. Cf. Dan 7–9; 1 Enoch 37–71.

18. Cf. 1 Enoch 62:9

19. Cf. 1 Enoch 45:3; 51:3; 61:8; 62:1–9; 63:11; 69:27

20. Burkett argues that understanding the origin and meaning of the Son of the Man in 3:13 helps one understand how it is used in the rest of the Gospel of John. He finds the origin of this title in Prov. 30:1–4 and goes to great lengths to show the connection (Burkett, *Son of the Man*, 76–92, also 51–75, 93–111). Although Burkett builds a substantial case for his argument, he misses many of the implications and origins of other aspects of the motif that are developed in early Judaism, and thus a fuller picture of the Son of Man in the Gospel of John is missed.

21. Cf. 1 Enoch 48:5–7 and 62:13–14. These two passages in the Parables show a somewhat implicit salvific nature of the son of man, as opposed to the Johannine Son of Man, which is quite explicit in the role that Jesus attributes to himself as the Son of Man (Reynolds, *Apocalyptic Son of Man*, 46).

22. Keener argues that the allusion to Jacob's ladder follows with 3:13, because it maintains Jesus as the Son of Man as the bridge between heaven and earth and the avenue for mankind to the heavenly and eternal world (Keener, *Gospel of John*, 561–63).

Moloney argues that the ascent and descent references have their origins in Jewish myth, where it was believed that certain individuals such as Enoch, Abraham, Moses, and Isaiah, ascended to heaven. They could not have had heavenly wisdom revealed to them unless they had ascended to heaven. He argues that the ascent and descent language here has to deal with the revelation of heavenly wisdom and the unique place of Jesus as the Son of Man to do so (Moloney, "*Parables of Enoch*," 281–82). See also Köstenberger, *John*, 127. Reynolds highlights the various ascent myths but makes the distinction that the Son of Man is different from the patriarchs and prophets, because his origins are heavenly and not an earthly ascent of one into heaven (Reynolds, *Apocalyptic Son of Man*, 106–8).

Kruse argues that this is polemical and Jesus speaks in a manner that rejects the Jewish belief of heavenly revealers (Kruse, *John*, 119).

concerning the son of man from the Parables, with which he likely was familiar.

The implications of the use of Son of Man in John 3:14 look toward crucifixion, exaltation, and salvation. The close proximity of verse 13 with 14 indicates that the heavenly knowledge revealed by the Son of Man is that his crucifixion is the culmination of his earthly glorification and the key piece of the salvation of humankind.[23] The notion of crucifixion in this verse is further supported by how the crowd responds to his statement in 12:32, when he says that he will be lifted up, to indicate the kind of death that he will die.[24] The crowd negatively responds, saying that their belief is that the son of man is supposed to remain forever. Exaltation of the Son of Man is further evidenced by Jesus's use of Son of Man in 12:23, where Jesus says that now is the hour of his glorification. Part of his reference looks toward his crucifixion and eventual resurrection and ascension. These three aspects become the redemptive part of his teachings of one of his main identities as the Son of Man; they are a main component of the heavenly knowledge that Jesus is teaching Nicodemus.[25] Jesus also references Num 21:6–9, where God sends serpents into the camp as a judgment against Israel for their sins. The people grumble, and God commands Moses to forge a bronze serpent to be lifted up in the camp; anyone who was bitten can look at the serpent and be saved. The illustration that Jesus is conveying is that the Israelites had been already judged for their sins. The only thing that the Israelites had to do was look up at the serpent and be saved. In John 3:14, Jesus speaks of himself in a similar manner. All mankind is already condemned, but the one who looks to the Son and believes will be saved (3:14–18).

---

23. Moloney, "*Parables of Enoch*," 282.
Keener notes that 3:14 is likely looking toward a dual meaning of lift up. He also notes that Wis 16:6 interprets the serpent as salvific. Jesus is using the same language for himself as one who will save all who look upon him and believe both in his crucified and glorified forms (Keener, *Gospel of John*, 564–66).

24. Tenney notes that the Aramaic term for lift up has a dual usage of lifting in exaltation from a low or bowed position or lifting up and crucifying (Tenney, *Gospel of John*, 49). Ellens also notes that there would have been a long, deep tradition of this term being used with crucifixion (Ellens, *Son of Man*, 51). Reynolds notes this dual meaning but says that the majority use in the OT and NT is of exaltion (Reynolds, *Apocalyptic Son of Man*, 117–18).

25. For further discussion on the redemptive event of the crucifixion and resurrection as the intended kerygmatic message of the text, see Beasley-Murray, *John*, 50–51; Morris, *Gospel According to John*, 198–200.

Ellens shows just how much impact the Son of Man sayings have in this passage as they directly relate to the message portrayed, observing:

> The Son of Man is not simply a man acting for humanity. Jesus' impending death is not to be just a saving human act of obedience to God, but rather it is God acting. God gives and sends (3:16–17). Consequently, those who really understand the Son of Man discern God, because Jesus, as Son of Man, is God acting. He has his origins outside the realm of humanity. John uses the themes of descent (3:13) and sending (3:17) to communicate the crucial Christological truth of preexistence in order to express clearly this divine heavenly reality.[26]

It is no mistake that John represents Jesus using Son of Man twice in back-to-back sentences and places the statement in the very center of his conversation with Nicodemus, so that his use of this title encompasses so much and such deep meaning. The use of Son of Man in John 3:13–14 encompasses all the rest of how Jesus will use the title in other more specific ways.[27]

John 5:27

The Son of Man usage in John 5:27 is in the midst of a response to Jewish leadership on the nature of true judgment, which contrasts the judgment that the Jews are passing on Jesus for healing on the Sabbath and judgment for how he speaks about his relationship with the Father. In 5:27, Jesus directly identifies himself as the Son of Man and directly indicates that all judgment has been given to him because he is the Son of Man.[28] This Son of Man saying gives direct reference to the Danielic one like a son of man and the Enochic son of man, as chapter 4 indicates that God passing the right to judge to the son of man was an early Jewish messianic expectation.[29] The

26. Ellens, *Son of Man*, 47.

27. Reynolds argues for an apocalyptic understanding of these Son of Man sayings with direct connection to Dan 7:13. He says that 3:13 draws one's attention to Jesus being the Son of Man as a preexistent heavenly being and as a revealer of heavenly wisdom, and 3:14 links his role in salvation and judgment (Reynolds, *Apocalyptic Son of Man*, 104–130).

28. Moloney argues that the context in this passage is a significant representation of realized eschatology (Moloney, "*Parables of Enoch*," 284).

29. The use of this Son of Man saying is the only anarthrous use in the Gospel of John. Some commentators argue that this anarthrous use indicates a direct link to Dan

Jesus's Representation as the Son of Man

Jewish leadership of Jesus's audience would have understood the messianic implications of not only this statement but also the words and phrases that he uses to further define his own role as messianic judge. Jesus uses the surrounding context to acknowledge that he knows what their messianic beliefs are concerning judgment and the role of the messiah in judgment. He also challenges their beliefs with his own teachings about his role as messianic judge, beliefs which are radically different from their preconceived beliefs.

John 6:27, 53, 62

The three Son of Man sayings in John 6 come in a discourse to Jesus's disciples and the Jewish people. This discourse comes right after Jesus performs two miracles of the nature of something that only God could do, feeding over five thousand people with five barley loaves and two fish and walking on water.[30] The sayings in 6:27 and 53 continue the theme of eternal life surrounding the Son of Man sayings in John 3:13–14. John 6:27 is a statement made because the crowd has followed him to the other side of the sea.[31] Interestingly, this is also in the context of the messianic expectation of the crowd that comes out right after the feeding of the five thousand, where the crowd believes him to be the prophet and are going to forcefully make him king (6:14–15).[32] Jesus takes this opportunity to teach the crowd about his

---

7:13, since Daniel's one like a son of man is anarthrous (Moloney, *Gospel of John*, 183; Morris, *Gospel According to John*, 283; Keener, *Gospel of John*, 654; Thompson, *John*, 131; Köstenberger, *John*, 189; Michaels, *Gospel of John*, 319–20), while others say that this is just stylistic and follows with John's representation of Jesus as the Son of Man (Ellens, *Son of Man*, 55–56; Beasley-Murray, *John*, 77). Reynolds notes that judgment and the Son of Man in early Jewish belief were very closely knit together. The main Jewish expectation of the Danielic one like a son of man was of one in a judgment role (Reynolds, *Apocalyptic Son of Man*, 139–40).

30. Burkett links the bread from heaven teaching to Sir 24:21, which says concerning the nature of wisdom, "Those who eat me will hunger again, those drink me will thirst again." He also links this discourse to Sir 15:3, Prov 9:5, and Isa 55:1–3 and 10–11, which are in addition to the manna allusions from Exodus (Burkett, *Son of the Man*, 129–41).

31. Reynolds observes that the Parables mention that the righteous will eat with the son of man after they receive their salvation and the kings of the earth are judges (1 Enoch 62:14). He says that this may or may not have been a piece of early Jewish tradition, but it is possible that the sharing of a meal with the self-proclaimed son of man may have conjured up this imagery in the minds of Jesus's audience (Reynolds, *Apocalyptic Son of Man*, 152–159).

32. McGrath makes connections not only to the Eucharist but also to the Mosaic

true purpose of coming as the Son of Man, which goes beyond performing signs and is rather to give eternal life to all who believe. Right after Jesus's statement in 6:27, the crowds ask Jesus what works of God they must do. Jesus responds similarly to how he did in 3:19–21 and 5:29 as to the nature of good versus evil deeds. He says that the good deed that is needed is belief in the one sent by the Father (6:29). Jesus associates the notion of one being judged according to deeds with the single deed necessary for a good judgment by the Son of Man: belief.[33] John 6:53 continues the theme of obtaining eternal life through belief in the Son of Man, but this saying comes toward the end of this discourse, when the teaching gets intense and causes many to leave him, based upon his teaching being too hard for them (6:60).[34]

Throughout chapter 6, part of what John is doing in his argument is linking Jesus to Moses and in fact showing him as a better Moses. Köstenberger shows how 6:52–58 mimics the Israelites grumbling and striving with Moses in the wilderness.[35] Thus, John links Jesus's Son of Man saying with Moses and the prophet to come, which conflates two different messianic expectations of his audience. The last Son of Man saying in this discourse is directed toward the disciples, who are having difficulty digesting Jesus's teachings. This phrase is also in the context of the Son of Man and his words as the giver of life, but the phrase itself alludes back to Jacob's ladder from 1:51 and 3:13, not only seeing the Son of Man as the mediator between heaven and earth, but now specifically mentioning his ascension (6:62), which looks toward his crucifixion and eventual exaltation.[36] Jesus's statement in 6:62 quite possibly references the Jewish belief that others such as Enoch, Abraham, and Moses have ascended into heaven. It appears that Jesus here forcefully rejects this notion. His rhetorical question concerns a

---

imagery with which the Jews would have been familiar. Jesus's self-portrayal as Son of Man in this passage directly reflects his ability to come down from heaven and give heavenly wisdom. He reveals God and does so in a way that is far superior to Moses (McGrath, *John's Apologetic Christology*, 174–78, 222).

33. Keener points out that works-based faith was a key part of early Jewish soteriology. He notes that Jesus redefines this notion to a faith-based system of salvation, which would have been a foreign concept to the Jewish people (Keener, *Gospel of John*, 676–79).

34. Ellens argues that this passage shows emphatically that Jesus as the Son of Man is a heavenly figure who descended to the earth to provide salvation and that only in him is spiritual nurture, vitality, and life (Ellens, *Son of Man*, 65).

35. Köstenberger, *John*, 215.

36. Ellens notes that 6:62 refers directly to the role of the Son of Man as the divinely exalted one and universal savior (Ellens, *Son of Man*, 68).

matter of what it would take his followers to actually believe his ascension.[37] Thus, Jesus's question concerning the Son of Man has in mind a Jewish belief with which his audience would have been familiar, but his intentions here are completely in the context of belief. The emphasis in Jesus's words also seems to indicate that the disciples' witness of his ascension will be the ultimate proof to them that Jesus truly is the heavenly Son of Man. His ascension will be the final piece that shows his disciples he is who he says he is.

John 8:28

The Son of Man saying in John 8:28 looks both back to Jesus's judgment discourse and his teaching about being the light of the world and forward to his eventual crucifixion, due to the lifting up language used.[38] In 8:24 and again in 8:28, Jesus makes two "I am" statements that link his identity with divinity, and in 8:28 there is an "I am" directly associated with the Son of Man. The purpose is to link his role as Son of Man not only to his messiahship, but also directly to his divinity. This self-identity culminates in 8:58, when Jesus explicitly identifies himself as "I am" in a manner similar to how God reveals himself to Moses (Exod 3:14–15).[39] Interestingly, there is an accusatory tone in 8:28 as he is talking to the Pharisees and says, "When *you* lift up the Son of Man" (italics added).[40] This is the prophetic proof that he is giving them to show the truth and accuracy of his words in this passage just prior to his statement about the Son of Man.[41] This saying is also

---

37. Moloney, "*Parables of Enoch*," 283–84

38. Keener notes the double entendre in the term, showing that by the Jews lifting Jesus up to crucifixion, they would also be lifting him up to be glorified. This lifting up would reveal his divinity (Keener, *Gospel of John*, 745).

39. Reynolds brings out multiple connections to Jesus's statements about his identity in John 8 with various "I am" passages throughout the OT that link Jesus's characteristics to God's (Reynolds, *Apocalyptic Son of Man*, 165–67).

40. Michaels notes the startling nature of this statement, since instead of having a passive sense like the previous verses, this has an active and accusatory sense (Michaels, *Gospel of John*, 491–92).

41. Burkett argues in depth for the direct connection of the "I am" statements of Amos 8:11–12, Isa 55:10–11, and Ps 107:20 to Jesus's "I am" statements in John 8:21–29 and how Jesus's self-identification as "I am" is directly linked to his Son of Man statement in both essence and purpose, with direct identification as God and as the one sent by God (Burkett, *Son of the Man*, 142–60). This would reinforce all the more Jesus's statement of his role as judge, which links God's role as judge in the OT with the messiah's role

linked to the theme of salvation that has already been seen in the previous Son of Man sayings and their contexts. This passage is in direct connection to his judgment discourse in chapter 5, which associates the Son of Man with the imminent and eschatological judge. The Son of Man whom the Jews will be judging and lifting up to crucify and kill is the one who will judge them according to their deeds and unbelief.[42]

John 9:35

The Son of Man saying in John 9:35 is in the second encounter that Jesus has with the man born blind. John 9:1–7 is Jesus's initial encounter with the man born blind and becomes a continuation of his teaching about himself being the light of the world and others being made free from sin upon belief in the Son (8:12–47).[43] Jesus's healing of the man born blind then becomes a teaching illustration and a parable to the Pharisees about their spiritual blindness and how they remain in their darkness and sin because of their refusal to believe in the Son. The Son of Man saying in 9:35 deals directly with belief in the Son of Man, for Jesus asks the man born blind (now healed) if he believes in the Son of Man. The man born blind demonstrates his willingness and desire to know who the Son of Man is, so that he can believe in him.[44] This question originally stems from the Pharisees investigating who healed the man and his not knowing the identity of who healed him. Instead of one response, Jesus gives two responses to the man who formerly was blind: "You have both seen Him, and He is the one who is talking with you" (9:37). Jesus uses verbs for both seeing and hearing. Originally, the man had only heard the voice of Jesus but now he also sees Jesus. Another interesting piece is that this is the only Son of Man saying in John in which Jesus directly identifies himself as the Son of Man.[45] This

---

as judge in early Jewish expectation.

42. Ellens links this Son of Man saying to Isaiah's suffering servant (Ellens, *Son of Man*, 73). See also Köstenberger, *John*, 260; Kruse, *John*, 93.

43. Burkett equates the Son of Man in this passage to the Son of God who is the light begotten from the light of God (Burkett, *Son of the Man*, 164–67).

44. Reynolds asserts that the theme of Johannine belief throughout the Gospel overlaps with recognition of the apocalyptic Son of Man in 9:35 (Reynolds, *Apocalyptic Son of Man*, 180).

45. Beasley-Murray notes that the emphasis of this saying is to show that Jesus as the Son of Man is not just the eschatological judge but also the one who mediates salvation (Beasley-Murray, *John*, 159).

Jesus's Representation as the Son of Man

self-identification causes the former blind man to worship Jesus.[46] This seems out of place, but the Parables of Enoch indicates that the Son of Man receives worship from the kings and the mighty (see 1 Enoch 62:9). The former blind man has the right reaction to the Son of Man, as opposed to the reaction that the Jewish leaders should have had.[47] This follows with the trend already seen in John of Jesus only directly identifying himself as the Messiah to the least likely people (see 4:25–26). Just like the previous Son of Man sayings, this saying is directly associated with belief that leads to salvation (9:35–38) and unbelief that leads to judgment (9:39).

John 12:23, 34

The Son of Man sayings in John 12:23 and 12:34 are contained within the context of Jesus's final entry into Jerusalem and the final week just prior to his crucifixion. John 12:23 comes right after two Greeks come to Philip seeking Jesus. This is a major turning point in the Gospel of John, because Jesus proclaims that the hour for which he came has come (12:23). The saying in 12:23 encompasses the themes of crucifixion, exaltation, and judgment that have been seen throughout previous Son of Man sayings. This passage has some of the most explicit connections to these three themes as compared to the implicit and indirect references in previous sayings. Crucifixion and salvation are seen in 12:24–26, when Jesus gives a parable about a grain of wheat falling to the ground and dying in order for it to bear much fruit (12:24).[48] This statement not only pertains to Jesus's death and resurrection, but also to those who believe in the Son of Man, who will have spiritual rebirth and bear spiritual fruit. Crucifixion and salvation are further seen in 12:32 when Jesus again says that the Son of Man will be lifted up and draw all men to himself, which causes the reaction of the crowd to ask the identity of the son of man, revealing their early Jewish

---

46. Reynolds notes that the word translated as worship is the same word used in John 4 during Jesus's conversation with the Samaritan woman regarding the true nature of worshipping God (Reynolds, *Apocalyptic Son of Man*, 181).

47. Ellens brings out that the Pharisees end up being their own judges because they have opportunity to see the divine will but behave as if blind to it. This follows what Jesus said previously about not coming to judge but that the actions of each person cause him or her to be condemned already (Ellens, *Son of Man*, 76).

48. Köstenberger notes that rabbinic literature uses the imagery of a grain of wheat as an illustration for the eschatological resurrection (Köstenberger, *John*, 378).

messianic expectation that the son of man would remain forever (12:34).[49] Exaltation in this passage is paired with the voice of the Father rumbling from heaven, confirming to Jesus that the Father's name is glorified and will be glorified again (12:28–30) because of the works of the Son. Judgment is seen in 12:31, and a stark contrast is given by Jesus concerning what he has said thus far concerning judgment, which is now that he did not come into the world to judge the world but that through him the world might be saved (cf. 3:17; 8:15). However, there is still an indirect sense in which Jesus says judgment has already come upon those that have chosen not to believe (cf. 3:18–19; 9:39). One interesting feature of the context here is the presence of two Greeks, gentiles, seeking Jesus. This links this passage to the Son of Man sayings in 3:13–14, which are in the immediate context of John 3:16, which indicates that salvation is for the world and not just for the nation of Israel. Thus, the Son of Man in John is linked to the salvation of the gentiles and not to their judgment and destruction, as seen throughout early Jewish texts.

John 13:31

The Son of Man saying in John 13:31 is spoken to the disciples and initiates Jesus's final discourse to his disciples in the upper room just prior to his crucifixion. The saying comes right after Jesus says that one of the disciples will betray him (13:21) and identifies that one as Judas (13:26–27). Right after Judas leaves, Jesus says, "Now is the Son of Man glorified and God is glorified in Him" (13:31).[50] This statement has the same exaltation language that was seen in 12:23, as it was associated with the voice coming from heaven of the name of the Father being glorified. This saying is also in close approximation to Jesus being lifted up in his crucifixion. Later in John 14, Jesus also uses salvation language, showing how he is the way to the father

---

49. Ellens notes the crowd understands the Christ as Son of Man and a Davidic figure, for he argues that the crowd makes the link between the Christ and the Son of Man spontaneously (Ellens, *Son of Man*, 78–80). However, Ellens seems to completely disregard the direct link of the messiah to the son of man in the Parables of Enoch; the crowd would likely have been familiar with this Enochic tradition.

Keener roots the idea of the messiah remaining forever in the OT, especially Isa 9:6 and Ps 110:4 (Keener, *Gospel of John*, 881).

50. Ellens argues that the emphasis of this saying shows that the Son of Man is directly identified with or as God (Ellens, *Son of Man*, 84).

(14:6) and he is going back to his Father to prepare a dwelling place for them (14:2–3).

CONCLUSION

The Son of Man in the Gospel of John surrounds many different characteristics that follow with the Danielic and Enochic traditions, such as being the Messiah, judgment, exaltation, heavenly origins, preexistence, and heavenly knowledge. John would have been well aware of the Enochic beliefs of his audience, which is why he chooses to present Jesus's own role as Son of Man in this manner. He purposefully uses verbiage and imagery with which they were familiar. The son of man was a messianic motif with which his audience was familiar. As was seen above, even the crowd, the common Jew, would have had beliefs formed about the identity of the son of man by the time Jesus starts using the title for himself. However, John represents Jesus completely redefining each preconceived characteristic of the son of man that his audience would have had from their Enochic tradition. This section not only shows that John knows what the beliefs of his audience are concerning the son of man, but it also gives a robust definition of how he shows how Jesus seeks to redefine the son of man as it pertains to himself. Eschatological judgment as imminent is one of the primary characteristics associated with the coming of the son of man in the Parables of Enoch. This is likely in the minds of his audience, as Jesus claims that the Father has given him all judgment because he is the Son of Man (John 5:22, 27). Although Jesus keeps his role as judge in the forefront of his redefined role of himself as the Son of Man, the above study reveals that his role as Son of Man encompasses so much more than what early Jewish belief allowed for. Jesus's main teaching on his role as the Son of Man switches from judgment to salvation, which includes not just the salvation of the Jews but the salvation of the entire world—which means the hated gentiles of the Parable of Enoch are included in the realm of salvation.

7

Jesus's Teachings on Judgment and Judgeship in the Gospel of John

INTRODUCTION

ONE OF THE MAIN things that John presents Jesus doing is redefining most if not all of the expected aspects of the messiah as they relate to judgment. Early Jewish literature indicates an eschatological judgment, but Jesus presents the time of judgment in both the present and in the last day. Later early Jewish texts identify the person who judges as the messiah or as one who receives the right to judge from God. Jesus identifies himself as this expected messianic judge, but this role is redefined by Jesus, since he is not the conquering messiah expected by the Jews, the one who was seen as a conquering Davidic warrior king or a heavenly one like a son of man who was going to defeat and judge the enemies of God and set up an eternal kingdom.

The Jews believed that the primary role of the messiah was to judge wicked men according to their evil deeds and reward the righteous for their good deeds and faithfully keeping the covenant.[1] John's Jewish audience had good reason for wanting judgment to come upon their enemies, as has been seen in chapters 2 through 4. Regardless of whether the Jewish belief was in a kingly messiah from the line of David or a heavenly messiah who looked like the Danielic one like a son of man, this messianic figure's

---

1. Cf. Sir 16:12, 14; 17:23; 28:1; Psalms of Solomon 2:7, 16, 34; 17:8; Wis 3:10, 18; 4:19–5:14.

primary responsibility was to bring judgment upon the enemies of God and salvation to the Jews. The coming of the messiah meant that they were in the eschatological age, and final judgment was about to take place.² Therefore, it is no surprise that Jesus addresses the belief that the messiah would take on the role of messianic judge. Although Jesus uses familiar verbiage and imagery concerning the messiah's role as judge, he redefines that role, redefines who would receive judgment, and redefines the Jewish view of good and evil deeds. The exposition of key passages below will demonstrate just how radically different Jesus's teachings about judgment and his role as judge are as they relate to the beliefs of his audience, especially in relation to their beliefs concerning their messianic expectations of the son of man as eschatological judge.

JUDGMENT AND JUDGESHIP IN THE GOSPEL OF JOHN

John 3:10–21

To the first-century Jew, much about Jesus's teachings in John 3:10–21 concerning the son of man and his role in judgment sounded familiar.³ This will also be the case with the other passages considered in this section. Jesus's teachings indicate that he was familiar with early Jewish belief concerning judgment and the messiah, evidenced in key words and phrases that he uses, which allude to certain early Jewish beliefs. Knowing early Jewish beliefs on judgment and messianic expectation helps one to better understand the nuanced complexities of Jesus's teachings about judgment and his role in it. It also helps one to understand why Jesus says what he says and just how radically different his teachings are to John's Jewish audience.

Much of the verbiage that Jesus uses in the Gospel of John alludes to the language of Daniel and the Parables of Enoch, but one also needs to keep in mind the views of judgment expressed in other early Jewish sources, because these give a more holistic view concerning the beliefs of John's Jewish audience (see ch. 2). The context of John 3:10–21 is when Nicodemus visits Jesus at night to inquire of Jesus who he is and by what authority he teaches (3:1–2). In this context, Nicodemus is Jesuss' immediate audience. As has been previously indicated, he was a Pharisee who would likely have studied

---

2. Cf. Psalm of Solomon 17; 1 Enoch 37–71; 90; Sibylline Oracles 3:652–56; 1QH VI, 12; II, 8–9, 13; V, 8–9; 1QpHab VIII, 1–3; 11QMelch; 4Q285.

3. Cf. 1 Enoch 45:3; 51:3; 61:8; 62:1–9; 63:11; 69:27.

Judge Jesus

or been familiar with many of the texts explored in chapters 2 through 4. The discourse that results is not at all the direction that Nicodemus thought the conversation would end up. Nicodemus entered the conversation with his own views on the son of man, judgment, and salvation, but Jesus challenges and redefines each of these beliefs, which will be evidenced in this discourse.

In John 3:12, Jesus indicates a contrast between earthly knowledge and heavenly knowledge.[4] Early Jewish belief indicates a few things concerning the revelation of heavenly knowledge to mankind. One belief was that one of the sins of the fallen angels was their revelation of heavenly knowledge to mankind, and this event impacted humanity and the earth to the extent that the cosmos no longer follows its God-given pattern.[5] There were also Jewish ascension myths surrounding various patriarchs and prophets, and these individuals would have had heavenly knowledge revealed to them. Also, certain Jewish texts made a distinction between heavenly and earthly wisdom, indicating the unattainability of heavenly wisdom. Concerning how this relates to the son of man mentioned in 3:13–14, the Parables of Enoch show that the Enochic son of man receives a revelation of heavenly knowledge.[6] One main aspect of Jesus's teachings throughout the Gospel of John is their heavenly source. Jesus teaches only what he has received from the Father (8:38). Early Jewish belief indicates that one of the expectations of the messiah was that he would have heavenly knowledge revealed to him. The heavenly knowledge revealed in this passage deals with salvation and judgment and the role that the son of man plays in both of these (3:14–21).

---

4. Burkett argues that heavenly knowledge refers to the fact that no human has yet experienced the heavenly aspect of eternal life (Burkett, *Son of the Man*, 78–87). However, by not considering early Jewish implications of heavenly and earthly wisdom, he misses the fuller picture of how Nicodemus would have likely understood his statement. Thompson poses that the earthly things to which Jesus refers are the things that were spoken of just prior to this statement, and the heavenly things are those that come after this statement (Thompson, *John*, 83–84). See also Beasley-Murray, *John*, 49–50. Michaels interprets heavenly and earthly knowledge as metaphoric or parabolic, due to how Jesus uses parable and metaphor in the Synoptics to reveal the hidden things of God (Michaels, *Gospel of John*, 193–94).

5. Cf. 1 Enoch 6–11; 68–69.

6. Cf. 1 Enoch 41–44; 51:3; 59–61; 71:1–4. Keener references 4 Ezra 4:5–9, 21 in regard to the Jewish tradition concerning earthly and heavenly wisdom, as opposed to a response to the gnostic tradition. He points out that the likely reference of Wis 9:15–16 (Keener, *Gospel of John*, 559–60). See also Thompson, *John*, 83–84.

Jesus's Teachings on Judgment and Judgeship

The focus of Jesus's discourse moves into his teaching on salvation and judgment (John 3:14–21). In order to understand the full force of Jesus's teachings on salvation and judgment, one must first know early Jewish views on these topics. The main Jewish view on salvation gleaned from early Jewish texts is that the righteous who kept the covenant and who practiced good works were those who would receive God's mercy at the final judgment and granted eternal life.[7] Jesus presents his own teachings on judgment according to deeds (3:19–21; cf. 5:29). The Pharisees and chief priests of Jesus's audience were among those who would have seen themselves as righteous and among those who would receive the mercy of God in the last day and be granted eternal life. They would have based this upon the fact that they strictly adhered to the law of Moses and even went above and beyond the keeping of the covenant by following all the traditions put into place so that they would not break the covenant. They would have seen their good works as outweighing those of all the rest of their fellow Jews. When Jesus teaches concerning good deeds that secure one eternal life, his teaching is shocking and unlike any belief that his Jewish audience holds. Jesus speaks of only one good deed that one needs to inherit eternal life: belief in the Son of Man. As has been seen previously, Jesus's self-identification as the Son of Man is also redefined and completely unlike what the Jews are expecting. This Son of Man, as Jesus identifies, is not just the expected Messiah but the incarnate deity himself, who has the right and ability to grant eternal life.

For the Jews, judgment would be upon those who practiced evil deeds.[8] The receipt of judgment was especially designated for those gentile kings and nations who persecuted the Jewish people, such as the Seleucids in the second century BC and the Romans in their present day. Later texts indicate that judgment would also be upon apostate Jews who forsook the covenant for positions of power and supporters of institutions that contradicted the law. The presence of the messiah is often associated with the coming eschatological judgment, whether the role of judge is God himself or the messianic figure. Inevitably, his coming would inaugurate the eschaton and final judgment. Thus, John's Jewish audience expects the messiah

---

7. Cf. 1 Enoch 40:9; 58:3–4; 71:15; see also concerning the reward of the righteous 1 Enoch 62:14–16; Psalms of Solomon 3:12; 14:9.

8. Psalms of Solomon 2:34–35, 38; 13:9–11; 14:4–7; 15:13–14; Wis 3:18; 5:1; 4:20–5:14; 11:9; 12:22; 16:5–14; 1 Enoch 11:7; 22:8–14; 45:3–6; 47:3–4; 51:3–5; 61:8; 62–63; 69:27–29; 95:5; 100:4–5; 104:5; 1QH IV, 20–21, 26; VI, 18–19, 29–30; 1QM XI, 16; 11QMelch; CD VII, 9, 11–12; VIII, 1–2; XIX, 6–16; 1QS II, 7–8; IV, 12–13.

to teach about judgment, salvation, and other eschatological themes as they relate Jesus's self-identification to the son of man. However, Jesus takes their known beliefs and redefines them in a radical way that is completely unexpected. The son of man is expected to mean eschatological judgment (per the Parables), but Jesus makes a contrary statement, saying that the Son of Man did not come to judge (John 3:17; cf. 8:15; 12:47) but to save. The implication is that Jesus is well familiar with the eschatological judgment beliefs of his audience, which is why he explicitly states that his role as the Son of Man is not judgment but salvation. He also defines evil deeds as unbelief.

A few elements of judgment are brought out in this passage. These elements are the one who judges, the mode of judging, the place of judgment, the recipients of judgment, and why they are being judged. These are the elements that frequently come up in the various passages, with a few of the passages adding an element or having a different or added aspect of judgment. The term judge, as far as eschatological judgment is concerned, is not explicitly used in this passage this way, but there are implications in this passage that show the above elements of divine judgment.[9] The one who judges the world is the Son (John 3:17); but, interestingly, the focus does not start off with condemnation but with salvation. For the Jews, the world represents the gentiles, those not part of the covenant, and the gentiles in Jewish thought were already condemned. The salvation of the world was something contrary to Jewish belief. The Jews believed that judgment was to come upon the gentile nations, especially those that directly oppressed Israel.[10] The salvation of the world would have been one of the farthest things from the minds of the Jews. Jesus turns the tables and shows that the desire of God is not to condemn the world (gentiles) but to save the world. For Nicodemus, this was likely a foreign concept, since the salvation of the world is the last thing he would have expected a teacher of Israel to have as the foremost priority for the sending of the messiah. The messiah was supposed to be the one to conquer the world and cause all the nations to submit to him and judge the world because of their sin. Jesus turns the

---

9. Carson notes that the verb *krino* can be translated as judge in this passage, but the context here and in other places in John shows it in the adverse sense of the word, which causes a better translation as condemn (Carson, *Gospel According to John*, 206). Beasley-Murray notes a dual meaning of separation and condemnation (Beasley-Murray, *John*, 51).

10. This is a prevalent theme in the Psalms of Solomon, esp. 2, 17, and 18; the Parables; and 4 Ezra.

Jewish notion of the messianic judge on its head as he redefines the purpose of the messiah.

The mode of judgment is also in view. Jesus places belief in himself as the determining factor of who will be saved and who will be condemned. Jesus is also judging in the present tense in this passage, when he says that the one that does not believe is already condemned (John 3:18).[11] There is an imminent judgment present, but it is passive. Jesus is in keeping with his word that he did not come to judge. This is also in keeping with the Jewish beliefs of one's fate being sealed upon death and of one being judged according to deeds.[12] Here Jesus presents the belief that the only good deed one needs to inherit eternal life is the belief in the name of the only begotten Son of God; anything else is considered an evil deed, which will garner judgment, especially the deed of unbelief.

There is also an aspect that judgment does come into the world with the coming of this Messiah—just not a judgment expected by the Jews. Unbelief causes one to be judged already.[13] In Jewish thought, the pervasive method of judgment, as for the earthly aspect, was something done by the messiah in his conquering of the nations and vindication of Israel, not something that had already happened.[14] In the place of eschatological judgment, condemnation was not supposed to happen until the last judgment. The *already* nature of this judgment shows that there is an aspect of present judgment as eschatological. The end-times judgment has already begun with the coming of the Son into the world.

The recipients of condemnation and salvation are not defined in the same way that the Jews would have viewed this. For the Jews, salvation was for the Jews and those proselytes who entered the faith. However, Jesus opens up salvation to whomever in the whole world (John 3:16). This goes against all Jewish nationalistic beliefs of salvation. There is also a

---

11. Carson notes that this is the reason for the mission of the Son, because the world already stands condemned (Carson, *Gospel According to John*, 207).

12. Keener notes that most Jews would have believed that judgment was mostly designated for the final judgment, not for the present. The emphasis in this passage is that there is a sense in which aspects of the final judgment are already taking place (Keener, *Gospel of John*, 571–74).

13. Beasley-Murray brings out the importance of Jesus's judgment being in the present, as opposed to future judgment (Beasley-Murray, *John*, 51).

14. Travis says that there is a deterministic feel to the passage yet also a stress on human choice and responsibility (Travis, *Christ and the Judgment*, 266). See also Keener's argument for how the Jews would have understood the tension between God's predestination and human responsibility (Keener, *Gospel of John*, 572–74).

contingency that Jesus places on salvation: it is for the one who believes in the Son and not based on righteousness and the deeds that people do, nor based on one's Jewish nationality.

Another thing that Jesus does is redefine good and evil deeds. Those who do evil are ones who love the darkness and hate the light (John 3:19–20).[15] They are condemned because they do not believe in the Son (3:18).[16] Thus, evil is redefined as one who does not believe in the Son, and good is redefined as one who has put one's faith in the Son.[17] The evil deeds that the Jewish leaders expected to bring condemnation would be blatant things such as murder, theft, adultery, idolatry, etc. On the other hand, Jesus says that the evil deed that causes condemnation is unbelief and rejection of the Son. Believing in the Son brings salvation and no longer condemnation. "The criterion for judgment is not righteousness or good works, but faith."[18] This also has nothing to do with a place in the Abrahamic covenant as a Jewish native. Carey notes that eschatological views of John repeatedly mention views of judgment and the afterlife, but the way to get to eternal life is through the Son.[19] This is a completely different view of salvation than just maintaining one's righteousness and good works. Although Jesus redefines good and evil deeds, he does not change the Jewish belief that all men will be judged according to their deeds. John presents Jesus as wanting to make sure that his audience truly understands what good deed garners one eternal life and not condemnation.

15. Fitzmyer surveys similar themes in Qumran literature compared to those in the Gospel of John such as creation, dualism, the spirit of truth, love of community members, and other parallels. His assertion is that the similarities link the Gospel of John to a thoroughly Jewish background (Fitzmyer, "Qumran Literature," 117–33). Bauckham also considers how light and darkness were understood at Qumran compared to how they are used in the Gospel of John. He argues that the uses between the two sources are completely dissimilar. The sources at Qumran are not needed to understand John in an early Jewish context, because there is enough information from other early Jewish sources to argue for an early Jewish background to John (Bauckham, *Testimony of the Beloved*, 125–36). Although this may be the case, understanding Jewish ideas concerning their own understanding of light and darkness will help one better understand the mindset of Jesus's audience, when Jesus gives his own definition of light and darkness and how the audience relates to his overall role as messianic judge.

16. Michaels notes that the condemnation of those who do not believe is self-inflicted; God has no need to judge one who is self-condemned (Michaels, *Gospel of John*, 203–4).

17. Michaels notes the explicit dualism in 3:18 to show an obvious distinction between the two categories (Michaels, *Gospel of John*, 204).

18. Michaels, *Gospel of John*, 204.

19. Carey, *Ultimate Things*, 118.

Jesus's Teachings on Judgment and Judgeship

In John 9:1–41 Jesus uses a real-life illustration of a man born blind to show how the Son of Man came into the world to save and to judge. In 9:37, Jesus directly identifies himself as the Son of Man to the former blind man, who immediately believes and proceeds to worship Jesus.[20] Jesus responds and says, "For judgment I came into this world, so that those who do not see may see, and that those who see may become blind" (9:39). Köstenberger notes that the judgment referred to here is a division of humanity into believers and unbelievers.[21] In the Jewish mindset, Jesus's response makes sense, because this was one of the primary objectives of the son of man in the Parables of Enoch. However, Jesus also indicates what that judgment practically and spiritually looks like; in the second half of that statement and in 9:41, he says, "If you were blind, you would have no sin; but since you say, 'We see,' your sin remains." This statement is directed right at the Pharisees, who expected the son of man to judge mankind according to their sins, but who saw themselves as righteous and ones that did not sin—or at least their good deeds far outweighed their sins. They also considered the man born blind as the sinner and one who would receive punishment because of his sin (9:34). However, Jesus completely reverses the recipients of judgment. The Pharisees, who saw themselves as righteous, are the ones who are blind in their sins and will be the ones who receive the judgment that Jesus says that he, the Son of Man, came into the world to execute.

John 5:21–30

Jesus's teaching about judgment in John 5:21–30 is contained within a much longer monologue (5:19–47). In order to understand what prompts this monologue, one must first consider the context of the events that just took place. These events took place in Jerusalem in an area of the city that would have been well known and received a lot of traffic. John tells the reader that these events took place on the Sabbath. All four Gospels make it a point to show that Jesus purposefully heals on the Sabbath in order to make a point about the nature of his identity and about the hypocrisy of the Jewish leadership (cf. Matt 12:1–14; Mark 2:23–3:6; Luke 6:1–11; 13:10–17; 14:1–5; John 9:1–34). The healing in John 5 serves the same purpose. The

---

20. Beasley-Murray notes that the Greek here "reflects the Eastern custom of prostrating oneself before a person and kissing his feet, especially of one viewed as belonging to the supernatural world, e.g., a deified king" (Beasley-Murray, *John*, 159).

21. Köstenberger, *John*, 295.

Judge Jesus

focus of Jesus's teaching comes as a response to the reaction of the Jews in 5:18, which says, "For this reason therefore the Jews were seeking all the more to kill Him, because He not only was breaking the Sabbath, but also was calling God His own Father, making Himself equal with God." Jesus's response shows that the Jews are being portrayed as illegitimate judges of Jesus. In the Synoptics, Jesus argues that it is lawful to do good on the Sabbath. None of Jesus's actions actually break any of the Levitical laws. Thus, the Jews are acting as illegitimate judges of Jesus and seeking to put him to death for breaking a law that he did not actually break. Their other accusation is that Jesus is making himself equal with God. John 10:33 reveals that the Jews consider this as blasphemy, and this is why they are seeking to kill him. Claiming to be equal with God was not something that was covered under the Levitical law of blasphemy. In 10:34–36, Jesus will argue the contrary, that the Scriptures do indicate that men are said to be gods and yet there is no contention with this passage (cf. Ps 82:6). Thus, John 5:18 shows two illegitimate reasons that the Jews are seeking to judge Jesus. The remainder of chapter 5 is a monologue in which Jesus claims to be the legitimate judge of all mankind, both imminent and eschatological, and provides four witnesses to prove this legitimacy.

The interesting thing about this passage is the amount of courtroom language that comes out of it. Morris notes that the emphasis of this passage is heavily on the comparison of the Son to the Father; Jesus's claims eventually show his oneness with the Father, and believing in the Son is equated to believing in the Father.[22] Jesus is seen to be both witness and judge, and the Father is also witness and judge. Jesus is on trial, and the Jewish leaders are also on trial. Jesus is acquitted based on testimony, and the Jewish leaders are condemned based on testimony.

John 5 is the main passage in John where Jesus speaks the most concerning his role as judge. The context of this passage starts with Jesus healing an invalid at the Pool of Bethesda in Jerusalem. This healing would have gone unnoticed, since the Gospels are full of healings; but John makes a point of telling his reader that it was the Sabbath on which Jesus healed this individual, and strict Jewish law forbade doing work on the Sabbath. This is the first thing that causes the Jews to want to persecute Jesus (John 5:16), but the thing that makes them want to kill him is that Jesus is calling God his own Father (5:17–18). The rest of this discourse contains Jesus's response to the Jewish leaders of how he does have authority from the Father

---

22. Morris, *Gospel According to John*, 275–98.

Jesus's Teachings on Judgment and Judgeship

to do the things he is doing and to say the things that he is saying.[23] Woven in this discourse is also a divine claim, which Evans notes:

> When Jesus claimed that he was "one" with the Father he was in fact claiming to be equal to God (John 5:18). In many places Jesus claims the prerogatives normally associated with God himself. Jesus will raise and judge the dead (5:28–29). He is able to grant eternal life (5:21; 10:28). No one but God can do these things. Accordingly, when Jesus says, "I and the Father are one," he surely means that he is equal to God. His accusers, therefore, are at least partially correct; Jesus has made himself God.[24]

One thing that should be noted is that the Jewish leaders were seeking to kill him prior to his claim as messianic judge. John does not indicate any more response from this section or from other parts of his Gospel that the religious leaders were seeking to kill him because of this claim as messianic judge. The thing for which they want to kill him is his claiming that God is his Father, which is equating himself with God and is seen as blasphemy by the Jewish leadership of Jesus's audience; blasphemy was punishable by death (cf. Lev 24:16). What Jesus does claim about judgment was already in the messianic traditions and expectations that Jesus is claiming for himself when he claims to be the Son of Man (John 5:27), but he also claims divine status as Son of God when speaking about the final judgment (5:25). Thus, Jesus conflates the two titles into one person—himself. Köstenberger notes:

> John also believes that God is a God of judgment and that this judgment will be executed in and through his Son, Jesus Christ (John 5:22–27, 30). John believes that Jesus, the crucified, buried, and risen one, will one day come again to bring about God's final judgment of unbelievers (5:28–29). In this way John identifies God, the Life-Giver and Judge of humankind, with Jesus as one in character and purpose (5:26; 10:30).[25]

The exposition of John 3:16–21 expounded on a few different elements that make up the office of messianic judge. John 5:16–47 reveals the same

---

23. Carson shows that there is a stark difference in Jesus's response compared to other Sabbath responses, since John writes that "Jesus answered them." He also notes that the verb is in the aorist middle instead of the aorist passive, which is in keeping with John wanting this passage to keep with the feeling of a legal proceeding (Carson, *Gospel According to John*, 247).

24. Evans, *Ancient Texts*, 335.

25. Köstenberger, *Theology of John's Gospel*, 280.

elements of judgment. However, Jesus adds to this office his role in the final resurrection (5:21, 25, 28–29). The Jews associated that final resurrection with the coming of the messiah, but Jesus makes four radical statements in this passage, indicating that he himself has the power of resurrection, just like the Father. Thus, Jesus indicates that the Son of Man encompasses far more than what was ever expected by his Jewish audience and is indeed coequal with the Father. This connects to the Jewish leaders' reasons for seeking to kill him.

Jesus starts his defense by telling the Jewish leaders that the only thing that he does is what he has already seen his Father doing, which includes raising the dead and judging (John 5:19–22).[26] The reason he says this is because he just finished telling them that he is at work on the Sabbath in the same way that his Father is at work on the Sabbath. The interesting thing about judgment here is that the Father is not the judge, but the Father has passed judgment to the Son (5:22).[27] Keener argues that Jesus's claim as judge would have shocked many of his hearers.[28] However, the context of this passage and all the other passages concerning Jesus's claim as judge does not see this reaction of his audience. The only thing that shocks his audience is Jesus calling God his Father. Thus, Jesus's claim of the Father delegating judgment to the Son of Man lines up with early Jewish tradition that God designates another with authority to judge. This verse identifies who will be judging, and the rightful place of judge falls in line with Enochic tradition. Jesus even identifies himself as the Son of Man, which is one of the titles given to the messiah in the Parables of Enoch. In this discourse, Jesus uses the Enochic tradition with which his audience was familiar to redefine his role as the Son of Man as imminent and eschatological judge. John 5:27 directly links the role of eschatological judge to the Son of Man. This reference is the most direct link to the Danielic one like a son of man and especially the Enochic son of man. As was seen in chapter 4,

---

26. Kruse notes that apprenticeship imagery is being used in 5:19–20, where a son would learn his exact trade from his father (Kruse, *John*, 174). See also Ridderbos, *Gospel of John*, 192.

27. Cf. 1 Enoch 61:5–8. Ellens references Testament of Abraham 13:2–3, where judgment is given to Abel to judge mankind, which reinforces the force of Jesus's statement in this passage (Ellens, *Son of Man*, 56–57). Köstenberger notes that other than the Parables as the most explicit representation and the Psalm of Solomon 17 of the messiah enacting God's judgment on his enemies, the messiah remains in the background as far as judgment is concerned (Köstenberger, *John*, 187–88).

28. Keener, *Gospel of John*, 651–54.

Jesus's Teachings on Judgment and Judgeship

the expectation of John's Jewish audience is that God would pass the role of eschatological judgment to the son of man. However, as was seen above, Jesus completely redefines what the expected son of man is supposed to look like. One of the main redefinitions that Jesus gives the idea of the son of man in this passage is that the eschaton is not being inaugurated at this time, but this is a time for salvation for all who believe in this Son of Man.

Life and death are also themes in this passage that help redefine the role of messianic judge. In Jewish thought, the judging of the living and the dead or the just and the unjust was designated to the final judgment. In part, Jesus shows himself in this role when he speaks concerning the final resurrection of the dead, which ushers in the final judgment of those who have done what is good and those who have done what is evil (John 5:28–29). Another interesting thing to note here is that Jesus claims to have the power of resurrection. Resurrection was closely associated with the son of man in both Daniel and the Parables of Enoch, but neither the son of man nor any other messianic figure associated with the final resurrection at the last judgment ever instigates the resurrection. Early Jewish tradition always puts the power of resurrection only with God at the final judgment. Jesus not only makes a claim to have the right of the eschatological messianic judge, but he also teaches that he has the eschatological power of resurrection, which would have been strictly something that only God himself could do. Thus, this is one more aspect of divinity that Jesus claims for himself.[29]

This passage not only puts Jesus in an eschatological role as judge but also in a present-tense role as judge. Jesus says that the time is now that the dead will hear the voice of the Son of God and receive life (John 5:25). Carson notes that it is the voice of God in the Old Testament that gives life (Isa 55:3).[30] This section hearkens back to John 3, where Jesus talks about being born of the Spirit (3:5–6) and the place of salvation being given to those who believe in the Son (3:16–18). Jesus again repeats the place of good and evil in the place of judgment (5:29). The place of good is for those who hear the voice of the Son and believe. Those who hear are the ones brought from death to life, which reflects back on spiritual rebirth (cf. Eph 2:1–10). Köstenberger rightly notes, "In an important sense, God's judgment was

---

29. Carson notes that the OT view of resurrection was something designated to God, and Jesus claiming this power takes this all-important divine quality upon himself (Carson, *Gospel According to John*, 252–53).

30. Carson, *Gospel According to John*, 256.

already brought about by the light's coming into the world in the incarnation of the Son (1:14). This coming of the light into the world, in turn, confronts people everywhere with the decision of whether to embrace the light or to go into hiding and persist in darkness."[31] This also speaks against where the Jewish leaders thought that life resided, which was in the law of Moses (John 5:39). Jesus shows them that it is this very law that condemns them, because the law speaks about Jesus, and the Jewish leaders do not believe him, even though he is standing right in front of them (5:39–40, 45–47). The receivers of condemnation are the Jewish leaders, because they do not listen to the mode of judgment, which is the voice of Jesus. Believing the voice of Jesus becomes the means of salvation. These Jewish leaders are among those who already have been condemned (3:18).

The dialogue in John 8 has similar judgment themes as John 5 and is yet another passage in which Jesus responds to the Pharisees' accusation that his testimony about himself is not valid. Bultmann points out the irony of their dialogue as he says, "At the very moment when they think they are passing judgment on him, he becomes their judge."[32] This passage hearkens back to chapters 3 and 5, where Jesus is talking again about light and darkness, testimony and judgment. Just like chapter 5, Jesus again uses courtroom language, showing that the Father's testimony and his testimony are enough to prove the true nature of his statements about himself. Jesus appeals to the highest possible witness, his Father (John 8:18). In this passage, Jesus makes two statements about judgment, the Jews and his, which he places in stark contrast with each other. His statements about judgment show that he does not judge by earthly standards but by heavenly standards (8:15–16).[33] Jesus continues this contrast between himself and the Jews in 8:21–30, where he indicates that he is from above and claims that the Jews are from below. Jesus then says that the ultimate proof that his statements about himself are true will be seen when the Jews lift up the Son of Man in crucifixion (8:28). This statement about judgment seems like an out of place statement because of what has been examined about where Jesus does claim to be a judge who passes judgment. Michaels thinks that this

---

31. Köstenberger, *Theology of John's Gospel*, 468–69.

32. Bultmann, *John*, 350.

33. Keener notes that Jesus was making this statement around the time of the Day of Atonement, when his Jewish audience would particularly be contemplating God's judgment (Keener, *Gospel of John*, 741).

Beasley-Murray notes the stark contrast of Jesus as the authentic and rightful judge compared to the Pharisees' superficial judgment (Beasley-Murray, *John*, 129).

statement is better understood with the insertion of "by myself," showing that Jesus is not alone in judgment but judges according to how the Father judges.[34] However, one must also take into consideration that Jesus does not have to pass judgment, because those who reject Jesus have already condemned themselves. Thus, Jesus has no reason to condemn them. The passage itself starts off with Jesus claiming to be the light of the world, so those who follow him never walk in darkness (8:12).[35] This again reiterates Jesus's redefinition of those who do good and those who do evil and by what standard all men will be judged. This would indicate that there are those who are walking in darkness, thus already condemned. Jesus also shows that his judging lies in contrast to how the Pharisees judge, which is by human standards, and how Jesus claims to judge, which is according to God's standards. The Pharisees would have judged according to one's works, as to whether or not one would be saved, and Jesus has already stated that he is the standard by which men are saved.

Jesus also pronounces a judgment upon the Pharisees when he says that they will die in their sins (John 8:24). This causes them to react even more by asking Jesus who he is (8:25). Jesus reiterates that this is something he has been spelling out to them from the beginning (8:26). Even through this dispute, many of the crowd were believing in Jesus during his conversation with the Pharisees. Thus, John is showing that Jesus is the one judging in the present. The crowd is seen as doing what is good and the religious leaders what is evil. Later in the passage, Jesus shows the contrast between himself and the religious leaders even more deeply as he judges them further by saying that the devil is their father (8:42–47). It is also in this chapter that Jesus makes his most controversial claim to being God in his "I am" statement, which directly links what he says to how God revealed his name to Moses (8:58). This claim gives Jesus even greater precedent of being seen not only as messianic judge but also the divine source of all judgment.

---

34. Michaels, *Gospel of John*, 480–81.

35. Carson explains how Jesus's statement is likely associated with the Feast of Tabernacles, where light was commonplace every evening of the celebration. The imagery of light is often tied to God's salvation in the OT, thus Jesus is claiming to be the place of salvation (Carson, *Gospel According to John*, 337–39).

Keener brings one's attention to the light of the world with reference to Jesus's mission to save the world (cf. 3:16) (Keener, *Gospel of John*, 739).

John 12:20–36

This is an intriguing passage because it serves as a transitional point in Jesus's ministry and is the last piece of his public teaching ministry. The rest of Jesus's teachings in the Gospel of John will be directed towards his disciples, as he prepares them for his crucifixion and departure from this world. This final piece is initiated by the coming of some Greeks who are seeking Jesus.[36] However, John does not record Jesus's interaction with the Greeks but only Jesus's statements upon the information that some Greeks are seeking him. The presence of the Greeks as a culmination of Jesus's ministry causes the reader to recall Jesus's words in John 3:16 that he came to save the entire world, which includes gentiles and not just Israel only.[37] As has already been seen, John's Jewish audience expected judgment to come upon the gentiles, but the presence of the Greeks here is in the context of salvation, not judgment. John shows that Jesus is again using his audience as a practical teaching tool of what he initially taught in John 3 and 5 concerning those that are saved and those that are already condemned. As was seen in the above Son of Man section, there is a Son of Man saying directly associated with the Greeks seeking Jesus. There is exaltation language directly associated with Jesus's death and crucifixion, which is completely contrary to the Jewish belief concerning the exalted and eternal position of the son of man. This is evidenced by the crowd's statement in 12:34, where the crowd says, "We have heard out of the Law that the Christ is to remain forever; and how can You say, the Son of Man must be lifted up? Who is this Son of Man?" As was seen above, the crowd had various messianic beliefs, and one of those beliefs stems from the exalted and eternal figure of the son of man in the Parables of Enoch. Thus, a messiah that comes to die by crucifixion makes no sense to the Jewish mindset (cf. Matt 16:22–23, Peter's response to Jesus saying that he must suffer many things), especially since the lifting up of one being crucified was an accursed position (cf. Gal 3:13).[38]

---

36. Bruner notes that "the hour has come" in v. 23, noting the reaction of the Greeks seeking Jesus, is in the perfect tense and shows a completed action. He links this to "it is finished," which is also in the perfect tense, as two endcaps to Jesus's passion week, marking the beginning and end of Jesus's redemptive work (Bruner, *Gospel of John*, 713).

37. Keener links the coming of the Greeks to the implication that their arrival emphasizes the importance of all humanity coming to know him for who he really is (Keener, *Gospel of John*, 872–81).

38. Burkett notes the possible connection of lift up to Isa 52:13, where glorification is

Jesus's Teachings on Judgment and Judgeship

In the context of the Greeks seeking Jesus, John presents Jesus making one of his final statements about judgment which John's Jewish audience would have had preconceived beliefs about. Jesus says, "Now judgment is upon this world; now the ruler of this world will be cast out" (John 12:31).[39] For the Jews, judgment upon this world was a good thing for them, because it meant their vindication and restoration. The Jews looked forward to the day that the messiah would come and cast out the ruler of this world.[40] This is a major piece of the judgment passages in various Jewish texts, such as the judgment on the kings and the mighty in the Parables and the judgment of the nations wrought by the warrior messiah in Psalm of Solomon 17. John's audience may have associated the coming of the Greeks seeking Jesus (John 12:31) with what they believed the messiah's purpose was. Jesus shows instead that there is a direct connection of the Greeks to his plan of salvation. Instead of on the gentiles, this judgment is on the rulers of this world. Interestingly, the Gospel of John only uses this term to refer to Jewish rulers and not to gentile rulers, as it relates to how this term is applied to a human figure (cf. 3:1; 7:26, 48; 12:42). Thus, one of the implications of this statement is that the Jewish rulers are the ones being judged because of their unbelief. This stands opposite to a Jewish view of the gentiles as the recipients of the messiah's judgment. There is also indication in the Gospel of John that the ruler of this world is referring to Satan as the one being judged (see also 16:8–11 for further context). The rebellious angels were also one of the entities who would receive judgment, as seen throughout early Jewish

---

seen in one's death. He also shows how this connection of terms connects the Son of Man in John to the suffering servant of Isaiah (Burkett, *Son of the Man*, 126–28).

39. Barret emphasizes the place of crucifixion that ultimately brings judgment upon the world and is also the place of Jesus' ultimate glorification (Barret, *John*, 426–27). It seems that Barret, as well as others, does not make much in connection to the coming of the Greeks and judgment.

40. The Parables indicate two different ruling entities who will receive judgment. The son of man in the Parables is the one who will judge heavenly beings (61:8) and mighty men on the earth, such as kings (48:8–9; 62:1–2).

Keener indicates many different possibilities that the ruler of this world might refer to an angelic or demonic figure such as Belial, prominent pagan deities, or the emperor. His main argument is that this is referring to Satan being defeated and dislodged from his authoritative position (Keener, *Gospel of John*, 879–80). Thompson notes that in the Dead Sea Scrolls, it is Belial who stands against the prince of lights (CD 5:18; 1QM 13:10; 15:2–3; 27:5–6) (Thompson, *John*, 271). Bruner completely links the ruler of this world to the devil, who receives his final judgment verdict because of the work of Jesus that overcame the power of the devil over this world up to this point in history (Bruner, *Gospel of John*, 717–18).

literature (cf. 1 Enoch 1–36). However, the main emphasis throughout the Gospel of John concerning imminent judgment are those who have already been judged because they do not believe in the Son. Jesus indicates that this judgment comes when the Son of Man is lifted up or crucified, which shows a contrast in the expected form of judgment from the messiah. Thompson says, "With the death of Jesus, it might appear that the forces of evil have conquered, that those who betrayed Jesus have won. But in fact, by means of Jesus' death, the 'ruler of this world' is judged, overthrown, cast out."[41] Regardless of whether the "ruler of this world" is spiritual or earthly rulers (or possibly both), it was expected that the messiah or son of man would judge them. Jesus's claim to judge them as the Son of Man was expected, but the means of judgment through defeat and death was unexpected in the mindset of John's Jewish audience.

CONCLUSION

The early Jewish eschatological beliefs of John's Jewish audience are key to better understanding the intensity and radical nature of Jesus's teachings on his identification as the messiah and his role as imminent and eschatological judge. Represented in the Gospel of John, Jesus's audience varied from the religious elite to the commoner. The chief priests were the religious elite, literalists, who strictly held to a literal interpretation of the Torah and did not believe in the resurrection of the dead. The Pharisees were the most predominant religious sect in the first century AD and are the main representation of Jesus's audience. Their greatest concern was to not break the Levitical law, and they had even built a hedge around the law in order to not break it. They had well-developed eschatological beliefs and also would likely have been familiar with the views of the other Jewish sects and the early Jewish literature produced in the Second Temple period. The Pharisees were seen as Jesus's main opponents, especially in relation to him doing or saying things that they considered unlawful or blasphemous. The Samaritans adhered only to the Torah and had their own views concerning Yahweh worship and messianic expectation. It was seen that they expected a prophet like Moses to arise and teach them all things. The last group represented in this study was the crowd and the disciples. This group was the common everyday people, identified as having a conglomeration of views, but it is quite evident from their words that they had developed messianic

41. Thompson, *John*, 271.

and eschatological judgment views. Jesus would have been quite familiar with each of his audiences, and the dialogues and monologues reflect this. Jesus speaks to his audiences with verbiage for which they already had definitions and preconceived beliefs.

Each sect and social group of Judaism held to a nuanced view of messianic expectation and how the messiah related to the eschatological judgment. Chapters 2 through 4 indicate that messianic expectation was not only at an all-time high during this era, but there were also numerous views on what the messiah would look like and the extent of his role in the eschaton. By the first century AD, messianic expectation was very well nuanced in a few of the later early Jewish texts. The three predominant views represented in the Gospel of John were that the messiah would be a prophet who also took on a kingly and teaching role, the promised Davidic king who would come in and defeat the Israel's enemies, and the heavenly son of man who would be handed the right to judge between the righteous and the wicked. In some of the passages in John, some of the roles were conflated, and it was observed that the people had multiple expectations concerning the messiah. Overall, the Gospel of John demonstrates that John's Jewish audience had robust and well-developed beliefs concerning judgment and the expected messiah.

John's representation of Jesus as the Son of Man is a major piece of how he presents Jesus as the rightful eschatological messianic judge. Chapter 4 represents the rise of the early Jewish belief surrounding the development of the son of man. John's Jewish audience likely had well-developed beliefs surrounding the messianic expectation of the son of man. This is evident in the verbiage that John uses and a few of the responses of the audiences he represents in his Gospel. The main thing that John does is show that Jesus redefines most, if not all, of his audience's preconceptions surrounding the son of man. A few of the redefinitions include the focus of his exaltation was on his crucifixion, which was also the place of belief to receive eternal life; Jesus as the revealer of heavenly knowledge; and his role as imminent and eschatological judge, where Jesus claims to not have come to judge, which was contrary to the Jewish belief that the main role of the son of man was as eschatological judge. The modern interpreter of the Gospel of John is well served to fully understand early Jewish beliefs surrounding the son of man in order to better understand the radical nature of Jesus's teachings concerning the redefinition of his self-identification as the Son of Man.

Early Jewish literature reveals that eschatological judgment was a major piece of Jewish belief throughout the Second Temple period, and some documents place judgment as the central theme or devote major portions to the theme. As messianic expectation intensified, a shift was seen in the diminished role that God would take as the eschatological judge. The role shifted to a messianic figure being given the right to judge. John 5:22 and 27 reveals that Jesus was well aware of this role and says that he is now the one taking it on. However, it was seen that Jesus completely redefines early Jewish preconceptions concerning the role of the messiah as the eschatological judge. Jesus indicates that his current role as judge is not to judge or at least not to judge in a manner expected by a first-century Jewish audience. He indicates that there is a present aspect of judgment that surrounds belief in his person and work, but there is also a coming eschatological judgment of the righteous and the wicked that is initiated at the final resurrection, which is instigated by the Son. Another piece of judgment that would have been shocking to John's Jewish audience is the recipients of judgment. The religious leaders saw themselves as among the righteous who would receive God's mercy and be granted eternal life. However, John shows that Jesus indicates that they are the ones who stand condemned; it is unexpected groups of people who receive eternal life, such as the Samaritans and the gentiles. John uses Jesus's teachings to radically redefine his Jewish audience's preconceived beliefs concerning Jesus's role as the messianic judge. Again, the modern interpreter of the Gospel of John will highly benefit from knowing John's Jewish audience's beliefs about judgment and the messianic judge, because they demonstrate the intensity and radical nature of Jesus's eschatological teachings.

It is evident that John's Jewish audience had well-developed messianic beliefs concerning the role that the messiah would take in judgment. John's verbiage in the Gospel of John indicates that he was quite familiar with the various beliefs of his audience. John uses familiar terms and definitions to define the true role of the Son of Man in imminent and eschatological judgment. The beliefs of John's Jewish audience reveal to the modern interpreter just how radical his redefinitions were to them. These differences aid the interpreter in showing the robust nature of Jesus's teachings about himself as they relate to all aspects of his person and work in the Gospel of John. When one knows and understands the contrasts, one gains a greater appreciation for what Jesus teaches concerning his own person and work.

8

Conclusion

SUMMARY AND CONCLUSION OF THIS STUDY

JUDGMENT IS A COMMON theme throughout many of the Second Temple documents. This study explored the early Jewish texts that had the topic of judgment as one of their major themes. The role of eschatological judge throughout the Old Testament and earlier Second Temple sources is revealed to be God. However, late first-century BC and first-century AD Jewish documents see a shift and a greater expectation of a messianic figure taking on a more active role as the eschatological judge or taking on certain aspects of eschatological judgment, and this role is delegated to the figures by God. Thus, by the time Jesus begins his ministry, there is an embedded Jewish expectation that the coming of the messiah would not only initiate the eschaton but that the messiah would also participate in the eschaton in a judgment role.

Throughout the Gospel of John, Jesus teaches concerning his own role as imminent and eschatological judge. The Gospel of John also reveals that Jesus's immediate Jewish audience had various messianic expectations that also reflect the beliefs of John's own Jewish audience. John wrote on topics that were familiar to his Jewish audience and thus used familiar terms and phrases when defining Jesus's messiahship. Chapters 2 through 4 sought to indicate the extent of the beliefs that his Jewish audience would likely have been familiar with concerning messianic expectation as it relates to judgment and the role of judge. More specifically, chapter 2 considered the criteria of deeds by which early Jews believed they would be judged, the identity of the righteous and the wicked, the extent of the judgment, and messianic beliefs and the messiah's role in the eschatological judgment, if present. This chapter observed that eschatological and messianic beliefs become more nuanced, with greater involvement of the messiah within the half century or so prior to the ministry of Jesus, which indicates that the Jews would have had well-formed eschatological and messianic beliefs by the time Jesus started his ministry. This chapter also observed the belief that the coming of the messiah meant that the eschaton was upon them and final judgment was very near. John's Jewish audience would have had or known about certain beliefs that the messiah would act as judge in some capacity. All of these themes and beliefs are reflected throughout the Gospel of John and have been thoroughly explored throughout chapters 5 through 7 of this study. Thus, John presenting Jesus as the messianic judge was not a foreign concept to his Jewish audience.

Chapter 4 focused primarily upon the identity of the son of man in early Jewish belief and what John's Jewish audience would have associated with the representation of Jesus's self-proclamation as the Son of Man in the Gospel of John. One of the objectives of chapter 4 was to demonstrate that there were an established early Jewish tradition and beliefs concerning the son of man, which would have been already present by the start of Jesus's ministry. This is evidenced in the Gospel of John as the represented audience reveals their own rebuttal to Jesus's teachings about the son of man (see John 12:34). Chapter 4 indicates that the early son of man tradition follows the Danielic tradition of the exalted one like a son of man in Dan 7:13–14. This is evidenced in the Parables of Enoch (1 Enoch 37–71) and 4 Ezra. This study concludes that the Parables were of great significance in helping shape what John's Jewish audience believed about the son of man. It is likely that both John and his Jewish audience were familiar with these teachings, due to many of the similarities found in John's presentation of Jesus' teachings compared to the themes found in the Parables. One of the main pieces of information from the Parables that informs this study is that the Parables speak to the fact that God passes judgment to the son of man (1 Enoch 61:5–8), and this is a claim that Jesus makes for himself in the Gospel of John (John 5:22, 27). This figure in the Parables is also seen to be the messiah, and Jesus closely associates his self-presentation as Son of Man with messianic expectation throughout his teachings in the Gospel

CONCLUSION

of John. John's Jewish audience was familiar with the traditions and beliefs concerning the son of man. They had a basis for when Jesus proclaims himself to be the Son of Man and teaches theological themes that were closely associated with the son of man that had already been established prior to Jesus's ministry.

Chapters 5 through 7 first considered the identity of the audiences that John represents in his Gospel and their relevant eschatological and messianic beliefs. The audiences would likely be similar to John's immediate Jewish audience. The background information aids the modern interpreter to understand Jesus's teachings through this particular Jewish mindset. Each social group inevitably had their own beliefs concerning various theological topics, but it was concluded that the different Jewish sects and social groups were familiar with the views that the others held. This meant that John's Jewish audience understood the theological implications of Jesus's teachings, since Jesus uses similar vocabulary to teach what he is seeking to convey about himself.

John represents Jesus as having the right to judge, because he is the Son of Man. Thus, this study explored the full implications of Jesus as the Son of Man as understood in the Gospel of John. It was observed that John represents a contrast of Jesus's teachings of himself as the Son of Man with what was believed by his Jewish audience. John nuances them in a way that would have caused his audience to reevaluate their own messianic expectations. The conclusion drawn is that John's representation of Jesus as the Son of Man is radically different from the preconceived beliefs of John's Jewish audience. Not only are Jesus's teachings about the Son of Man radically different, but his teachings about his role as judge are also unexpected, especially when he claims that the Son of Man did not come to judge, since Jewish belief saw the revelation of the son of man directly associated with the final judgment. Another radically different aspect of judgment that Jesus teaches is judgment according to deeds, where the only deed that leads to eternal life is belief in the Son, as opposed to a weighing of good and evil deeds. Jesus also indicates that those who believed themselves to be righteous were lost. He taught that salvation was for the world, which went against Jewish nationalistic beliefs. Overall, chapters 5 through 7 sought to show just how radically different John's representation of Jesus's teachings are compared to the preconceived beliefs of his Jewish audience. These conclusions will aid the modern interpreter of the Gospel of John to see Jesus's teachings in light of the beliefs of John's first Jewish audience.

The purpose of this study was not just to demonstrate how radical Jesus's teachings are concerning his role as messianic judge in light of the beliefs of his immediate audience, but to argue that knowing the views of John's Jewish audience on any given theological theme will help one understand and interpret Jesus's words more fully. This study has sought to consider how John's immediate audience heard and possibly reacted to the words of Jesus. This study also reveals that Jesus's teachings were quite radical to the ears of John's Jewish audience. John represents Jesus using the vernacular and familiar Jewish beliefs, but his teachings were unlike anything else that would have been taught by any of the other religious leaders. This leads to the hermeneutical implications, which argue for a more amplified and illuminated way to interpret the teachings of Jesus in the Gospel of John.

HERMENEUTICAL IMPLICATIONS

One of the hermeneutical implications of this study is to amplify the meaning and demonstrate the benefit of hearing Jesus's teachings from the perspective of John's initial Jewish audience. His Jewish audience had centuries of traditions and beliefs, which influenced how they heard and understood Jesus's teachings and ultimately how they responded to his words. The modern interpreter starts to understand why it was so difficult for early Jews to accept the teachings of Jesus. In essence, his teachings are radically different from the traditions and beliefs that were common to many early Jews. Although the meaning of the text does not change, having a sufficient understanding of early Judaism will illuminate nuances in Jesus's teachings that are easy to miss if one is not familiar with the beliefs of a first-century Jewish audience. When one understands the beliefs of John's Jewish audience, one will start to better understand why Jesus says some of the things that he says. In some cases, Jesus completely argues against a certain belief, and in others he nuances it in a different direction, thus redefining how something was originally understood. However, if one is not familiar with the said Jewish belief, then one will miss out on the full implications of Jesus's teachings. Thus, understanding the beliefs of John's Jewish audience will add hermeneutical amplification and illumination to the interpretation of the Gospel narrative.

Another hermeneutical implication of this study is it helps one understand the words of Jesus in their first-century AD Jewish context. Jesus does

CONCLUSION

not teach in a vacuum. Jesus uses words and phrases and teaches concepts already familiar to his audience. The eschatological topics such as judgment, resurrection, salvation, messianic expectation, and others had deep rooted backgrounds in Judaism. These beliefs were mainly rooted in the Old Testament, but there are many nuances that were influenced by the surrounding nations and their cultures, which do not find their origins in the Old Testament. This study has sought to reveal just how widely the early Jewish beliefs on the topics of judgment and messianic expectation actually span. Jesus's teachings speak on topics with which first-century Jews were quite familiar. Thus, when Jesus claims that all judgment was passed to him because he is the Son of Man, early Jewish literature reveals that this was not a foreign concept to them. Their own Jewish traditions allowed for God to pass judgment to a messianic figure. From this example and the many others in this study, one can clearly see that having a background in early Judaism helps one to understand Jesus's teachings in their early Jewish context.

WHY STUDY SECOND TEMPLE LITERATURE?

Background Information

Second Temple literature provides immensely valuable background information for New Testament biblical studies.[1] Over the past thirty years, especially, there has been a significant influx in Second Temple Jewish and Christian studies. The trend in New Testament interpretation has been to get its biggest portion of background information from the Old Testament and a few other historical texts that help fill in some of the gaps. This is where study of Second Temple literature needs to come in—not just surface level but deep study. The goal is to get the interpreter to see the usefulness of Second Temple literature to New Testament study.

---

1. Two key sources are a good starting place for Jewish texts that stand behind various NT passages. For a focus on Gospel studies, see Bock and Herrick, *Jesus in Context*. This book gives the Gospel passage and title and then quotes the entirety of the Jewish text that relates to it. The editors also include historical sources such as Josephus, as well as rabbinic literature that informs certain aspects of the Gospels. Evans provides lists and descriptions of texts that inform NT study and also extensive bibliographies of secondary sources, which aid the interpreter regarding the given ancient text. One of the most helpful features is a list of NT passages and verses with possible parallels to various ancient texts (Evans, *Ancient Texts*, 342–423).

Theological and Religious Belief

Theological and religious belief is one of the main background features that is helpful to understanding the Jewish setting of Jesus' day.[2] One of the main things with which this helps is understanding what a first-century Jewish audience believed while reading or hearing the teachings of Jesus. Understanding the beliefs of the original Jewish audience will cue the interpreter in understanding why Jesus says some of the things that he does. Also, Jesus would have known many of the beliefs from these texts, which becomes evident in much of his teaching. Thus, an understanding of Second Temple literature will help the interpreter have a fuller understanding of what Jesus is teaching the people, and the interpreter will be able to give a more informed interpretation of the text.

Most of the theological themes in the teachings of Jesus have a parallel in Jewish literature. However, Jesus also presents many of his teachings that have a radically different nuance from what his contemporary Jewish teachers were teaching. Most of the time, this difference of nuance is not very noticeable from the New Testament text alone. Jewish literature aids the interpreter to see this difference.

Interpretive Keys

Until recently, many if not most interpreters have largely ignored the impact that Second Temple Jewish literature has had on the development of the New Testament. One of the reasons that interpreters have ignored this body of literature is because both Jews and Christians consider this material non-canonical (and for good reasons).[3] Although it is not inspired Scripture, this does not mean that it is not extremely useful in helping one to understand inspired Scripture. One of the goals of hermeneutics is to understand the text as fully as possible and to understand everything in it and surrounding it before seeking to establish a final interpretation. Unfortunately, many books on hermeneutics still do not treat the usefulness

---

2. There are several introductions to Second Temple Judaism that will aid the interpreter with theological background information. See Docherty, *Jewish Pseudepigrapha*; Nickelsburg and Stone, *Early Judaism*; VanderKam, *Introduction to Early Judaism*.

3. This is probably the main excuse I have heard as to why fellow students will not even consider reading any of this body of literature. In fact, I have heard people call it heresy, even though they are completely ignorant of its contents.

Conclusion

of Second Temple literature in the interpretation of the New Testament.[4] The Gospels alone are not enough to understand the rich dynamic that lies behind much of the teachings in the Gospels concerning resurrection and eternal life. This is one place where Jewish texts can play a major role in helping the interpreter better understand the Gospels.

---

4. Although the following texts aid the interpreter in proper biblical hermeneutics, they do not give much, if any, treatment to the usefulness of Second Temple literature for NT interpretation. See Klein et al., *Introduction to Biblical Interpretation*; the latest edition does give more attention to Second Temple background. Also see Duvall and Hays, *Grasping God's Word*. Osborne is one of the few who does give treatment to the influence of Second Temple literature (Osborne, *Hermeneutical Spiral*, 158–72).

Appendix

An Example of Further Study
Sheol, Hades, and Hell

ONE OF THE DISCONNECTS between the Old and New Testaments is the place where the dead end up. The Old Testament is quite vague on the afterlife. Those places in the Old Testament which interpreters say point to a belief in the afterlife often read into the text something that may not have been intended by the original author. This is another place that Second Temple literature is extremely helpful in understanding the development of the concept of hell. Second Temple literature is especially helpful when seeking to understand what Jesus means when he says there is a place with "weeping and gnashing of teeth" and what he means with his references to Gehena or Hades.[1]

The New Testament concept of hell is not as explicitly described as it is in Second Temple Jewish literature. This is likely the case because a first-century Jewish audience would have had a preconceived picture of hell as it is described in Second Temple literature. The problem comes in New Testament interpretation, when the interpreter does not know what that picture is.

Second Temple literature sees a significant increase in the development of the doctrine of hell. Russell says that one of the biggest changes between the Old Testament and Second Temple period is a radical change

---

1. Papaionnou gives a very thorough and in-depth treatment on the background of the references in the NT on the place where the unrighteous dead go upon death (Papaionnou, *Geography of Hell*, 3–26).

Appendix A

in the survival of the individual soul or spirit after death.[2] There is a greater certainty for the Jew on what will happen to him when he or she dies.[3] Overall, Second Temple literature provides the backdrop for Jesus's teachings on hell, which greatly helps the interpreter understand what Jesus means and what a first-century Jewish audience understood. It is likely that Jesus does not go into much detail about hell and what eternal punishment looked like because he does not have to. A study of the Second Temple background of hell compels the interpreter to understand just how serious Jesus is when telling his audience what was waiting for those who did not put their faith in him.

The study of Second Temple Jewish literature is an absolutely essential part of New Testament interpretation. The interpreter can gain in his or her understanding of the New Testament through a deep study of Second Temple sources. One thing still lacking in this field is more focused work on the parallels between Jewish literature and New Testament passages and themes. Unfortunately, this study can only do so much, due to its constraints. Thus, a more comprehensive work will need to be completed to explicitly show the parallels and differences between the two. Present scholarship does well at descriptive works but often falls short in moving toward interpretation of New Testament passages in light of Second Temple texts and in understanding the words of Jesus in light of how a first-century Jewish audience would have understood them.

---

2. Russell, *Method and Message*, 358–59.

3. Oesterley notes that Sheol is the typical place in the Apocrypha as a place where the soul goes upon death, but these are earlier Second Temple writings that have not yet seen the deep developments witnessed by the Jewish audience of Jesus (Oesterley, *Introduction to the Books*, 100–101).

Bibliography

Arcari, Luca. "A Symbolic Transfiguration of a Historical Event: The Parthian Invasion in Josephus and the Parables of Enoch." In *Enoch and the Messiah Son of Man: Revisiting the Book of Parables*, edited by Gabriele Boccaccini, 478–86. Grand Rapids: Eerdmans, 2007.

Argall, Randall A. *First Enoch and Sirach: A Comparative Literary and Conceptual Analysis of the Themes of Revelation, Creation and Judgment*. Atlanta: Scholars Press, 1995.

Ashton, John. *Understanding the Fourth Gospel*. 2nd ed. Oxford: Oxford University Press, 2007.

Assefa, Daniel. "Matthew's Day of Judgment in Light of 1 Enoch." In *Enoch and the Synoptic Gospels: Reminiscence, Allusions, Intertextuality*, edited by Loren T. Stuckenbruck and Gabriele Boccaccini, 199–214. Early Judaism and Its Literature. Atlanta: SBL, 2016.

Bampfylde, Gillian. "The Similitudes of Enoch: Historical Allusions." *JSJ* 15 (1984) 9–31.

Barrett, C. K. *The Gospel According to St John: An Introduction with Commentary and Notes on the Greek Text*. 2nd ed. London: SPCK, 1978.

Bartlett, John R. *The First and Second Books of Maccabees*. Cambridge, UK: Cambridge University Press, 1973.

Bauckham, Richard. "Apocalypses." In *The Complexities of Second Temple Judaism*, edited by D. A. Carson et al., 135–87. Vol. 1 of *Justification and Variegated Nomism*. Grand Rapids: Baker Academic, 2001.

———. *Gospel of Glory: Major Themes in Johannine Theology*. Grand Rapids: Baker Academic, 2015.

———. *The Jewish World around the New Testament*. Tübingen, Germ.: Mohr Siebeck, 2008.

———. *The Testimony of the Beloved Disciple: Narrative, History, and Theology in the Gospel of John*. Grand Rapids: Baker Academic, 2007.

Bautch, Kelley Coblentz. "Adamic Traditions in the Parables? A Query on 1 Enoch 69:6." In *Enoch and the Messiah Son of Man: Revisiting the Book of Parables*, edited by Gabriele Boccaccini, 352–62. Grand Rapids: Eerdmans, 2007.

Baynes, Leslie. "The Parables of Enoch and Luke's Parable of the Rich Man and Lazarus." In *Enoch and the Synoptic Gospels: Reminiscence, Allusions, Intertextuality*, edited by Loren T. Stuckenbruck and Gabriele Boccaccini, 129–52. Atlanta: SBL, 2016.

Beasley-Murray, George R. *John*. 2nd ed. Nashville: Thomas Nelson, 1999.

Bibliography

Ben Zeev, Miriam Pucci. "Jews among Greeks and Romans." In *Early Judaism: A Comprehensive Overview*, edited by John J. Collins and Daniel C. Harlow, 367–90. Grand Rapids: Eerdmans, 2010.

Ben-Dov, Jonathan. "Exegetical Notes on Cosmology in the Parables of Enoch." In *Enoch and the Messiah Son of Man: Revisiting the Book of Parables*, edited by Gabriele Boccaccini, 143–52. Grand Rapids: Eerdmans, 2007.

Berthelot, Katell. "Early Jewish Literature Written in Greek." In *Early Judaism: A Comprehensive Overview*, edited by John J. Collins and Daniel C. Harlow, 228–52. Grand Rapids: Eerdmans, 2010.

Betz, Otto. "Jesus and the Temple Scroll." In *Jesus and the Dead Sea Scrolls: The Controversy Resolved*, edited by James H. Charlesworth, 75–103. New York: Doubleday, 1992.

Beutler, Johannes. *A Commentary on the Gospel of John*. Grand Rapids: Eerdmans, 2017.

Bird, Michael F. *Are You the One Who Is to Come?: The Historical Jesus and the Messianic Question*. Grand Rapids: Baker Academic, 2009.

Black, Matthew. "The Messianism of the Parables of Enoch: Their Date and Contribution to Christological Origins." In *The Messiah: Developments in Earliest Judaism and Christianity*, edited by J. H. Charlesworth, 145–68. Minneapolis: Fortress, 1992.

Blomberg, Craig L. *Historical Reliability of John's Gospel: Issues and Commentary*. Downers Grove, IL: InterVarsity, 2001.

———. *Matthew*. Nashville: Broadman, 1992.

Boccaccini, Gabriele, ed. *Enoch and the Messiah Son of Man: Revisiting the Book of Parables*. Grand Rapids: Eerdmans, 2007.

———. "Finding a Place for the Parables within Second Temple Jewish Literature." In *Enoch and the Messiah Son of Man: Revisiting the Book of Parables*, edited by Gabriele Boccaccini, 263–89. Grand Rapids: Eerdmans, 2007.

———. "Forgiveness of Sins: An Enochic Problem, a Synoptic Answer." In *Enoch and the Synoptics: Reminiscence, Allusions, Intertextuality*, edited by Loren T. Stuckenbruck and Gabriele Boccaccini, 153–67. Atlanta: SBL, 2016.

Bock, Darrell L. and Gregory J. Herrick, eds. *Jesus in Context: Background Readings for Gospel Study*. Grand Rapids: Baker Academic, 2005.

Borchert, Gerald L. *John 1–11*. Nashville: B&H, 1996.

Boyarin, Daniel. "Was the Book of Parables a Sectarian Document?: A Brief Brief in Support of Pierluigi Piovanelli." In *Enoch and the Messiah Son of Man: Revisiting the Book of Parables*, edited by Gabriele Boccaccini, 380–85. Grand Rapids: Eerdmans, 2007.

Brown, Raymond E. *An Introduction to the Gospel of John*. Edited by Francis J. Moloney. Anchor Yale Bible Reference Library. New York: Doubleday, 2003.

———. *The Gospel According to John (I–XII): Introduction, Translation, and Notes*. Garden City, NY: Doubleday, 2006.

Bruner, Frederick Dale. *The Gospel of John: A Commentary*. Grand Rapids: Eerdmans 2012.

Bultmann, Rudolph. *The Gospel of John: A Commentary*. Philadelphia: Westminster, 1971.

Burkett, Delbert Royce. *The Son of Man Debate: A History and Evaluation*. Cambridge, UK: Cambridge University Press, 1999.

———. *The Son of the Man in the Gospel of John*. Sheffield, UK: JSOT, 1991.

Capon, Robert Farrar. *Kingdom, Grace, and Judgment: Paradox, Outrage, and Vindication in the Parables of Jesus*. Grand Rapids: Eerdmans, 2002.

Bibliography

Carey, Greg. *Ultimate Things: An Introduction to Jewish and Christian Apocalyptic Literature.* St. Louis: Chalice Press, 2005.

Casey, Maurice. *The Solution to the "Son of Man" Problem.* London: T&T Clark, 2007.

Carson, D. A. *The Gospel According to John.* Grand Rapids: Eerdmans, 1991.

Charlesworth, James H. "Can We Discern the Composition Date of the Parables of Enoch?" In *Enoch and the Messiah Son of Man: Revisiting the Book of Parables*, edited by Gabriele Boccaccini, 450–68. Grand Rapids: Eerdmans, 2007.

———. "The Dead Sea Scrolls and the Historical Jesus." In *Jesus and the Dead Sea Scrolls: The Controversy Resolved*, edited by James H. Charlesworth, 1–74. New York: Doubleday, 1992.

———, ed. *Jesus and the Dead Sea Scrolls: The Controversy Resolved.* New York: Doubleday, 1992.

———. "Jesus as 'Son' and the Righteous Teacher as Gardener." In *Jesus and the Dead Sea Scrolls: The Controversy Resolved*, edited by James H. Charlesworth, 140–75. New York: Doubleday, 1992.

———, ed. *The Messiah: Developments in Earliest Judaism and Christianity.* Minneapolis: Fortress, 1992.

———, ed. *The Old Testament Pseudepigrapha.* 2 vols. Peabody, MA: Hendrickson, 1983.

Chester, Andrew. *Messiah and Exaltation.* Tübingen, Germ.: Mohr Siebeck, 2007.

Chiala, Abino. "The Son of Man: The Evolution of an Expression." In *Enoch and the Messiah Son of Man: Revisiting the Book of Parables*, edited by Gabriele Boccaccini, 153–78. Grand Rapids: Eerdmans, 2007.

Cohen, Shaye J. D. *From the Maccabees to the Mishnah.* 3rd ed. Louisville: Westminster John Knox, 2014.

Collins, Adele Yarbro. "The Secret Son of Man in the Parables of Enoch and the Gospel of Mark: A Response to Leslie Walck." In *Enoch and the Messiah Son of Man: Revisiting the Book of Parables*, edited by Gabriele Boccaccini, 338–42. Grand Rapids: Eerdmans, 2007.

Collins, Adela Yarbro and John J. Collins. *King and Messiah as Son of God: Divine, Human, and Angelic Messianic Figures in Biblical and Related Literature.* Grand Rapids: Eerdmans, 2008.

Collins, John J. *The Apocalyptic Imagination: An Introduction to Jewish Apocalyptic Literature.* 2nd ed. Grand Rapids: Eerdmans, 1998.

———. "The Date and Provenance of the Testament of Moses." In *Studies on the Testament of Moses*, edited by G. W. E. Nickelsburg. Septuagint and Cognate Studies. Cambridge, MA: Society of Biblical Literature, 1973.

———. *The Dead Sea Scrolls: A Biography.* Princeton, NJ: Princeton University Press, 2013.

———. "Early Judaism in Modern Scholarship." In *Early Judaism: A Comprehensive Overview*, edited by John J. Collins and Daniel C. Harlow, 1–29. Grand Rapids: Eerdmans, 2010.

———. "Enoch and the Son of Man: A Response to Sabino Chiala and Helge Kvanvig." In *Enoch and the Messiah Son of Man: Revisiting the Book of Parables*, edited by Gabriele Boccaccini, 216–27. Grand Rapids: Eerdmans, 2007.

———. "The Heavenly Representative: The 'Son of Man' in the Similitudes of Enoch." In *Ideal Figures in Ancient Judaism*, edited by John J. Collins and George W. E. Nickelsburg, 111–33. Chico, CA: Scholars Press, 1980, .

———. *Jewish Wisdom in the Hellenistic Age.* Louisville: Westminster John Knox, 1997.

BIBLIOGRAPHY

———. "Messianism in the Maccabean Period." In *Judaisms and Their Messiahs at the Turn of the Christian Era*, edited by Jacob Neusner et al., 97–110. New York: University of Cambridge Press, 1987.

———. "Pre-Christian Jewish Messianism: An Overview." In *The Messiah in Early Judaism and Christianity*, edited by Magnus Zetterholm, 1–20. Minneapolis: Fortress, 2007.

———. *The Scepter and the Star: Messianism in Light of the Dead Sea Scrolls*. 2nd ed. Grand Rapids: Eerdmans, 2010.

———. "The Sibylline Oracles." In *The Old Testament Pseudepigrapha*, edited by James H. Charlesworth, 1:317–472. Peabody, MA: Hendrickson, 1983.

Collins, John J. and Daniel C. Harlow, eds. *Early Judaism: A Comprehensive Overview*. Grand Rapids: Eerdmans, 2010.

———. *The Eerdmans Dictionary of Early Judaism*. Grand Rapids: Eerdmans, 2010.

Colwell, E. C. "A Definite Rule for the Use of the Article in the Greek New Testament." *Journal of Biblical Literature* 52, no. 1 (Apr. 1933) 12–21.

Davenport, Gene. "The 'Anointed of the Lord' in Psalms of Solomon 17." In *Ideal Figures in Ancient Judaism: Profiles and Paradigms*, edited by George W. E. Nickelsburg and John J. Collins, 67–92. Atlanta: Scholars, 1980.

Davies, W. D. and Dale C. Allison. *The Gospel According to Saint Matthew*. 3 vols. Edinburgh: T&T Clark, 1988–2000.

DeSilva, David A. *Introducing the Apocrypha: Message, Context, and Significance*. 2nd ed. Grand Rapids: Baker Academic, 2018.

———. *The Jewish Teachers of Jesus, James, and Jude: What Earliest Christianity Learned from the Apocrypha and Pseudepigrapha*. Oxford: Oxford University Press, 2012.

DiTommaso, Lorenzo. "The Apocalyptic Other." In *The "Other" in Second Temple Judaism: Essays in Honor of John J. Collins*, edited by Daniel C. Harlow et al., 221–46. Grand Rapids: Eerdmans, 2011.

———. "Deliverance and Justice: Soteriology in the Book of Daniel." In *This World and the World to Come: Soteriology in Early Judaism*, edited by Daniel M. Gurtner, 71–86. London: T&T Clark, 2011.

Docherty, Susan. *The Jewish Pseudepigrapha: An Introduction to the Literature of the Second Temple Period*. Minneapolis: Fortress, 2015.

Dodd, C. H. *The First Epistle of John and the Fourth Gospel*. Manchester, UK: Manchester University Press, 1937.

———. *The Interpretation of the Fourth Gospel*. Cambridge, UK: Cambridge University Press, 1968.

Doran, Robert. *Second Maccabees: A Critical Commentary*. Minneapolis: Fortress, 2012.

Dunn, James D. G. "Messianic Ideas and Their Influence on the Jesus of History." In *The Messiah: Developments in Earliest Judaism and Christianity*, edited by James H. Charlesworth, 365–81. Minneapolis: Fortress, 2010.

Duvall, J. Scott and J. Daniel Hays. *Grasping God's Word: A Hands-On Approach to Reading, Interpreting, and Applying the Bible*. Grand Rapids: Zondervan, 2012.

Eckhardt, Benedikt. "The Psalms of Solomon as a Historical Source for the Late Hasmonean Period." In *The Psalms of Solomon: Language, History, Theology*, edited by Eberhard Bons and Patrick Pouchelle, 7–30. Atlanta: SBL, 2015.

Ellens, J. Harold. *The Son of Man in the Gospel of John*. Sheffield, UK: Sheffield Phoenix, 2010.

BIBLIOGRAPHY

Enns, Peter. "Expansions of Scripture." In *The Complexities of Second Temple Judaism*, edited by D. A. Carson et al., 73–98. Vol. 1 of *Justification and Variegated Nomism*. Grand Rapids: Baker Academic, 2001.

Eshel, Hanan. "An Allusion in the Parables of Enoch to the Acts of Matthias Antigonus in 40 B.C.E.?" In *Enoch and the Messiah Son of Man: Revisiting the Book of Parables*, edited by Gabriele Boccaccini, 487–91. Grand Rapids: Eerdmans, 2007.

Evans, Craig A. *Ancient Texts for New Testament Study: A Guide to the Background Literature*. Grand Rapids: Baker, 2005.

———. "Opposition to the Temple: Jesus and the Dead Sea Scrolls." In *Jesus and the Dead Sea Scrolls: The Controversy Resolved*, edited by James H. Charlesworth, 235–53. New York: Doubleday, 1992.

Falk, Daniel. "Psalms and Prayers." In *The Complexities of Second Temple Judaism*, edited by D. A. Carson et al., 7–56. Vol. 1 of *Justification and Variegated Nomism*. Grand Rapids: Baker Academic, 2001.

Fitzmyer, Joseph A. "Qumran Literature and the Johannine Writings." In *Life in Abundance: Studies of John's Gospel in Tribute to Raymond E. Brown*, edited by John R. Donahue, 117–33. Collegeville, MN: Liturgical Press, 2005.

Frey, Jörg. *Theology and History in the Fourth Gospel: Tradition and Narration*. Waco, TX: Baylor University Press, 2018.

Fröhlich, Ida. "The Parables of Enoch and Qumran Literature." In *Enoch and the Messiah Son of Man: Revisiting the Book of Parables*, edited by Gabriele Boccaccini, 343–51. Grand Rapids: Eerdmans, 2007.

Fruchtenbaum, Arnold G. *Yeshua: The Life of Messiah from a Messianic Jewish Perspective*. 4 vols. San Antonio: Ariel Ministries, 2017.

Gieschen, Charles A. "The Name of the Son of Man in the Parables of Enoch." In *Enoch and the Messiah Son of Man: Revisiting the Book of Parables*, edited by Gabriele Boccaccini, 238–49. Grand Rapids: Eerdmans, 2007.

Gowan, Donald E. *Bridge Between the Testaments: A Reappraisal of Judaism from the Exile to the Birth of Christianity*. Eugene, OR: Pickwick, 1986.

———. "Wisdom." In *The Complexities of Second Temple Judaism*. Edited by D. A. Carson et al., 216–239. Vol. 1 of *Justification and Variegated Nomism*. Grand Rapids: Baker Academic, 2001.

Grabbe, Lester L. *Judaic Religion in the Second Temple Period: Belief and Practice from the Exile to the Yavneh*. London: Routledge, 2000.

———. "The Parables of Enoch in Second Temple Jewish Society." In *Enoch and the Messiah Son of Man: Revisiting the Book of Parables*, edited by Gabriele Boccaccini, 386–402. Grand Rapids: Eerdmans, 2007.

———. "'Son of Man': Its Origin and Meaning in Second Temple Judaism." In *Enoch and the Synoptics: Reminiscence, Allusions, Intertextuality*, edited by Loren T. Stuckenbruck and Gabriele Boccaccini, 169–97. Atlanta: SBL, 2016.

Greenfield, Jonas C. and Michael E. Stone. "The Enochic Pentateuch and the Date of the Similitudes." *Harvard Theological Review* 70 (Jan–Apr 1977) 51–66.

Grindheim, Sigurd. *God's Equal: What Can We Know about Jesus' Self-Understanding in the Synoptic Gospels?* London: T&T Clark, 2011.

Gurtner, Daniel M., ed. *This World and the World to Come: Soteriology in Early Judaism*. London: T&T Clark, 2011.

Bibliography

Hannah, Darrell D. "The Book of Noah, the Death of Herod the Great, and the Date of the Parables of Enoch." In *Enoch and the Messiah Son of Man: Revisiting the Book of Parables*, edited by Gabriele Boccaccini, 469–77. Grand Rapids: Eerdmans, 2007.

Harkins, Angela Kim et al., eds. *The Watchers in Jewish and Christian Traditions*. Minneapolis: Fortress, 2014.

Harlow, Daniel C. "Early Judaism and Early Christianity." In *Early Judaism: A Comprehensive Overview*, edited by John J. Collins and Daniel C. Harlow, 391–419. Grand Rapids: Eerdmans, 2010.

Harlow, Daniel C., et al., eds. *The "Other" in Second Temple Judaism: Essays in Honor of John J. Collins*. Grand Rapids: Eerdmans, 2011.

Heger, Paul. *Challenges to the Conventional Opinions on the Qumran and Enochic Issues*. Leiden, Neth.: Brill, 2012.

Helyer, Larry R. *Exploring Jewish Literature of the Second Temple Period: A Guide for New Testament Students*. Christian Classics Bible Studies. Downers Grove, IL: IVP Academic, 2002.

Henze, Matthias. "The Parables of Enoch in Second Temple Literature: A Response to Gabriele Boccaccini." In *Enoch and the Messiah Son of Man: Revisiting the Book of Parables*, edited by Gabriele Boccaccini, 290–98. Grand Rapids: Eerdmans, 2007.

Higgins, A. J. B. *The Son of Man in the Teaching of Jesus*. Cambridge, UK: Cambridge University Press, 1980.

Horsley, Richard A. *Revolt of the Scribes: Resistance and Apocalyptic Origins*. Minneapolis: Fortress, 2010.

Hurst, L. D. "Did Qumran Expect Two Messiahs?" *Bulletin for Biblical Research* 9, no. 1 (1999) 157–80.

Isaac, Ephraim. "First (Ethiopic Apocalypse of) Enoch." In *The Old Testament Pseudepigrapha*, edited by James H. Charlesworth, 2:5–12. Peabody, MA: Hendrickson, 1983.

Jackson, David R. *Enochic Judaism: Three Defining Paradigm Exemplars*. London: T&T Clark International, 2004.

Johnston, Philip. *Shades of Sheol: Death and Afterlife in the Old Testament*. Downers Grove, IL: InterVarsity, 2002.

Keddie, G. Anthony. "Judaean Apocalypticism and the Unmasking of Ideology: Foreign and National Rulers in the Testament of Moses." *Journal for the Study of Judaism* 44 (2013) 301–38.

Kee, Howard C. "Membership in the Covenant People at Qumran and in the Teaching of Jesus." In *Jesus and the Dead Sea Scrolls: The Controversy Resolved*, edited by James H. Charlesworth, 104–22. New York: Doubleday, 1992.

Keener, Craig S. *The Gospel of John: A Commentary*. 2 vols. Peabody, MA: Hendrickson, 2003.

Kim, Kyoung-Shik. *God Will Judge Each One According to Works: Judgment According to Works and Psalm 62 in Early Judaism and the New Testament*. Berlin: De Gruyter, 2011.

Klein, William W., et al. *Introduction to Biblical Interpretation*. Grand Rapids: Zondervan, 2017.

Koch, Klaus. "Questions Regarding the So-Called Son of Man in the Parables of Enoch: A Response to Sabino Chiala and Helge Kvanvig." In *Enoch and the Messiah Son of Man: Revisiting the Book of Parables*, edited by Gabriele Boccaccini, 228–37. Grand Rapids: Eerdmans, 2007.

BIBLIOGRAPHY

Köstenberger, Andreas J. *John.* Grand Rapids: Baker Academic, 2004.

———. *A Theology of John's Gospel and Letters.* Grand Rapids: Zondervan, 2009.

Köstenberger, Andreas J., and Richard Patterson. *Invitation to Biblical Interpretation: Exploring the Hermeneutical Triad of History, Literature, and Theology.* Grand Rapids: Kregel, 2011.

Kruse, Colin G. *John.* Rev. ed. Downers Grove, IL: IVP Academic, 2017.

Kugel, James L. *A Walk through Jubilees: Studies in the Book of Jubilees and the World of Its Creation.* Leiden, Neth.: Brill, 2012.

Kugler, Robert A. "Testaments." In *The Complexities of Second Temple Judaism*, edited by D. A. Carson et al., 189–213. Vol. 1 of *Justification and Variegated Nomism*. Grand Rapids: Baker Academic, 2001.

Kvanvig, Helge S. *Primeval History: Babylonian, Biblical, and Enochic: An Intertextual Reading.* Leiden, Neth.: Brill, 2011.

———. "The Son of Man in the Parables of Enoch." In *Enoch and the Messiah Son of Man: Revisiting the Book of Parables*, edited by Gabriele Boccaccini, 179–215. Grand Rapids: Eerdmans, 2007.

Lucass, Shirley. *The Concept of the Messiah in the Scriptures of Judaism and Christianity.* New York: T&T Clark, 2011.

Mazzinghi, Luca. "The Antithetical Pair 'To Punish' and 'To Benefit' (κολάζω and εὐεργετέω) in the Book of Wisdom." In *Wisdom for Life*, edited by Nuria Calduch-Benages, 237–49. Berlin: de Gruyter, 2014.

McCready, Wayne O. and Adele Reinhartz. "Common Judaism and Diversity within Judaism." In *Common Judaism: Explorations in Second Temple Judaism*, edited by Wayne O. McCready and Adele Reinhartz, 1–10. Minneapolis: Fortress, 2008.

McGrath, James F. *John's Apologetic Christology: Legitimation and Development in Johannine Christology.* Cambridge, UK: Cambridge University Press, 2001.

Michaels, J. Ramsey. *The Gospel of John.* Grand Rapids: Eerdmans, 2010.

Michalak, Aleksander R. *Angels as Warriors in Late Second Temple Jewish Literature.* Tubingen, Germ.: Mohr Siebeck, 2012.

Milik, J. T. *The Books of Enoch: Aramaic Fragments of Qumran Cave Four.* Oxford: Clarendon, 1976.

Mlakuzhyil, George. *The Christocentric Literary Structure of the Fourth Gospel.* Rome: Pontifical Bible Institute, 1987.

Moloney, Francis J. *The Gospel of John.* Collegeville, MN: Liturgical Press, 1998.

———. *The Johannine Son of Man.* Eugene, OR: Wipf and Stock, 1978.

———. "The *Parables of Enoch* and the Johannine Son of Man." In *Parables of Enoch: A Paradigm Shift*, edited by Darrell L. Bock and James H. Charlesworth, 269–293. London: Bloomsbury, 2013.

Moore, Anne. "The Search for the Common Judaic Understanding of God's Kingship." In *Common Judaism: Explorations in Second Temple Judaism*, edited by Wayne O. McCready and Adele Reinhartz, 131–44. Minneapolis: Fortress, 2008.

Morris, Leon. *The Gospel According to John.* New International Commentary on the New Testament. Grand Rapids: Eerdmans, 1995.

———. *Jesus Is the Christ: Studies in the Theology of John.* Grand Rapids: Eerdmans, 1989.

Neusner, Jacob, et al., eds. *Judaisms and Their Messiahs at the Turn of the Christian Era.* Cambridge, UK: Cambridge University Press, 1987.

Neyrey, Jerome H. *The Gospel of John in Cultural and Rhetorical Perspective.* Grand Rapids: Eerdmans, 2009.

Bibliography

Nickelsburg, George W. E. *Ancient Judaism and Christian Origins: Diversity, Continuity, and Transformation*. Minneapolis: Fortress, 2003.

———. *Resurrection, Immortality, and Eternal Life in Intertestamental Judaism and Early Christianity*. Exp. ed. Cambridge, MA: Harvard, 2006.

———. "Salvation without and with a Messiah: Developing Beliefs Ascribed to Enoch." In *Judaisms and Their Messiahs at the Turn of the Christian Era*, edited by Jacob Neusner et al., 49–68. New York: University of Cambridge Press, 1987.

———. "The We and the Other in the Worldview of 1 *Enoch*, the Dead Sea Scrolls, and Other Early Jewish Texts." In *The "Other" in Second Temple Judaism: Essays in Honor of John J. Collins*, edited by Daniel C. Harlow et al., 247–61. Grand Rapids: Eerdmans, 2011.

Nickelsburg, George W. E. and Michael E. Stone. *Early Judaism: Texts and Documents on Faith and Piety*. Minneapolis: Fortress, 2009.

Nickelsburg, George W. E. and James C. VanderKam. *First Enoch 2: A Commentary on the Book of 1 Enoch Chapters 37–82*. Minneapolis: Fortress, 2012.

Novenson, Matthew V. "Jesus the Messiah: Conservatism and Radicalism in Johannine Christology." In *Portraits of Jesus in the Gospel of John*, edited by Craig Koester, 109–124. London: T&T Clark, 2019.

Oegema, Gerbern S. *The Anointed and His People: Messianic Expectations from the Maccabees to Bar Kochba*. Sheffield, UK: Sheffield Academic, 1998.

———. *Apocalyptic Interpretation of the Bible: Apocalypticism and Biblical Interpretation in Early Judaism, the Apostle Paul, the Historical Jesus, and Their Reception History*. London: T&T Clark, 2012.

———. "'The Coming of the Righteous One' in Acts and 1 Enoch." In *Enoch and the Messiah Son of Man: Revisiting the Book of Parables*, edited by Gabriele Boccaccini, 250–62. Grand Rapids: Eerdmans, 2007.

Oesterley, W. O. E. *An Introduction to the Books of the Apocrypha*. Berkeley, CA: Apocryphile, 2006.

Orlov, Andrei A. "Roles and Titles of the Seventh Antediluvian Hero in the Parables of Enoch: A Departure from the Traditional Pattern?" In *Enoch and the Messiah Son of Man: Revisiting the Book of Parables*, edited by Gabriele Boccaccini, 110–36. Grand Rapids: Eerdmans, 2007.

Osborne, Grant R. *The Hermeneutical Spiral: A Comprehensive Introduction to Biblical Interpretation*. Downers Grove: IVP, 2006.

Papaionnou, Kim. *The Geography of Hell in the Teaching of Jesus: Gehenna, Hades, the Abyss, the Outer Darkness Where There is Weeping and Gnashing of Teeth*. Eugene, OR: Pickwick, 2013.

Patte, Daniel. *Early Jewish Hermeneutic in Palestine*. Missoula, MT: Scholars, 1975.

Percer, Leo. "War in Heaven: Michael and Messiah in Revelation 12." PhD diss., Baylor University, 1999.

Phillips, J. B. *The New Testament in Modern English*. New York: Macmillan, 1958.

Piovanelli, Pierluigi. "'A Testimony for the Kings and the Mighty Who Possess the Earth': The Thirst for Justice and Peace in the Parables of Enoch." In *Enoch and the Messiah Son of Man: Revisiting the Book of Parables*, edited by Gabriele Boccaccini, 363–79. Grand Rapids: Eerdmans, 2007.

Pomykala, Kenneth E. *The Davidic Dynasty Tradition in Early Judaism: Its History and Significance for Messianism*. Atlanta: Scholars, 1995.

Bibliography

Purvis, James D. "The Samaritans and Judaism" in *Early Judaism and Its Modern Interpreters*, edited by Robert A. Kraft and George W. E. Nickelsburg, 81–98. Atlanta: Scholars, 1986.

Reiser, Marius. *Jesus and Judgment: The Eschatological Proclamation in its Jewish Context*. Translated by Linda M. Maloney. Minneapolis: Fortress, 1997.

Reynolds, Benjamin E. *The Apocalyptic Son of Man in the Gospel of John*. Tübingen, Germany: Mohr Siebeck, 2008.

———. "The Enochic Son of Man and the Apocalyptic Background of the Son of Man Sayings in John's Gospel." In *Parables of Enoch: A Paradigm Shift*, edited by Darrell L. Bock and James H. Charlesworth, 294–314. London: Bloomsbury, 2013.

———. "Jesus the Son of Man: Apocalyptic Interpretations and Johannine Christology" in *Portraits of Jesus in the Gospel of John*, edited by Craig Koester, 125–40. London: T&T Clark, 2019.

Rhea, Robert. *The Johannine Son of Man*. Eugene, OR: Wipf and Stock, 2017.

Ridderbos, Herman. *The Gospel of John: A Theological Commentary*. Translated by John Vriend. Grand Rapids: Eerdmans, 1997.

Rogers, Cleon L., Jr. "The Promises to David in Early Judaism." *Bibliotheca Sacra* 150, no. 599 (July 1993) 285–302.

Russell, D. S. *The Method and Message of Jewish Apocalyptic: 200 BC–AD 100*. Philadelphia: Westminster, 1964.

Sacchi, Paolo. *The History of the Second Temple Period*. London: T&T Clark, 2000.

———. "Recovering Jesus' Formative Background." In *Jesus and the Dead Sea Scrolls: The Controversy Resolved*, edited by James H. Charlesworth, 123–39. New York: Doubleday, 1992.

Sanders, E. P. "Common Judaism Explored." In *Common Judaism: Explorations in Second Temple Judaism*, edited by Wayne O. McCready and Adele Reinhartz, 11–26. Minneapolis: Fortress, 2008.

———. *Jesus and Judaism*. Philadelphia: Fortress, 1985.

———. *Judaism: Practice and Belief 63 BCE–66 CE*. Eugene, OR: Wipf and Stock, 1992.

———. *Paul and Palestinian Judaism: A Comparison of Patterns of Religion*. Phildelphia: Fortress, 1977.

Schnackenburg, Rudolf. *The Gospel According to St John*. 3 vols. New York: Seabury, 1980.

Scott, J. Julius, Jr. *Jewish Backgrounds of the New Testament*. Grand Rapids: Baker Academic, 1995.

Seeman, Chris and Adam Kolman Marshak. "Jewish History from Alexander to Hadrian." In *Early Judaism: A Comprehensive Overview*, edited by John J. Collins and Daniel C. Harlow, 30–69. Grand Rapids: Eerdmans, 2010.

Segal, Michael. *The Book of Jubilees: Rewritten Bible, Redaction, Ideology, and Theology*. Leiden, Neth.: Brill, 2007.

Skehan, Patrick W., and Alexander A. Di Lella. *The Wisdom of Ben Sira*. New York: Doubleday, 1986.

Stone, Michael E. "Enoch's Date in Limbo; or, Some Considerations on David Suter's Analysis of the Book of Parables." In *Enoch and the Messiah Son of Man: Revisiting the Book of Parables*, edited by Gabriele Boccaccini, 444–49. Grand Rapids: Eerdmans, 2007.

Stuckenbruck, Loren T. "Apocrypha and Pseudepigrapha." In *Early Judaism: A Comprehensive Overview*, edited by John J. Collins and Daniel C. Harlow, 179–203. Grand Rapids: Eerdmans, 2010.

BIBLIOGRAPHY

———. *The Myth of Rebellious Angels: Studies in Second Temple Judaism and New Testament Texts.* Grand Rapids: Eerdmans, 2017.

Stuckenbruck, Loren T. and Gabriele Boccaccini, eds. *Enoch and the Synoptic Gospels: Reminiscence, Allusions, Intertextuality.* Atlanta: SBL, 2016.

Suter, David W. "Enoch in Sheol: Updating the Dating of the Book of Parables." In *Enoch and the Messiah Son of Man: Revisiting the Book of Parables,* edited by Gabriele Boccaccini, 415-43. Grand Rapids: Eerdmans, 2007.

———. *Tradition and Composition in the Parables of Enoch.* Missoula: Scholars, 1979.

Talmon, Shemaryahu. "Waiting for the Messiah: The Spiritual Universe of the Qumran Covenanters." In *Judaisms and Their Messiahs at the Turn of the Christian Era,* edited by Jacob Neusner et al. New York: University of Cambridge, 1987.

Tenney, Merrill C. *Gospel of John.* Grand Rapids: Zondervan, 1981.

Thompson, Marianne Meye. *John: A Commentary.* Louisville: Westminster John Knox, 2015.

Tigchelaar, Eibert. "The Dead Sea Scrolls." In *Early Judaism: A Comprehensive Overview,* edited by John J. Collins and Daniel C. Harlow, 204-27. Grand Rapids: Eerdmans, 2010.

Tiller, Patrick A. *A Commentary on the Animal Apocalypse of 1 Enoch.* Atlanta: Scholars, 1993.

Trafton, Joseph L. "What Would David Do?: Messianic Expectation and Surprise in Ps. Sol. 17." In *The Psalms of Solomon: Language, History, Theology,* edited by Eberhard Bons and Patrick Pouchelle, 155-174. Atlanta: SBL, 2015.

Travis, Stephen H. *Christ and the Judgment of God: The Limits of Divine Retribution in New Testament Thought.* Peabody, MA: Hendrickson, 2008.

VanderKam, James C. *The Book of Jubilees.* Sheffield, UK: Sheffield Academic, 2001.

———. "The Book of Parables within the Enoch Tradition." In *Enoch and the Messiah Son of Man: Revisiting the Book of Parables,* edited by Gabriele Boccaccini, 81-99. Grand Rapids: Eerdmans, 2007.

———. *An Introduction to Early Judaism.* Grand Rapids: Eerdmans, 2001.

———. "Jubilees and the Priestly Messiah of Qumran." *Revue de Qumran* 13 (Oct. 1988) 353-65.

———. "Judaism in the Land of Israel." In *Early Judaism: A Comprehensive Overview,* edited by John J. Collins and Daniel C. Harlow, 70-94. Grand Rapids: Eerdmans, 2010.

———. "Righteous One, Messiah, Chosen One, and Son of Man in 1 Enoch 31-37." In *The Messiah: Developments in Earliest Judaism and Christianity,* edited by James H. Charlesworth, 169-91. Minneapolis: Fortress, 1992.

VanLandingham, Chris. *Judgment and Justification in Early Judaism and the Apostle Paul.* Peabody, MA: Hendrickson, 2006.

Vermes, Geza. *The Complete Dead Sea Scrolls in English.* 7th ed. London: Penguin, 2012.

———. *Jesus in the World of Judaism.* London: SCM, 1983.

———. "Methodology in the Study of Jewish Literature in the Greco-Roman Period." *Journal for the Study of Judaism* 36 (1985) 145-58.

Venter, Pieter M. "Spatiality in the Second Parable of Enoch." In *Enoch and the Messiah Son of Man: Revisiting the Book of Parables,* edited by Gabriele Boccaccini, 403-14. Grand Rapids: Eerdmans, 2007.

Von Wahlde, Urban C. *The Gospel and the Letters of John.* 2 vols. Grand Rapids: Eerdmans, 2010.

BIBLIOGRAPHY

Waddell, James A. *The Messiah: A Comparative Study of the Enochic Son of Man and the Pauline Kyrios*. New York: T&T Clark, 2011.

Walck, Leslie W. "The Son of Man in the Parable of Enoch and the Gospels." In *Enoch and the Messiah Son of Man: Revisiting the Book of Parables*, edited by Gabriele Boccaccini, 299–337. Grand Rapids: Eerdmans, 2007.

———. *The Son of Man in the Parables of Enoch and in Matthew*. New York: T&T Clark, 2011.

Whitacre, Rodney A. *John*. Edited by Grant R. Osborne. Downers Grove, IL: IVP, 1999.

Williams, Catrin H. "Jesus the Prophet: Crossing the Boundaries of Prophetic Beliefs and Expectations in the Gospel of John." In *Portraits of Jesus in the Gospel of John*, Edited by Craig Koester, 91–108. London: T&T Clark, 2019.

Winston, David *The Anchor Bible: The Wisdom of Solomon*. New York: Doubleday, 1979.

Wintermute, O. S. "Jubilees." In *The Old Testament Pseudepigrapha*, edited by James H. Charlesworth, 2:35–142. Peabody, MA: Hendrickson, 1983.

Wise, Michael, et al. *The Dead Sea Scrolls: A New Translation*. San Francisco: Harper Collins, 1996.

Wright, R. B. "Psalms of Solomon." In *The Old Testament Pseudepigrapha*, edited by James H. Charlesworth, 2:639–70. Peabody, MA: Hendrickson, 1983.

Wylen, Stephen M. *The Jews in the Time of Jesus: An Introduction*. New York: Paulist, 1996.

Yinger, Kent L. *Paul, Judaism, and Judgment According to Deeds*. Cambridge, UK: Cambridge University Press, 1999.

Zacharias, H. Daniel. *"Raise Up to Them Their King": Psalms of Solomon 17–18 in the Context of Early Jewish Messianism*. Saarbrücken, Germ.: VDM, 2008.

Zetterholm, Magnus. *The Messiah in Early Judaism and Christianity*. Minneapolis: Fortress, 2007.